8/23/05

To Mary Kay:

Hope you enjoy

The Coterian Retreat

The Coterian Retreat

GROWING UP IN HAMILTON, OHIO

Timothy S. Simer

VANTAGE PRESS
New York

FIRST EDITION

Published by Vantage Press, Inc.
419 Park Ave. South, New York, NY 10016

Manufactured in the United States of America
ISBN: 0-533-14869-3

Library of Congress Catalog Card No.: 2004090945

0 9 8 7 6 5 4 3 2 1

To Coleen Armstrong, who convinced me I was a writer and devoted several years to helping to make me one; and to my wife, Liz, who gently nudged and patiently abided me as I gave literary birth—I dedicate this book.

Coterie *(ko'ta-ree): An intimate group of persons with a unifying common interest or purpose.*

Coterian *(ko'teer ian): No definition found in the English language. Speculative definition: a member of a coterie.*

Coterian Retreat: *Weekend retreat held in early fall at Camp Luella May by members of the High Street Christian Church, Hamilton, Ohio.*

Contents

Preface

Our family moved to Hamilton, Ohio, in the fall of 1961—and from that moment forth, it was forever to be my hometown. The world that I observed and lived in during the 1960s and early 1970s was a far cry from what exists as my reality today. Hamilton was an invulnerable world unto itself—survival was less complicated and people not nearly as disillusioned. I was allowed to grow up at a leisurely pace and could roam my neighborhood without fear of harm.

Neighbors were numerous and far-reaching, and you felt comfortable on their front porches or in their homes. They were willing to lend a hand whenever there was a need. Life was challenging, but rarely overwhelming. When a problem appeared insurmountable, members of the community came to the rescue. Your community was your family and your church, your neighborhood and your school. With these formidable reinforcements, one rarely felt alone.

The Coterian Retreat is a series of reminiscences about my childhood and adolescence growing up in Hamilton. The stories are arranged nearly in chronological order and are self-contained. Many people will make appearances in more than one story, and might bring back images of forgotten faces of your own youth.

The stories are as factual as my memory allows them to be. To the reader the details may sometimes prove tedious, but the book necessarily has a diary quality. It is real life, with honest accounts of actual events. The entries provide an opportunity to view these events through a child's eyes—but from an adult's perspective. For those who were fortunate enough to share the decades with me, the book has been written so that you might return to a different place and time—to re-experience sensations and prod emotions that you perhaps have not felt in years. For the younger reader, the book will transport you to an era that you will only be able to visit. But I believe you will find that although the world is now vastly different—our innermost thoughts and feelings have not changed nearly as drastically.

The book is not a tell-all account of my childhood, and it spends little time in critical analysis of its cast of characters. It is a book of hope, friendship and community—so the slant, if there is one, is decidedly upbeat. My childhood and Hamilton, Ohio, were certainly not idyllic, and although darker observations and characters abound, they will come to life in works more suited to them.

The stories are connected only through repetition of characters and settings—so be prepared for a game of hopscotch through most of my formative years. The setting is almost always my hometown, but we will manage an escape for a few summer vacations. The journey will be a bumpy, but hopefully enriching exploration. Our adventure begins on the day that I first cross the city's limits. Welcome to Hamilton, Ohio. If you are at all like me, you will want to return quite often.

Acknowledgments

As I tentatively took the baby steps and missteps necessary to complete and publish this book, I became increasingly aware of angels by the wayside (albeit sometimes very irritating angels) who assisted, nudged, prodded, coaxed and sometimes even carried me toward the finish line. Without their support, I would still be rattling on about a memoir that I had "somewhere inside of me." Instead, I will now rattle on about how grateful I am to all of them.

I wish to thank my parents, Scott Simer and Mona Bennett—and my sisters, Emily, Becky and Laurie—for their endless encouragement. They listened patiently when I began reading them excerpts over the phone and urged me on throughout this process. I appreciate their tolerance in accepting my interpretations and their insistence that my manuscript should see the light of day.

How do I begin to thank my wife, Liz? She has been a facilitator, a confidante and a loyal advocate. Regrettably, she took a few lumps along the way for offering me opinions when I solicited them. While I still insist that I am always right, I now readily admit that a few of her suggestions made me just a little "righter." I am extremely fortunate to have Liz by my side. She is a true companion in every sense of the word.

I also wish to gratefully acknowledge my mother-in-law, Dorothy Ogilvie, for exhibiting faith in the book and in me. Because of her kind assistance, substantial obstacles were removed. Her wholehearted support will not be forgotten.

My sincere appreciation also goes to Ralph Pinkerman and Bob and Linda Ashbrook. Without their skills and contributions, the photo insert section of the book would have been sorely lacking. And to the congregation of the Disciples Christian Church in Hamilton, Ohio—many thanks for allowing me to use those precious photographs taken at the Coterian Retreat in 1963. The church has a proud and rich history, and I am honored to be a small part of it.

The book's cover art and photo insert section are due primarily to the fine pen-and-ink drawing by my wife Liz (yes . . . she's disgustingly talented) and the contributions of our friend and graphic artist extraordinaire, Mike McCormick. What did I ever do to deserve these associations?

I'd also like to acknowledge the efforts of Mary Alicia Lemon, Lois Hill, Mike Sparks—and my lifelong friend, Mike Engel. They offered information, forwarded photographs, arranged get-togethers and almost always pointed me in the right direction. When I think of each of them, I now feel a strong connection to both my past and my present.

And finally, there is Coleen Armstrong. Although she will forever be my ninth-grade English teacher, she is also my mentor, my editor and my forever friend. Simply put, without her influence there would have been no book. From the encouragement she offered to me as a fifteen-year-old, to the concrete and always willing assistance she offers to this day, Coleen has once again demonstrated her innate ability to positively change people's lives. I was extremely blessed to intersect paths with her and was thankfully smart enough to never completely let her out of my sight. I will be eternally grateful to her.

The Coterian Retreat

1

The Audition

I was seven years old when I first set eyes on Hamilton, Ohio. My father was a minister in the Christian Church/Disciples of Christ denomination and had maintained a ministry in New Philadelphia (near Cleveland) for nearly all of my young life, and for as long as I had any personal recollections. By 1961, my parents' desire for a change in scenery had become apparent even to me, and they had learned that an affiliated congregation in the downstate city of Hamilton was actively seeking a pastor.

When my mother and father, three sisters and I packed into our beige Studebaker Lark station wagon to make our initial visit to Hamilton, we were fully aware that the overnight expedition was a trial of sorts. We would scout the church and the community, while the congregation contemplated hiring my father as their new pastor.

The day-long intrastate trek concluded in the late afternoon as we approached the town amidst waves of gently rolling green hills, on a two-lane highway that eventually paralleled the course of the Great Miami River. The river cleaved the city into two distinct sections, separated not only by the tributary's steep banks, but also by stark social class differences. As our shiny new Studebaker hugged the lightly traveled winding pavement, trees and signs whizzed by within the frame created by the car window. They zoomed into view and just as quickly vanished from sight, all at a breakneck pace that taxed our over-curious eyes. Eventually a two-legged metal road sign proclaimed the city limits, and landmarks crept across the window at a more moderate tempo.

The Columbia Bridge soon commanded my attention, as it stretched out as the link between the west banks of the river and the town that invitingly dominated the horizon. To my young eyes, Columbia seemed an awesome construction, surely as expansive as any of the renowned American bridges I had seen on my 3-D Viewmaster slides. As we traversed the seemingly endless span, our arrival into East Hamilton was unknowingly

1

momentous. This was where my family and allegiance would reside until well into my adolescence. We were soon to discover that this was where the bitter half lived—where factory workers punched time clocks while pounding out a living, all the while cursing their more affluent crosstown neighbors. The contrast between the two regions was not quite black to white, although the racial segregation often was. The river represented a formidable canyon that was rarely traversed.

On this day, our immediate plan was to locate a diner where we might silence our growling bellies. After eating, we would register and change clothes at our motel, before finally attending a welcoming reception scheduled at the church hall. Our eyes nearly overwhelmed us with exposition as Hamilton unfolded like a storybook—with each sight offering clues to the town's personality.

Our short search for sustenance ended at Frisch's Big Boy Restaurant, located on a busy thoroughfare known as Dixie Highway. It appeared that the settling dusk had recently energized this lively stretch of road. There were streams of cars, intricate neon signs and dazzlingly bright lights—many more than I was accustomed to in New Philadelphia. I remember how completely fresh and overwhelming it all seemed to me. It was my first realization that people actually resided in other areas of the country. Suddenly it dawned on me that these citizens went to school or work, shopped, ate and had acquaintances in surroundings that were completely foreign to me. Of course I had been in other towns before, but we had either just been passing through or were there to visit someone we knew. In those instances, the townspeople seemed one-dimensional—like hired background characters in a movie telling someone else's tale. But I might be moving to Hamilton, so I was convinced that these people had to be real.

The Big Boy was a warm and spacious eatery with an imposing flashing street sign that featured the "Big Boy" himself. The restaurant had a natural grey multi-stoned facade with large glowing raised letters which read "Coffee Shop" in a bold and showy script. I had heard tell of coffee shops on television and the radio, but to the best of my knowledge had never seen one. An entire building where people met to indulge in such a uniquely adult activity intrigued me. We were to eat dinner out at Frisch's, an escapade so glamorous and grown-up that my sisters and I neglected our obligatory spats so that we might fully appreciate the culinary experience.

The menu was the Sears Catalogue of edibles, including pictures of delectable sandwiches piled high with fixins, and perfectly prepared and photographed main courses. I finally settled on the Big Boy Platter so that I might experience what the remainder of the planet's population was already raving about. After all, it was clearly disclosed in writing throughout the L-shaped room that the sandwich was world-famous. Our meal was capped off with a complimentary comic book, priced at ten cents, but labeled "free to our guests." Ah, those extra subtle touches one receives when dining at an elegant restaurant!

After ingesting the lion's share of a double-deck burger dripping with tartar sauce, I reluctantly bade the Big Boy good-bye as we continued to the Motel Capri—our evening's lodging. This was the Simer siblings' first stay at a motel, and although to the seasoned traveler the Capri might not have been the most luxurious of accommodations—to our family it was the Waldorf Astoria. I was certain that the exotic name alone would lend itself to some prolonged bragging at my next second-grade show-and-tell session. The front of the motel was evenly sectioned and paneled with each segment painted a brilliant rainbow hue. The gaudy but impressive glitzy signage proudly revealed two amenities that truly represented the good life to youth in the 1960s—air-conditioning and color television. Air-conditioning was a drug-free, mood-altering sensation that was rarely experienced and completely savored. And to watch a rare color television broadcast was a rite of passage to be discussed gratingly often among the privileged few.

Once all the cots had been unfolded, our motel room more closely resembled an army barracks. Almost immediately and quite willingly we commenced the monumental task of showering and sprucing up for the evening's audition. Showering was a divine event that we had experienced only at our grandparents' home in Illinois, so the usual parental coaxing normally associated with required bathing was unnecessary.

I recall how completely special I felt lounging in a motel shower in an unknown town, while being a closed door away from the protection that the people in that motel room afforded me. For the first time, I truly recognized what my immediate family meant to me. We were striking out on an adventure—leaving the only world we knew and entering a realm that was unfamiliar to all of us. Our unity would provide our only support. To an untested, shielded and theretofore unharmed child, it was unbridled exhilaration.

I recognized that the night was a critical one, and that my father would not be the only one evaluated. Seven years as a minister's son had taught me that I always cast a reflection on my parents, and on this occasion any slip-up could affect a move that they were quite excited about. I was nervous, but eager for the drama to begin.

* * *

High Street Christian Church was located on the main downtown four-lane boulevard on the east end of the city. It was situated only a block away from a major rail line that regularly slowed traffic to a standstill when mighty and seemingly endless freight trains lumbered through town. These lengthy road delays would later prove a source of periodic diatribes from my father as he impatiently waited to get to some church event. The church, built in 1883, was a cream-colored multi-level building with two prominent slender spires that extended a graceful reach into the sky. The frontage wore a beautiful circular stained glass window on its face and held an expression of pride in its rich history.

This area of the city had deteriorated somewhat, and the church was now situated across the street from a coin-op laundromat with several low-rent apartments located on the second floor. If one ventured farther down the street, he would encounter a dreary blue-collar tavern known simply as The Oasis. Nestled next door to the church were the yellow-bricked Dorona Apartments that housed dozens of less-than-affluent seniors. The people of Hamilton had already begun a slow migration away from the downtown shopping area, and even in 1961 the city seemed a lonesome monument to what once was. Major retail stores such as Penney's, Grant's and Kresge's were still there, but not quite thriving— and although there was more than occasional vitality and commotion on High Street, the talk was of new shopping centers being built in the surrounding suburbs.

On our opening night, we entered through a pair of hefty double doors into a cavernous foyer where smiling faces and outstretched hands said welcome. I observed a set of identical staircases on both side walls that I later discovered ascended to the sanctuary and a long block of single stairs that led into the church basement. An entourage promptly escorted us to the lower level to an already buzzing reception. There was a noisy yet friendly din that echoed through the spacious linoleumed basement. The hall was filled with rows of long lacquered wooden folding tables with paper tablecloths. Dishes clanked in the kitchen, and there was the clearly distinguishable aroma of freshly brewed coffee.

Directly across the room from the staircase was a small stage complete with footlights and a semi-drawn theatre curtain. This stage would be the site of many impromptu performances when inhibiting adults were meeting elsewhere in the building. The footlights were wired so they could either be turned on all at once or by separate color banks. This phenomenon never ceased to delight and amaze us, and when left unsupervised we would create alternating color explosions that may have rivaled the finest psychedelic light shows of the '60s.

There was a fire-engine red Coke machine, shuffleboard courts and worn beige curtains that could be drawn from the walls to separate areas for Sunday school meeting rooms. These curtains were also ideal for wrapping a friend (and an occasional enemy) into a giant cocoon that rendered him or her totally defenseless. In the back of the hall and to the right of the stage was a huge kitchen filled with friendly, laughing women dishing cake onto dessert plates and sending trays of the frosted treats through the built-in serving window. The atmosphere was animated and genuine, the recreation hall relaxed and fascinating. I was entranced.

The next two hours were a blur of activity. There were so many people to be introduced to, so many kids to size up, delicious homemade cake to devour, and my inaugural soda from the kid-captivating Coke machine to drink. That night I was apprised that Hamilton was the eleventh largest town in Ohio, and that Randy King and Greg Guthrie were about my age and attended church regularly. I discovered that there was a genuine bonafide fire escape that went from the junior high Sunday school room on the top floor to the lawn near the side entrance of the church. And I was provided the vital information that Coca-Cola had printed photographs of Cleveland Browns players beneath the cork linings of their bottle caps. When the deep trough that caught caps beneath the machine's bottle opener was full, you could bury your fingers into it and pull out a few that were within reach.

Most importantly, I learned that there were lots of nice people in Hamilton. As I sat on the stage with my three sisters, and people walked through a reception line to greet us, many of them spoke and looked directly at me. Under most circumstances, when an adult stood and addressed you while you remained seated, it was not a pleasant encounter. But these giant faces had kindness in their eyes. Most appeared earnestly happy to be there—as if they were simply getting together with some good friends. That night I met many people who would have a deep and enduring impact on my life. There were Don and Waneta Anderson, Red and Eva Lemon, Seborn and Pat Wilhoit, among many others. On that evening, they were just pleasant faces in the crowd—but they were to become important and everlasting forces in my life and in my soul.

Some of the names could have comprised the players in a W.C. Fields movie: Rolla Coyle, Everett McElyea, Ellsworth Blossom, the Peters Sisters (Florence and Gladys), Bertha Betscher, Sis Fath, George Pippert, Carl Maupin, Daisy Pottinger, Nellie Carter and Vernon Grathwohl, to name a few. Fiction could not improve on this cast of characters. But these names had faces, and these faces surrounded me with a warmth that felt as cozy as a down comforter on a winter's night.

* * *

I was convinced that evening that Hamilton was where I wanted to be. It seemed that life would go on forever, and I was once again at its beginning. I wasn't afraid of leaving what I had, and I looked forward to my rebirth with great anticipation. It was a feeling of time suspended; there was no need to say good-bye, and tomorrow was forever.

Later that evening we returned to the Motel Capri. The audition had been a smashing success, and we reveled in entering a world that was new to all of us. Our parents even permitted us to watch Candid Camera, a program I usually heard only from my upstairs room, well after my bedtime. We would leave the next day never to visit Hamilton again. From that day forth, I would belong to it.

2

Mike

We had lived in Hamilton for only two days, but were already pleased with our spacious new home on Pleasant Avenue. The full backyard accommodated nearly every imaginable lawn game, and there was a steady stream of children near my age who roamed the neighborhood. The outside porch offered ample space to horse around on rainy days and was elevated several stairs from ground level—thus making it easier to defend against ambush from unnamed marauders.

The house had a fireplace in the living room, and although the flue was boarded up and a pair of time-honored logs held permanent residence in the hearth—the accompanying mantel was quite impressive. There were large bookcases on either side of its cream-white bricks, and the projecting shelf was ideal for hanging Christmas stockings. A mail slot opened directly into the house, and the floor furnace registers were adjustable grids that blew hot air, keeping our fannies toasty when we perched atop them on winter's coldest nights. On the second floor there were three bedrooms, one of which had been awarded to me alone. Privacy was a newly discovered freedom that I now fought for vigorously.

The outside cellar doors were the spitting image of those that Dorothy had tugged on to escape a Kansas twister. There was a tall maple tree to climb and a hollowed-out lilac bush near the alley that was an ideal place to hide—or for a clubhouse if any recruits became available. The alley connected the homes on Pleasant with Clinton and Corwin Avenues and was the path most traveled by wayfaring children. It provided direct access to backyards, which were our true domain, and the location where most activities of any real significance took place. We were still unpacking a few moving boxes when the doorbell chimed, and my mother went to answer.

Standing on the porch was a blond boy who appeared older and was considerably taller than I. As I peered out the French doors in the living room, I recognized the caller's identity immediately. My mother had al-

7

ready spilled a great deal of vital information about him. Soon her voice rang out, announcing that he had come to pay me a visit. I swallowed nervously, but quickly collected myself. Trying to look as formidable as possible, I tightened my muscles and made my way to the front door. Our eyes locked, then he grinned sheepishly and introduced himself. He was Mike Engel—the boy who lived next door.

I reluctantly invited him to come in. Our conversation began slowly and awkwardly, but steadily gained momentum and enthusiasm with each passing minute. We talked about the Cincinnati Reds, who had just won the National League pennant and were his favorite team. And I talked about the Cleveland Indians, who never won anything and were mine. I discovered that he had an older brother named David and a younger sister named Julia. He attended Taylor Elementary, which was on the other side of Pleasant Avenue, instead of Pierce where I would be going, because his mother was a sixth-grade teacher at Pierce.

Just when it seemed that we were getting along famously, a devastating bombshell was dropped—he was nine years old and in the fourth grade. I was certain that this would curse any potential relationship. Fourth-graders only fraternized with second-graders when no one was looking. It happened only in public, when a parent or other adult demanded it, and even then was done grudgingly. But Mike Engel was different. He appeared unfazed by this revelation and wasn't relating to me as if he were older and bigger than I.

Mike took me into his backyard and showed me his rope swing. We explored a pile of flat rocks that were to be used to make a stone path and found a spectacular collection of slugs and roll-em-up bugs underneath. I showed him my hiding place in the lilac bush, and we commiserated about the trials and tribulations of having brothers and sisters. He briefed me on the neighborhood's children and asked me about my old home in New Philadelphia. When he left to eat dinner that evening, I felt as if I had made a good friend.

Over the next few months, I came to know him much better. I grew to admire his discipline and organization. His room was crammed with fascinating goodies but was invariably immaculate. His shirt tail was always tucked in and his shoe laces tied. He was an honor student who scheduled time for his studies—and when he was assigned a chore, it was done promptly and properly. Mike's yard work was impeccable. Mowing was an art form to him, and he raked leaves with the precision of a hair stylist.

When he had put the final touches on a lawn, it actually appeared as if it had been combed.

Unfortunately none of these admirable traits ever rubbed off on me, but I was in awe of his ability to do all these good deeds unapologetically and without appearing prissy about it. Mike was well-liked by his peers, big for his age and imposing enough that his work habits were rarely questioned. He maintained a bright, wide-eyed look and an unrestrained grin on his face—and always appeared as if he was amazed and pleased that God had put him here.

He came to defend me steadfastly and never excluded me, in spite of my being a scrawny eight-year-old. I, in turn, became completely loyal to him. His brother David became a sometime-enemy, not because of who he was or how he treated me, but because he and Mike were often at odds. I avoided his younger sister Julia for years—although she was closer to my age than he—simply because she was his little sister.

As time progressed, we became inseparable and patrolled our neighborhood of Lindenwald daily—on foot and by bicycle. Everyone recognized us, because we were so visually unforgettable. We looked like Mutt and Jeff, Fred and Barney or Wally and the Beaver. Mike and I shared an avid interest in baseball cards and Marvel comics. Both of us loved sports and rooting through piles of useless statistical information. Our bedrooms showcased collections of Matchbox cars, old coins and plastic dinosaurs. And we delighted in penny candies, aquariums and his ever-expanding train set.

But what we shared most was laughter. We devised a complete repertoire of physical and inside word-humor that was hilarious to us and unmitigatingly irritating to our parents. Each of us found the other to be uproariously funny, and we could find the humor in almost all that we observed and experienced. This often provided us collective strength in coping with the inherent pain of growing up. Even if there was turmoil in our homes, we always had our friendship to lean on.

We eventually developed a series of weekly rituals, none more important than those performed during summer daylight hours on Saturdays and Sundays. This was the time that we reserved to run our required errands and make all the rounds that reinforced our commitment as best friends.

Mike arrived at our house late Saturday morning and would immediately inquire what had been served for breakfast. As he well knew, Pillsbury cinnamon rolls were usually the Saturday morning food fare and were also one of his few culinary weaknesses. If any of the pastries remained uneaten, he would graciously clean off the plate, often washing them down with nearly a quart of milk. We would then loll for about an hour, watching cartoons and attempting to irritate one or more of my sisters. But we had a full slate of activities scheduled, and the road beckoned. So we were soon off, mounting our bicycles and pedaling furiously toward Herman's Grocery Store—clutching a list from either or both of our mothers, along with a substantial chunk of our weekly allowance.

Herman's was two blocks away and was a privately owned corner grocery store that was not much larger than our living room. They had an impressive array of candies and treated us with a tolerable amount of respect. We would take care of the mandatory family shopping, then salivate at the cash register, where Herman's wide selection of penny candies was prominently displayed atop the checkout counter. Each of us would purchase one or two packs of baseball cards and spend the remainder of our allotted budget on a painstakingly individualized collection of our preferred confectionery tastes. This would include various assortments of agreed-on favorites such as Caramel Creams, red-hot dollars, Pixy Sticks, Hot Tamales, red licorice and the multi-functional and fruit flavored wax lips.

As soon as we set foot outside Herman's doors, we tore into the baseball cards. Mike had converted me into an avid Reds follower, so it was necessary to immediately uncover the treasures hidden inside the plastic wrappers. Were there any Reds or other favorite players within? A pack that contained two or more Reds would be tantamount to acquiring a winning lottery ticket. Even if the pack was devoid of cards of any perceived value, each would still temporarily carry the fresh scent of bubble gum that distinguished it as a new card. The bubble gum itself was neither fresh nor new and was usually stale enough that it was chewed only if we were desperate for literally anything sweet, and our funds were utterly depleted.

After making a speedy home delivery of requested grocery items, we set off for Avenue Pharmacy, which functioned as our personal mini-department store. In the early years of our childhood, the pharmacy housed a soda fountain where we would spend leisure time twirling on counter stools while sipping phosphates or nibbling hot dogs. Avenue Pharmacy was little more than a block away, and on our regular weekend agenda because it was the nearest dealer of Marvel comic books. Each Saturday we would religiously check for any new issues or purchase comics that we had coveted, but had been unable to afford.

Nearly everything a young boy needed or wanted could be purchased there—including last-minute birthday and Christmas gifts, school supplies, the latest 45 RPM hit singles and a decent selection of inexpensive toys. The owner, who would be our family's landlord in later years, was a casual friend of our parents, and most of his employees knew us by name. Therefore, we were always on our best behavior—because whenever we stopped there, our parents later seemed to know all the particulars of our visit.

Upon completion of our shopping or extended browsing, we would take a short bike ride down Pleasant Avenue to the business district of Lindenwald. If necessary, we would make an expeditious stop at Bartel Pharmacy, but only to search for particular comic books that we had been unable to find. Diversions were usually avoided, because our next required stops were Tom's Tropical Fish and Don's Hobby Shop—our two favorite specialty stores.

Tom's Tropical Fish was a tiny store that carried all sizes, shapes and colors of tropical fish, and a full line of necessary equipment and supplies. This was where Mike conducted all of his aquarium-related business. Although my parents had not allowed me to purchase my own tank, it was nearly as gratifying to help Mike with his. We rarely made a new acquisition immediately—it was much more fun to return for three or four weeks to ogle the exotic species that we desired. Wishing for something that you might someday be able to obtain was often more enjoyable than actually receiving it. If Mike was adopting a new addition to his underwater family, an often flustered employee would wildly swirl the water with a small net while attempting to nab the fugitive fish. The prize catch was then placed in a clear plastic bag filled with lukewarm water for the transport home. The show alone was nearly worth the purchase price.

Don's Hobby Shop was a popular Saturday hangout for children and where we purchased our Matchbox cars. Their long glass counter was filled with a collection of finely crafted Matchbox vehicles and a number of perfectly assembled and painted model cars and planes. No model that I ever purchased even vaguely resembled these works of art. Instead, each usually remained a cardboard box filled with spare parts—but now also included a poorly assembled grill or chassis and a slightly used tube of Testor's glue that had been frustratingly tossed in. The hobby shop was a dream store for young boys—with Aurora race car sets, electric trains, walkie-talkies, chemistry kits and an owner who was as enthusiastic as the children who attended her one-room store. The hobby shop was also where Mike bought accessories for his train set. Most often we searched diligently for landscaping such as grass, trees, buildings, etc. that would make his rail town ever more realistic.

A token stop at Roemer's Hardware store was often in order, primarily because Bertha Betscher—a friendly woman who attended our church—worked there. If we had earned extra money or had birthday or Christmas cash that had been given us, we might stop in at the Linden Lanes for a game or two of bowling, or to the Linden Theater for a Saturday matinee.

We normally rushed home, though, to watch Big Time Wrestling on television. Wrestling was sponsored by Rink's Bargain City, and their commercials featured the local semi-celebrities, The Bargain City Kid and Willie Thall. The Bargain City Kid sported a slick cowboy hat, and Willie Thall bore a striking resemblance to Charlie Weaver. I never did find out how The Kid got his nickname, or what Willie Thall had done to warrant his regional fame—but each week they would belt out their "We're the Kids From Bargain City" theme song, and we were exceedingly amused. We caught an hour of jam-packed, wall-to-wall action as the crazed Sheik gnawed on opponents' faces, the evil Wild Bull Curry foamed at the mouth, or Wild Bull Curry's estranged and heroic son, Flying Fred Curry, felled his current challenger with eight consecutive flying drop kicks. Wrestling was hilarious and intriguing, in a comic-book sort of way.

After watching wrestling, it was time to make our weekend bicycle rounds. We buzzed the houses of a short list of friends, as we methodically zigzagged our way through the streets of the neighborhood. Our ultimate destination was Freeman Hill, the steepest incline in Lindenwald for downhill biking. This modest slope was located in a large subdivision of modern homes where some of our more affluent friends resided. Approximately one block before reaching the Hill one would encounter the largest puddle of standing water within biking range. It rarely dried up completely and seemed like a small pond after a substantial rainstorm.

On an ideal weekend, we would build up a head of steam, fling our legs as high up on our bicycles as possible and coast through the high waters with a fountain spraying on both sides of our wheels. We would then rebuild speed and finally fly down Freeman Hill with the wind blowing in our faces and whistling past our ears. It was an awesome and unforgettable adventure.

After our death-defying trip, we would make a speedy hard right and slowly roll past the homes of Kurt Robinson and Brandon Smith—two schoolmates of mine. Then quite suddenly, my heart would plummet to my stomach as the street dead-ended into Bedford Ave. This was the street where Jill Wolsefer lived.

Jill was the love of my life through nearly all of elementary school, and even a glimpse of her parents' car would make my heart race. She was a blond beauty with gloriously curly hair and dimples that got a regular workout. Jill was a silky smooth tap dancer, the best gymnast in school, and had a smile and laugh that transformed me into a blathering idiot. I was occasionally her boyfriend, but she was always my obsession.

*   *   *

It was mandatory that we pass her house at least twice, although we almost never caught even a glimpse of her. So we would take a repeat run down the hill, this time cautiously inching past the home of Keith Schrader—a teenager who had done something to Mike's brother that we did not approve of. We would bellow out a few choice names—calling him a creep or rat fink—and wait with feet firmly planted on our bike pedals, hoping that he would bolt from his house and chase us down the street. Exactly what this poor fellow had done to Mike's brother has remained a mystery to me, but he suffered dearly for it with semi-regular harassment for nearly two years.

After our mandatory routines had been completed, we would either wind our way home or continue down Freeman Avenue to River Road. On the other side of this busy roadway was Joyce Park, where we might find a baseball game that was commencing. Or we could opt to go it alone, combing the neighborhood, searching for unsuspecting participants to organize our own game. No matter what option was taken, we would always milk the daylight hours. It was a boy's duty to squeeze out the last minutes of dusk. And we usually obliged, either playing whiffle-ball in Mike's backyard or gathering with other roving and restless neighborhood youths for a game of tag—or an elaborate three-lawn contest of hide and seek.

*   *   *

Sunday was a less active day, since Mike and I each attended church, and most businesses still honored the old blue laws and were closed. We would partake of an early dinner and eat together if we could finagle it. After the meal, we would again mount our trusty bicycles and follow Pleasant Avenue in the opposite direction that we had taken the day before.

Located two blocks from home was a Sohio Service Station. Sohio was the state's Standard Oil affiliate and for much of the year ran a license plate jackpot, with winners posted each Sunday at the dealership. Mike and I had taken on the task of visiting the station each week to see if we had become millionaires. After recovering from the routine disappointment of having to wait at least one more week for our fortune, we would check the tire pressure on our two-wheeled vehicles and continue our journey—comfortable in the knowledge that we were now properly inflated. We might stop at the A&P, primarily to loiter, or King Kwik Food Mart for a flavored Icee—but our true objective was to bicycle two or three more blocks and cross the city limits into Fairfield. For some reason, entering Fairfield gave us a feeling of grand accomplishment and made us feel that we had ridden an impressive distance. We would venture only a little further onto this foreign soil, stopping at Twin Fair (the poor man's K-Mart) to see what new records had arrived and to do some additional meandering.

The remainder of the afternoon was usually spent at Joyce Park, involved in some sporting event befitting the number of colleagues we were able to round up. Or we might be found at George Washington Swimming Pool, where we spent countless hours because both the Simers and the Engels had annual family passes. Our day would conclude at home—usually in his living room—as we watched whatever happened to be on television and sipped on ice-cold glasses of his mother's famous home-brewed iced tea.

I often felt then that life could not be better, and the passage of time has proven that my childhood analysis was accurate. The days of our youth were endless. There was so much to see and so many new things to experience. Each day was a series of discoveries, and it seemed our lives transpired in a plastic bubble where no serious harm could come to us. We were in a state of constant anticipation.

*   *   *

Mike Engel remained my close friend throughout my years in Hamilton. He was there to support me when I entered junior high school as a frightened seventh-grader. And he stood by my side when my mother and father divorced, and I moved down the street and finally across town. Mike double-dated with me when I went out with my high school sweetheart for the first time. And he continued to date and eventually married her closest friend. Mike served as a groomsman in my wedding in 1977 and remains a true friend to this day.

There are so many emotions, so many stories and so much loyalty and history uniting us that it is impossible to describe the impact that he has made on my life and my character. All I know is that to this day, when I see his wide-eyed expression and that unrestrained grin takes over his face, it is as if the sun has just burst through the clouds. My world appears new again, and for a while life becomes a little more bearable.

3

The Golden Boy

I had spent only two weeks in the second grade at Pierce School before my teacher, Mrs. Tracy, took me aside to inform me that I would be transferred into Miss Hester's class. She tried valiantly for several minutes to convince me that I would be much happier in this class of more advanced pupils. I was dead set against the idea. It was an emotional setback to be transferred so soon after we had moved to Hamilton. I had just begun to acclimate, and the reassignment meant that I would have to begin the process again. But the decision had already been made, and I silently accepted my sentence.

The next morning, I took the excruciating walk into another classroom of new faces. After Miss Hester formally introduced me to the group and pointed out my desk, I could feel the same cold alienation I had confronted only two weeks earlier. The students who now eyeballed me had to adjust to only one unknown face in their otherwise familiar surroundings. I had to grow accustomed to a whole new world.

Miss Hester was an extraordinary teacher. She had been afflicted with polio, but none of her students saw this as her distinguishing feature. We were certainly aware of the fact that she used crutches, but we saw them as tools she made use of—as one would eyeglasses or a hearing aid. She was slight and pale, but pretty, and could generate a smile that warmed the room. That was the only source of heat that emanated from these four walls, however, as young gapers beamed icy stares through me as if I were a visiting circus freak. And after undergoing this second once-over, I had begun to feel like one.

*　　*　　*

Unfortunately, my approach to gaining approval from my classmates was dangerously naive. My parents told me that if I wanted to be accepted, all I had to do was be myself. Well, "myself" was an inquisitive, earnest

16

and sincere young man. This combination of traits was an ideal recipe—if I wanted to be eaten alive. My experience in Mrs. Tracy's class had taught me to distinguish the big fish from those merely along for the swim. Although I spotted several potential predators lying in wait, it was obvious from day one that Ken Simmons was the most intimidating shark in this ocean.

Ken Simmons was a tough kid. He walked tough, he talked tough, he even cracked his knuckles tough. He was about my height, but much bulkier, and had light brown hair that became blond with increased exposure to sunlight. Ken was the classic adorable rascal, with dark mischievous eyes and frequently bronzed skin.

Just about everything I did seemed to irritate him. I had a sometimes overzealous hunger for knowledge, and was often completely absorbed by my zest for life. Because I had been raised in a household of women, with few male influences, both my knowledge of and exposure to juvenile males was limited. I had yet to be taught the cruel lesson that scholastic enthusiasm was often frowned upon. Even worse, I bore the label of being a preacher's kid—a cursed title that I might just as well have had branded on my forehead.

Ken addressed me simply as "Brain," which was some serious name-calling, considering it was disgraceful to be evaluated as intelligent by your peers. His abhorrence of me was not passive; Ken was on a mission to make my life miserable. He made a habit of publicly ridiculing me and almost single-handedly made my road to acceptance an arduous one. Fighting him seemed out of the question. My father had instructed me in passivity, and even if I defied him and stood up to Ken, I probably wouldn't have been standing for long. So instead I deferred to him and secretly wished that I could be more like him.

Ken lived on Freeman Avenue, in a subdivision of modern homes that I longingly visited on my bicycle. I envied the fact that he had three older brothers and a mother who was heavily involved in PTA and other school functions. He dressed fashionably—sporting button-down collars and Hush Puppies long before they became mundane. And he was, without question, the standout athlete in our class. In other words, Ken Simmons was the indisputable kingpin of the second grade, and the kind of person that I wouldn't want to offend in any way. Unfortunately, he had reached the conclusion that I was rampantly offensive.

That year our non-relationship was limited to verbal confrontations, or more accurately, verbal lashings. I would try to approach him as a friend, and he would crack his whip and return me to my role of submission. The tensions between us had not become physical, but the anguish I suffered was much more continuous and non-healing. And although I made breakthroughs with other students during that school year, my most successful moments with Ken were when he simply ignored me.

During our third-grade school year, our class took part in a school pageant. Ken's mother had sewn a collection of elegant costumes in the style of the American Revolution, to be used for our portion of the pageant program. Ken handpicked the approximately ten participants who would do an intricately choreographed minuet on stage. The boys wore powdered wigs and were even allowed to pencil moles onto their faces. I, of course, remained wigless and mole-free, and instead sang some forgettable patriotic number with others who had been blackballed from this Colonial dance party. Ken bowed properly before gliding about the stage with Jill Wolsefer—clearly the belle of the pageant ball. And I looked on with resentment, as the elementary school aristocracy executed their well-rehearsed and stately steps in three-quarter time.

*   *   *

As I continued to participate in organized sports, I developed into a pretty respectable athlete. Ken and I were both shooting up like weeds, and whatever tests of manhood we engaged in were settled in gym class. The ultimate confrontation was a game called artillery. Utility balls were lined up at the center of the gym, and our class was divided into two teams. When the whistle blew, the teams battled for possession of these balls (the artillery), while remaining on their side of the gym floor. The artillery was then heaved at opposing team members. If a ball struck an opponent, he was ruled out and exiled to the risers until the game was completed. If the opponent caught the ball, the thrower was banished to the benches.

When the game began, third-graders scattered—as the lambs sought refuge in distant corners of the gym, while the wolves made short work of those resigned to seats as early spectators. One would hear an occasional yelp as those in defensive postures were slapped with high-velocity rubber. As the opposing packs of participants dwindled, the timid were herded from the safety of their no-combat zones into the fray of battle, where they sacrificially met their demise. When the floor was nearly cleared, Ken and I usually remained on the front lines, and our showdown was brief, but gritty. The mano y mano would generally end with one of us palming a ball and hurling it at the other with all the strength that he could muster. If the ball was caught, the thrower would wince and take the long walk from the floor. But if the ball connected and ricocheted to the ground, the victor would glare at his fallen victim and retain bragging rights until the next encounter. The tensions between us were forever worsening.

By the beginning of the fourth grade, we had both matured enough that a fight seemed an inevitability. Hamilton had toughened me up, and I now had my own collection of friends. I had resigned myself to the fact that Ken Simmons was never going to accept me.

Whatever civility existed between us was decimated when Jill Wolsefer, now the dimpled darling of Miss Banker's class, added me to her long list of suitors. Ken and she were usually an item, so he angrily issued a challenge to fight me. My father's demands of pacifism had provided me nothing but headaches and relentless harassment. No longer able to live with his mandate, I went home one evening and discussed my dilemma with my mother. Her remedy was not what I had expected. She contacted school officials without first consulting me.

The next day, Ken and I were asked to report to the principal's office. Mr. Matthews was a tall, imposing, bespectacled gentleman of Southern roots. When he was smiling, he seemed to be a proper and genteel grandfather—but when angered, his face tightened, and only his formidable jowls remained void of tension. On this morning, he was definitely not smiling.

We walked into his office as if we were approaching the gallows, and his angry glare convinced us that he would have gladly slipped the nooses around our necks. His speech to us was short and to the point. He would not tolerate fighting on school grounds, and if we decided to disobey him, we would be paddled for our defiance. We were both well aware of the legendary tales of Mr. Matthews' mighty assaults on mischief-makers' rumps, so a schoolyard face-off was out of the question. He would, however, allow a boxing match to be held after school that would be refereed by Mr. Van Ness, our gym teacher.

Ken and I looked at each other in disbelief. This after-school encounter would only be witnessed by Mr. Van Ness. No one else could be present. The intimidation of losing and the exhilaration of winning would thus be almost entirely removed. We would only be fighting for the joy of beating each other around the gymnasium. Although we both made a feeble attempt at machismo by declaring that we were not afraid to participate, we eventually concurred that we would decline the opportunity. For some reason, this meeting and the fact that we had faced a shared dilemma had created a temporary and tenuous bond. We shook hands and carried our truce with us into the classroom.

Ever so slowly, Ken began to exhibit behavior toward me that could not be interpreted as loathing. Mr. Matthews' open invitation to us to engage in a supervised battle had eliminated all the rhetorical traps and egging-on that might have cornered us into a spontaneous clash. Suddenly when we lined up and counted-off in gym class for a game of artillery, we no longer strategically positioned ourselves so we would be on opposing teams. His friends, sensing the unspoken truce, became more congenial, and the chasm between us seemed to narrow. We began to speak without baring our teeth—then actually started talking and enjoying our conversations.

Once this pleasant breeze broke the years of animosity, it seemed to swirl and then quickly accelerate into a virtual whirlwind that one day shockingly found us walking home from school together. It seemed almost too good to be true, but Ken had requested that I accompany him. And although we lived in nearly opposite directions—I enthusiastically accepted. As a child, it seemed so easy to forgive and forget. After all, it was an honor to call Ken Simmons a friend.

*   *   *

By the time we entered the fifth grade we had a comfortable relationship. Ken and I were never best buddies, but were always on good terms. Not even Jill Wolsefer could come between us. She alternated boyfriends regularly, and we grew to accept that we were competing with a wide circle of admirers—and the honor would eventually return to each of us.

I still occasionally walked home with him, and we would speak on a broad range of topics. Ken was intelligent and surprisingly self-aware. He was tough because he had to be—it was not easy being the youngest of four boys. His brothers had unknowingly schooled him in the art of intimidation, and he had learned his lessons well. Although on the surface, our personalities appeared to be nearly diametric—there was more commonality than either of us had realized. As we came to trust each other, we frequently let down our guards and tested our newfound friendship. We usually dropped by his favorite candy stop, a tiny one-room grocery store on Freeman Avenue, where we would purchase a handful of red-hot dollars. We would then tread slowly until we reached St. Clair Avenue, where we parted company. I would then inconspicuously scoot back to Pleasant Avenue and return in the same direction that I had come. It was a lengthy but gratifying detour.

We began eating lunch together and would collectively consume up to six peanut butter sandwiches—although his were always on brand-name bread. His mother also scraped the excess peanut butter from the knife onto the inside edge of his sandwich halves. It was a subtle but creative touch that truly impressed me. His friends became my friends and vice versa. I would have spent time with him simply because of his elevated stature among our peers, but I found I really liked him anyway.

*　　*　　*

As we entered sixth-grade, it finally became our turn to rule Pierce Elementary. The inmates were now in charge as we were placed on the safety patrol and paraded around school wearing our ceremonial belts and safety badges. All the events and activities reserved for those who reached the top of the grade school totem pole were ours to enjoy and gloat about.

In the early spring of the year, Ken asked me to team up with him for a talent show that our French class was presenting. I was, of course, thrilled to be asked and came up with the inspiration of drafting two of our friends to form a pretended rock group that we called the Frenchies. We grew thin mascara moustaches and wore Girl Scout berets, as I crooned the Beatles, "Do You Want to Know a Secret?" or more appropriately, "*Voulez-vous Savoir un Secret?*" My "amis" sang or shouted background vocals while strumming cardboard cutouts of electric guitars. We were a smash, primarily because we performed our number with such romantic flair—while appearing so laughable. I was convinced of our suave coolness and envisioned a Ricky Nelson-like personal appearance at an upcoming birthday party, where Jill Wolsefer would squeal when she heard the sound of my sultry voice and French interpretations.

The remainder of the school year seemed like a downhill coast to George Washington Junior High. There were numerous skating parties, a big sixth-grade field trip to LeSourdsville Lake Amusement Park and a couple's outing to the Putt-Putt Miniature Golf Course—when Ken again won out and took Jill Wolsefer. We remained respectful friends and survived the remainder of our public schooling without having a rift of any kind.

*　　*　　*

There are fewer stories to be told about our junior high and high school days together. Ken and I were rarely in the same classes, and our interests took us in different directions. Because our last names were so close alphabetically, we were usually seated next to each other in homeroom and used the time to renew our friendship and discuss each other's extracurricular activities. Ken was always popular in school. He was an outstanding football player and an excellent student, and the process of puberty never put a dent in his good looks. He still struck fear in the hearts of those who crossed him and always had an adoring throng of females from which to select his current girlfriend.

The boxing match we had both earlier managed to sidestep finally occurred in the ninth-grade when we were forced to spar against one another in Mr. Vilkoski's gym class. I was elated that I more than held my own, and although I masked my enthusiasm, it did wonders for my masculine self-image. Ken was appropriately congratulatory, and it made us feel a little more bound by history, with the memories of our elementary school feuds still fresh in our minds.

I was always aware that Ken Simmons was destined for center stage. He never demanded it, but the spotlight seemed to shift to wherever he was standing. The spring science fair was a major annual event that heralded the end of a ninth-grader's junior high career. Each student was to conduct a science project and assemble an exhibit to be displayed in the school gymnasium. The gym was teeming with junior scientists for the evening show and an afternoon-long tour by younger students. I had spent weeks toiling on a series of experiments displaying the many properties of sound. The centerpiece of my exhibit was eight Pepsi bottles, each filled with an increasing amount of water. I spent hours blowing into the bottles in succession so that they would play a simple scale. This crowd-pleaser drew a steady stream of curious spectators to my booth, and I demonstrated the phenomenon until I became lightheaded, and the exhibits around me began to spin.

My project was highly regarded, but again Ken had outdone me. He had teamed with three neighbors and had constructed a simulated space capsule in one of the participants' basements. They conducted a weekend mission, locking themselves in the capsule with rations and closely following a detailed and regimented agenda. The creativity of the experiment caught the eye of the Hamilton *Journal-News*, and we read several days of updates on the cellarnauts' exploits. Naturally, they won the competition and the adoration of adults and children alike. It was vintage Ken Simmons—everything seemed to come easily for him.

*   *   *

Ken went on to become the captain of our high school football team and a class officer. We continued to touch base in homeroom, but because we were not in courses together, and our after-school pursuits were different—we rarely ran into each other. He was always supportive about my activities in choir and theater, and I was admiring of his continued athletic prowess. On the final day of school, I remember thinking that he was an individual who had been a part of my life for over ten years. We had grown up together, and as of graduation day our relationship would probably be abruptly terminated. He would go his way, and I would go mine. Time would prove me right.

Ken and I completely lost contact with each other—our paths did not cross on the street or in social situations. As happens with so many high school associations, it became a case of "Whatever happened to . . . ?" I rarely received answers to my queries. We finally saw each other very briefly at our ten-year high school reunion and exchanged pleasantries. I wanted to talk to him longer, but someone aggressively pulled me aside, and by the time I could escape, he was nowhere to be seen.

*   *   *

In the spring of 1990, my mother sent me a newspaper clipping that told of Ken's death in an automobile crash. He was to participate in a Tough Man Competition outside Ross, a neighboring community, and was involved in a head-on collision. I was shocked and could not get him out of my mind.

I have experienced the death of many people much closer to me than Ken Simmons. But a profound sadness consumes me when I realize that this person who lives so powerfully in my memories no longer walks this earth. I can see now that he was and still is important to me—that we almost inadvertently helped to shape each other's personalities, and his death places a finiteness on my own existence.

Ken was never a bosom buddy. Our association was not particularly complex or remarkable, yet I find its effects intense and life-spanning. It was the first friendship that I ever really worked at—and there is obvious significance in the fact that we managed to come to terms rather than

23

blows. But the magnitude of this lesson runs far deeper. Our compromise offered benefits that neither of us had anticipated—it brought understanding on a much deeper level. Ken and I discovered more than civility on our middle ground. We found that although we had often taken seats on opposite ends of the fence—our reasons for hunkering down made much more sense than we had originally realized. Our differing backgrounds had given us each something that the other wanted and had not yet found. Simply put, I had been the "Brain" and he the brawn. Our relationship brought the two together—in both of us.

Although the paths of our lives ceased to follow parallel directions years ago, I grieve for those who were still traveling with him when he left this world. But to the extent that he touched any of us, our lives reflect his influence. His departure affects only where he will sow his future seeds. The impact he made on those he met is already deeply rooted and flourishing. Over this life, death has no power.

4

T.W. & Annabel

My last name is pronounced sigh-mir, like timer with an "S." The name seems uncomplicated, yet it never ceases to amaze me how many people bungle its pronunciation, and how violated I feel each time the dreaded dagger named Simmer is confidently and matter-of-factly drawn from someone's lips. Granted, the mistake is unintentional, but the speaker, who obviously pretends familiarization, manages in just two syllables to destroy his deception and instead displays that he clearly knows nothing about me.

The name's simplicity lures people into attempting its challenge without consultation or verification, and the thoughtful few who logically and correctly decipher its great mystery are immediately elevated in stature. After all, the word "Simer" is music to my clan's ears and is a precious word that is rarely uttered anywhere in North America. Simers are as rare as they are unusual, and if you ever meet one you'll probably consider yourself either fortunate or snake-bitten—or perhaps both.

The name is of German derivation, and the only Simers that I have ever met were traceable kin. I have heard of other Simers and have even seen the name in print, but these alleged individuals remain unsubstantiated and uninvestigated rumors, my passive recognition allowing me to envision them as uncommonly captivating characters. My known relatives fit this description to a tee, providing a deluxe assortment of personalities and peculiarities—a collection of colorful stray pieces that don't seem to fit this world's puzzle.

*　　*　　*

My earliest memories of Simer influence are of my grandparents, Thamer Waldo and Annabel Simer. My grandfather, like my father, was a minister in the Christian Church/Disciples of Christ denomination. He

25

seemed a man not of this planet—a dreamer who spent much of his life with his head not in the clouds, but instead in a universe well beyond them.

Thamer Waldo Simer was orphaned at an early age. In young adulthood, he became an undefeated featherweight boxer before a life-threatening bout with pneumonia precipitated a spiritual revelation which led him into the ministry. My grandfather was a muscular man of average size, with eyes that appeared fixed on something that I could not see. His lips were slight and delicate, yet doggedly determined. His nose was a piece of work created by laced-gloved artisans, who had made drastic adjustments with total disdain for subtleties. He had a surprisingly smooth and gracefully chiseled face; his white-grey hair wavy, but receding—a natural process of aging that he would not tolerate. His vanity demanded that he grow what hair he had to great lengths and then comb it forward to disguise nature's indiscretion. It was then doused with hair spray so it remained brittlely in place, except in a great gust of wind when it would flip up like a giant cranial lid before resetting atop his barren expanses. Later in life, he would wear hair nets at outdoor events, thus maintaining his "do," but forfeiting a degree of his savoir-faire.

*   *   *

My grandfather was an uncommon man. He was a lifelong civil-rights advocate and the pastor of the first organized racially integrated Disciples church in the state of Illinois. He marched with Dr. Martin Luther King, Jr. in Alabama, and stood tall against the powerful racial bigotry of his day.

But this was not the grandfather I saw through my youthful eyes. I saw a man whose speech was often poetry, as his Southern Illinois dialect danced delicately through carefully crafted words and sentences that were captivating to listen to. I watched a spry clown, who could walk on his hands when I urged him to, creeping up and down the sidewalk like some mutant human insect and delighting both family and friends. My grandfather was a living contradiction—easy to like and impossible to get close to, prone to both pensive quietude and lengthy pontification.

He could steal center stage at public gatherings by deftly performing his renowned jig or flaunting his resounding tenor singing voice. Or he could withdraw to the degree that his body no longer seemed to hold him. The only time he seemed truly in tune with his surroundings was in his beloved Canada. He returned to the province of Ontario at least once a year, where he would fish for muskie, northern pike and walleye, and behave like a dog that had been lost, but had rediscovered his home. His friends called him T.W. or strangely enough "Bill," a nickname that seemed as irrational as his curious marriage to my grandmother.

Annabel Simer was a pixie of a woman, with densely thick auburn hair and eyes that breathed a life of their own. During the years that I shared with her, her face was heavily lined—bearing the remnants of countless smiles and a neverending pluck. Her deep exaggerated furrows betrayed years of ponderous thought and personal struggle—and a sometimes almost cold resolve. The gentle creases that emanated from her purposeful lips seemed to soften them like petals on a flower.

She, like my father, suffered from a curvature of the spine, which left her almost magnetically diminutive. Grandma Simer was able to delicately enter and touch people's lives—partially because she appeared so non-threatening. Her involvement in her church and community was a full-time endeavor. She offered her time and services to those in need, and kept track of the goings-on of any number of families who considered her a precious friend.

Her mind was brimming with quotes and family history, birthdays and anniversaries, great thoughts and an endless collection of seemingly meaningless data. Letters from her had their margins filled with postscripts, arrows, afterthoughts and smiley faces. Any unused area of a sheet of paper became her scratch pad, and some of her finest writing can still be found jotted on ancient mimeographed church bulletins or postmarked envelopes and on the periphery of the pages of a well-read magazine. There was little about her that resembled a traditionally idealized grandmother. Her cooking was barely average and done only reluctantly. Her house was cluttered with stacks of books and magazines. Although passably clean, it always appeared as if it were considered only temporary headquarters.

Annabel Simer was an independent and strong-willed woman. Although they remained married and never separated, T.W. and Annabel seemed only to tolerate each other. Their mutual passion had dissolved by the time I entered the family photo album, and all that remained was grudging respect for each other and the institution of marriage. Grandma Simer diligently carried out her agenda and went about her own ministry. She worked steadfastly to keep our extended family close and served as the hub of updated information and the glue that kept us feeling a part of each other.

As a child, I recognized her tenaciousness and was sometimes intimidated by her fire. She spoke to me person-to-person, asked direct questions and stored away the answers to be recalled months and even years later. I loved her cackling laugh and bird-like mannerisms. And I adored the large glass jar that she kept filled with marbles, coins, trinkets and memorabilia. I respected and loved her, but only came to truly appreciate her as I reached adulthood. At the end, she was the grandparent that I felt closest to.

*   *   *

My first powerful recollection of a day spent with them takes me back to a small farm in Sherburnville, Illinois—a tiny community on the northern Illinois and Indiana border. It was a sweltering sun-dried Saturday afternoon during the summer of 1962, and for lack of anything better to do, my sisters and I were waging battle over control of a single hammock. The conflict had begun amid a collection of unmatched lawn furniture on a vast lawn surrounding my grandparents' small rented farmhouse. Grandma had poured each of us an icy, cherry Kool-Aid served in a tall, brightly colored aluminum tumbler that quickly collected chilly condensation in the high humidity. Just clutching the wet frigid metal provided psychological relief from the heat, and I imagined that the drink was a powerful elixir that would provide me additional strength to catapult anyone who dared recline upon my green canvas throne.

My grandfather was playing with Pepper—an ebony-black, medium-sized dog that was as much a beagle as anything else. Pepper was pantingly adoring of his master and properly polite to the remainder of the human population. Grandpa was dapper as usual, wearing a dark pair of crisply pressed pants and a black long-sleeved shirt with the sleeves neatly folded back to the elbow. Style superseded comfort, as my grandfather prided himself on his extensive immaculately maintained wardrobe. My grandmother leaned back on her lawn chair, magazine in hand, dressed in a comfortable print smock. She tried to concentrate on her reading, but was frequently interrupted to chide us for our incessant bickering.

*   *   *

My mother and father had left midmorning with Bob Bahr, who was a long-standing pal of my dad's and lived in a nearby community. The afternoon was ours to explore the property's boundaries, but the punishing heat had left us cranky and sapped our desire for any civil social recreation.

I had thoroughly explored the grounds earlier, while carefully avoiding the chicken coop and a particular hen that seemed to have a personal vendetta against me. Whenever we crossed paths, she would speed-strut in hot pursuit of me, squawking and flapping her wings until I sought refuge in the house. I had never knowingly done anything to warrant this assault, and I wonder to this day what sort of bizarre altercation would have resulted if she had ever caught up with me. But for the time being, I was feeling far too lethargic to dodge a vindictive chicken, so instead I draped myself across the entire hammock and scowled at my sisters, suspicious that they were plotting to unseat me. I was simply starving for a break in the tedium of this seemingly endless afternoon.

*   *   *

My grandparents did not actually farm the land that they lived on. The house had been rented for them as a parsonage, while my grandfather was pastoring at the Sherburnville Christian Church and at the newly founded and integrated church in Markham. The killer chicken and the remainder of the more passive poultry were theirs, but the accompanying land was tended and harvested by others. We usually spent a week there each summer, occasionally sightseeing in nearby Chicago and experiencing the relaxation and occasional dreariness of rural living. There were no boys my age anywhere nearby, and the only female who was a potential playmate was a neighbor whose family attended Sherburnville Church. Beth Fowler was a year or more older than I, and our tenuous relationship had ended as far as I was concerned. We had tangled during prior summers, and she had trounced me on more than one occasion. I was weary of the thorough embarrassment and wary of additional headaches, for it seemed that my noggin inevitably collided with the unforgiving turf whenever she mightily hurled me to the ground. As hard as it is for me to admit it, she had regularly beaten the stink out of me. For several years I had plotted my revenge, but by the time I had bulked up and stretched out enough that I could take her, male-female grappling had taken on a whole new meaning. I was the reigning king of the hammock on this Saturday, though, and I assured myself that Beth would want no part of me when I was this rankled. I'd had my belly full of women in general and sisters in particular.

I knew that we would spend most of the next day in church-related activities, and there would be little time for recreation. Sherburnville Church was a picture postcard—a small historical one-room wooden church, with a tall narrow steeple bell tower. It was a piece of Americana, an alabaster

29

man-made gem that glistened against the green and blue horizon. Located on a lightly traveled paved country road, the scene was pacific and spiritual, and when standing alone outside the building, hushed breezes felt like brushes with the spirit.

But the activities that would occur beyond the tall green double doors that led into the sanctuary were what made me dread the next day. There would be a circle of unfamiliar faces in Sunday school—and Dutch head rubs, bear hugs and sloppy kisses from overly sentimental and heavily perfumed ladies. I would hear endless stories about myself as a baby, and countless conversations which began, "You probably don't remember me, but . . ." Most of the time I didn't. Sunday morning and early afternoon would be a young boy's social nightmare, and as I thought about it—it made me even more anxious and edgy. The afternoon was almost over. The time was ripe for something wonderful to happen.

*　　*　　*

Just when I felt like I was going to drown in the stagnation of monotony and oppressive heat, Bob Bahr's car pulled up to the farmhouse. My parents exited the back seat, while Bob and his wife Eleanor swung open the front doors and crawled out lugging several red-and-white cardboard boxes. They had come bearing a snack called caramel corn—a sensational and still warm treat that they had purchased at a small shop dealing exclusively in this recent food fancy. I had never had caramel corn, and the sweet sugary smell of the butter-based coating enticed me immediately. But before digging into the delectable goodies, I ran over to offer obligatory thanks to our guests.

Bob Bahr was a generous man who genuinely liked children. He had a broad face with a prominent nose, friendly cheeks and an eternal crew cut that never seemed to vary in length. His wife was a shy, thin, silky-skinned woman with large dark glasses that took over her face. She was considerably younger than Bob and unusually silent for an adult.

I was as polite as a ravenous young boy could be, but eventually I drifted over to the folding table and began gorging myself with what I considered to be a taste of heaven. The conversation picked up, and laughter and animation soon replaced the stifling silence. Many playful verbal darts whizzed over my head, and soon a reference was made to my regulation-size rubber ball and pint-sized bat that lay next to a nearby tree.

Almost instantaneously, the three men formed a triangle and began

30

lobbing the ball back and forth as I looked on—anxiously waiting to be invited to join in. Granddad must have seen my puppy-dog eyes and motioned me over, before tossing the ball softly in my direction. To my everlasting pride, I caught it easily and winged it to my dad.

Our game of pitch gradually evolved until a miniature pine tree was officially designated as "first," and we searched for three more makeshift bases. A game of two against two followed, and I watched in amazement as my grandfather sprinted from base to base, made effortless and deft defensive plays and swung the bat like a natural. My father was a much better athlete than he realized and was taking the good-natured competition quite seriously. I found myself enthralled with watching these men in my life play baseball—a game I was growing to love. For one of the first times in my life, I felt like a man, and could almost sense myself maturing as I stood in the blazing sunshine. It was much too hot to play baseball, and only blockheads would voluntarily exert such energy in this oppressive heat. But what happened transcended logic. For some unknown reason, this game among generations seemed exactly right.

*   *   *

Decades have passed since we chased after that silly rubber ball and dashed around the lawn at my grandparents' home in Sherburnville. And during that time, I have only grown prouder of the fact that my name is Simer. Passing time and circumstances have brought the Simer family closer together, and as the years race past us, the age discrepancy between myself and my aunts and uncles becomes far less significant.

My father has three sisters, and I have grown to appreciate each of them as the intriguing people that they are. His sisters, like my own, are each charged with incredible talent and colored with their own distinctive shade of Simer lunacy. They are beautiful women, not only because they are attractive to look at and exude charm, but because they are burdened with excruciating sensitivity and have a basic and highly uncommon sense of personal morality.

And as the Simer tree branches out, it becomes no less interesting. Spouses, cousins, nieces and nephews are people whom I am proud to call my family. Simer reunions are taxing, not because of the lack of bounty, but because of an overabundance of it. It is mental overkill. I'm often initially overwhelmed by relatives' razor-sharp minds before I've had an opportunity to dust off my own brain and jump-start it.

31

*   *   *

My grandmother passed away of liver failure in 1982. And my grandfather, whose mind was failing him, unexplainably committed suicide in 1989. The incident sent shock waves through our collective souls. It was a seemingly senseless act from a sworn pacifist who had sent no distress signals that had been received. But experience has taught me that much of life appears irrational, and the picture will become clearer when I am prepared to see it. For now, our family can only draw closer, and allow the memories of those who have left us to remain vital in our minds.

My grandparents are buried together in a small cemetery adjacent to the Sherburnville Christian Church, with their names and life dates carved into the marker. The inscription reads, "Ministers of Christ." When I have stood alone by that marker and felt the gentle breeze caress my face, I have sometimes felt a force more powerful than a simple brush with the spirit. If I listen closely, I can hear the angels sing.

32

5

Downtown

Easter was fast approaching, and my mother had reluctantly agreed that it was time to buy each of us the new outfits we would be wearing on Easter Sunday. Since my father showed disdain for family shopping, it was decided that he would drop us off downtown and return after he had completed some work at the church. It was rare for all of us to spend time together browsing High Street. So I looked forward to the visit—in spite of the embarrassment I might endure if I were seen publicly with four female family members.

In 1963, downtown Hamilton stretched out over only a few municipal blocks, but gave the city some of its great visual character. Our town's centerpiece was a proud old courthouse, complete with a tall clock tower. The clock's wide four-sided face was encircled with Roman numerals and had hefty black hands that seemed too massive to set. The enormous illuminated timepiece was a low-riding second moon after sunset and cast a serene light on the quiet city streets. Butler County's courthouse occupied an entire block, and because the building and lawn were slightly elevated, there was a chair height ledge that met the sidewalk. Retirees donning gentlemen's hats would take a load off here—chatting with friends and watching nine-to-five traffic whisk by.

Due west on High Street toward the river was the Soldiers, Sailors and Pioneers Monument, where a gun-toting statue of an infantryman held vigilance on the roof. It was a striking edifice, but one that Hamiltonians rarely entered. I had never knowingly seen a tourist in town, so one would not encounter a crowd of people clamoring to get in. A bit west of the monument was the Miami River and the Main Street Bridge. The river was slow-moving and its level usually down, so the bridge served more to traverse the ravine than to protect those crossing from deep and dangerous waters.

Across High Street on the first block west of the courthouse was the

33

aptly named Court Theater, the premier first-run movie house in town. This was the hot spot where all major film events took place. On a Saturday afternoon, it was not unusual to see a line of children a block long waiting to see the latest Walt Disney offering. Their refreshment counter was second to none, with all the finest chocolate bars and boxed sweets attractively displayed in an immaculately clean glass case. Candy stored in this transparent treasure chest tasted even more delectable and provided satisfaction similar to the adult delight of purchasing a fine watch from a locked jeweler's case.

Due east of the courthouse was the eight-story Rentschler Building, the tallest structure in Hamilton. As a younger child I had inaccurately but proudly proclaimed it to be one of the largest buildings in the state. It housed several doctors' and lawyers' offices and a music store on the ground level, where shiny brass and woodwind instruments were showcased in broad picture windows.

The main shopping district was primarily east of the courthouse and included such established stores as Penney's, Grant's and Kresge's, which came to represent American small-town shopping in the 1960s. Hamilton was a blue-collar town, so pedestrians were dressed in casual and functional attire. People were there to accomplish a task or shop with friends, rather than to be seen or make acquaintances. Passersby looked you in the eye, and invariably you would run into someone you knew or recognized, giving a true community feeling to the bustling streets. Townspeople did not visit downtown Hamilton—it was considered home turf.

A substantial percentage of Hamiltonians had migrated from the Bluegrass State and other southern climes, prompting the locals to jokingly call the town "Hamiltucky." This contingent gave the city a strong and lovable southern grace, as well as a rough and crude "hills of Kentucky" edge. The rural mountain mentality had a subtle to powerful impact on all the neighborhoods of Hamilton. Raw emotion often motivated actions, which was both intimidating and oddly appealing.

The general effect on the town was to give it a no-nonsense attitude. The people lived hard and played hard—maintaining a dogged pride in their straightforwardness. People were fiercely loyal and generally honorable, and as a child I felt protected by their unpretentious simplicity. They became and remained a part of my character and influenced what I have sought in people throughout my adult life.

On that day, as always, my sisters outnumbered me, so we began our wardrobe search at The Lerner Shop—a women's clothing store near Penney's and Grant's. I accompanied my family inside the store, but spent most of our visit anchored by the front door, trying to salvage my masculinity by appearing uninterested. It seemed that we remained there for hours as my sisters tried on various outfits. They posed and pivoted, while my mother pulled on hemlines and carefully examined fabrics and price tags. All eyes were fixed on the world inside the mirror, as they scrutinized their images and complained about the fit or some deficiency in their physique. My youngest sister Laurie—still too young to have transformed into a shopping she-monster—looked calmly on. She was probably absorbing nasty habits like a sponge—storing shopping protocol for use and abuse at a future date.

Slipping away, I discovered a half-hexagon of full-length mirrors on the wall near a dressing room. When no one was looking, I ambled over to them—contorting my facial expressions and self-consciously evaluating my head and body from all angles. I felt fortunate that some perspectives could normally be seen only through another person's eyes.

Finally the Simer brood was ready to move on, and I was relieved to see that Laurie and Becky had made their Easter selections. My mother toted two shopping bags, and both sisters wore the confident smiles of satisfied customers.

J.C. Penney's was our next stop, where we briefly looked for my Easter apparel. We found an acceptable pair of charcoal-grey Levi trousers, but came up empty on a shirt smart enough to be worn on such an important holiday occasion. However, after noticing that Emily was still flipping through clothing racks, I decided to take refuge in another part of the store.

Penney's had a basement level, where most of its non-clothing items were displayed. I went into hiding, wandering through an electronics department filled with wood-cabinet console televisions, and imagining that I would someday have a color TV set of my own. I fantasized about languishing in my living room and admiring the NBC peacock in the glory of living color. A salesclerk eyed me suspiciously, realizing my presence in his department without an accompanying adult offered him nothing but a nuisance. Realizing that I was moments away from a snipped, "May I help you?" intended to drive me away, I voluntarily took my dreams elsewhere.

The tool department was convenient and appropriately masculine, so I began to examine various hammers and saws. This was a curious habit that I had developed, considering I had no knowledge about either item. The craftsmanship was impressive, though, and I hand-inspected a few as if testing their durability. I was gripping a claw hammer which had a lifetime guarantee, when my sister Becky bounced toward me and gleefully reported that my mother wanted me upstairs immediately. It was time to go. Becky was thrilled to perform this duty, since it gave her the opportunity to indirectly order me to do something. I rolled my eyes and moved at a snail's pace toward the stairs—providing her as little satisfaction as possible.

Emily left the store empty-handed, so my mother warned that Wilmer's would be our final destination. Wilmer's was the finest and most complete department store in Hamilton and was located across High Street and a block east of the courthouse. As we left Penney's, I heard the clanks and squeals of a moving freight train and could see it rumbling along the tracks near our church. I caught sight of the intricate neon advertisement atop the First National Bank Building, which now flashed with a green background. This was a color-code indication that fair weather was in the offing. Laurie, not yet three, had now become restless and cantankerous. She sometimes refused to walk and was consistently whining unless her attention could be diverted. I was amazed that so much stubbornness could be contained in so small a body.

It was mid-afternoon, and we were all hungry, but knew that we would have to wait until we got home to eat. We passed the Brown Bar Restaurant, where a heavily male clientele lined up on fountain stools and huddled in cramped booths, while streams of cigarette smoke snaked toward the ceiling. When we passed Kresge's, my suggestion of snacking at their soda fountain fell on predictably deaf ears. I found that my hunger pangs even kept me from pleading to spend time browsing at both Kresge's and McCrory's, two of my favorite stops for useless products that were within my limited budget. It was pleasing to see countless items that I did not need, yet knew I could afford.

I then endured the pure agony of walking past the entrance of The Country Kitchen, because the distinct odor of grilled hamburgers and fried crinkle-cut potatoes permeated the air. The Country Kitchen was nearly always busy and was the most popular eatery in downtown Hamilton. Its prominent sign dominated the corner at Third and High. On it was a cartoon depiction of a reposed country boy, dressed in stereotypical straw hat, checkered shirt and bib overalls. This freckled hayseed looked like a cross between Howdy Doody and Alfred E. Newman. The sign heralded the restaurant as the home of the world-famous Country Boy double-deck hamburger. It never ceased to amaze me that there was such global interest in the foods of Hamilton.

We finally arrived at Wilmer's and separated to save time—with Emily escorting Becky and Laurie, and my mother accompanying me. When we reached the boys' wear department, it was only a matter of minutes before my eyes fixed and then locked on a rainbow plaid short-sleeved shirt with a button-down collar. As if it were a sign from above, this technicolor dreamshirt was also in my size. It was the most beautiful piece of clothing that I had seen in my entire life, and I knew immediately that I wanted it. I began imagining my heartthrob, Jill Wolsefer, staring at me in adoration—awestruck by my impeccable taste in fashion. The shirt had been made for me, and I had to have it.

It turned out to be an easy sell. My mother must have seen my face light up, and was probably overjoyed that I hadn't become attached to some hideous garment that she had to talk me out of. We made the purchase, and as we went back to find Emily, I kept a tight grip on the bag that contained my key to Jill's heart. I then remained with the rest of the family as Emily painfully eliminated three dresses and finally settled on her selection for the gala Easter Sunday service. I heard rhythmic intermittent chimes echo throughout the store, sending mysterious messages to employees and a subliminal message to my brain to record the moment. I would not forget this event or day—for some reason my mind wanted to remember. Fifteen minutes later my father picked us up outside the store, and we headed home. The Simer children recalled the trip and our purchases in rambling quadrophonics. It had been a full afternoon.

Often there is no rhyme nor reason to what we remember and what we forget. Perhaps I recall this early spring day because my mother, sisters and I ventured out together as a family unit. Or perhaps it is because Hamilton was so alive and vibrant, and I simply delighted in it being my hometown. But I think that it's more likely that I recall this snippet of my history for the same reason that I so distinctly remember the rainbow plaid shirt that I purchased that day. Memories become a part of our very identity: a defining of our character and our experiences. We wear these memories with pride, shame or indifference, and they help to mold the image that we present to others. We wear them because we like the way they look or feel, or because we have nothing else to wear—but most importantly we wear them because they fit us.

And if the fondness of my recollections is any indication, it was as if I received two rainbow plaid shirts on that extraordinary day. The one I took home in a shopping bag was first worn at an Easter Sunday service at High Street Christian Church in 1963. The other, I've never outgrown. Every time I slip it on, it hangs on me just right—with plenty of room to breathe.

6

Hoop Dream

My brief but illustrious basketball career began at the Hamilton Central YMCA when I was almost nine years old. High Street Christian Church fielded a junior league team, and since my father was the pastor, I felt obligated to participate in this church-sponsored activity. The only glaring obstacle to my becoming a member of this squad of elementary school cagers was that I knew absolutely nothing about the game of basketball. My father, though somewhat of a sports fan, had never taught me the game, and I had somehow managed to avoid the embarrassment of any gym class instruction or playground pickup games. But my arm was now being twisted, and I knew it was time to cry, "Uncle!"

I walked into the YMCA on the day of my first game, bewildered and fidgety. I had never seen a facility quite like this one. It was located in the core of downtown Hamilton and was frequented mostly by kids whom I had never laid eyes on before. As I entered the youth department, there were two large rooms jammed with boys of various ethnic backgrounds, engaged in games of pool, bumper pool and Ping-Pong. It was one-on-one, full-scale confrontation.

Through the doors by the service desk was a short hallway, which led past a set of long observation windows that had been built into one side wall. The windows overlooked an indoor swimming pool situated one story below. There was always a tepid-steambath feel to the hallway, with a strange odor that combined perspiration and chlorine. If the window curtains were drawn, it usually meant that someone was swimming "au naturel," a discovery that would have been much more intriguing had this been a unisex pool. When the drapes were open, we would press our noses against the pane-glass and investigate the activity, enjoying the fact that the swimmers were generally oblivious to us.

The hallway led to a gymnasium where the game preceding ours was already in progress. I sat down on a row of wooden risers with two of my new teammates and studied the game, hoping to pick up some tips that might later help me save face. The approximately fifteen minutes that I had available to conduct my research project helped me to draw the following three conclusions:

1. The object was to put the ball into the basket.
2. You could bounce the ball or pass the ball, but you could not run with the ball.
3. I still had no idea how to play the game of basketball.

I gained a little encouragement from watching an Asian boy who had developed a nasty habit of kicking the ball downcourt to his teammates. But I couldn't stop thinking that if this was, indeed, a church-related function, God should intervene by making certain that I didn't get into this game. Basketball was far too confusing to absorb in one day. The competition seemed to be continually halted by mysterious infractions, and the players' concentration was regularly disturbed by the obtrusive sounds of loud whistles and buzzers. I did not need this aggravation.

I was becoming flustered and felt a little clammy as we left the game to suit up. But because I was too old to run away, I bravely paid my twenty-five cents for a gym basket in which to deposit my street clothes, and marched like a good Christian into the lion's den.

Upon arrival, I was handed a pair of shiny royal-blue trunks and a gold jersey with matching blue trim and number identification. Meanwhile, my teammates were outfitting themselves with knee and elbow pads, color-coordinated stirrup stockings and Converse All-Star tennis shoes. When I donned my modest white ankle-socks and grass-stained sneakers and compared myself to these athletic-wear poster boys, I felt grossly underdressed. But of course that was not possible, since my shirt hung nearly down to my knees, thereby dressing much more of me than the manufacturers had originally intended.

We received a rousing pep talk from our coaches Mr. King and Mr. Anderson and then charged up the stairs to our pre-game warmups. I felt highly motivated, but was not quite sure exactly what I was motivated to do. As I loped up the staircase two steps at a time, my jersey straps kept slipping off my shoulders. This made me aware that if I didn't quickly become motivated to keep my shirt on, I would lose it from the top down.

The team went through a series of choreographed drills on the gymnasium floor, and I hopelessly tried to mirror the moves of my teammates. I would have experienced nearly as much success performing a kick-routine with the Rockettes. The scene was classic comedy, except that I was not in on the joke. My antics were nobly performed straight-faced, which probably could not be said of those who witnessed my sad attempt to blend in. Finally, a buzzer sounded, compassionately signaling that the cartoon was over. It was time for the feature presentation.

I hid behind our pre-game huddle, but was quite impressed when the starting lineup formed a giant hand sandwich by placing one player's hand upon another until all ten were carefully stacked. The head coach then palmed the players' hands, thus forming the sandwich buns, and the pile was thrust suddenly downward and quickly separated by the cry, "Let's go!" I wanted to try this right away, finding it much more pleasurable and less frustrating than the sport itself.

The game was close throughout the first half, but gradually the Presbyterian team we were playing began to pull away. There were about two minutes remaining when Mr. King ordered me to the scorer's table, so that I could report into the contest. I was no longer experiencing embarrassment or frustration. My stress gauge had soared to the level of total terror.

I don't recall much of what occurred after that moment, but I have been told that I spent most of the remainder of the game straddling the mid-court stripe with my mouth agape. My nightshirt-length jersey rode below my trunks, making it look as if I were wearing only a mid-length shift with extra long straps. When I finally went into motion, the jersey exposed nothing but my head, upper chest, shoulders, and what appeared to be jointless legs. On several occasions I would line up outside the lane when free throws were being shot, but invariably a referee would move me like a chess piece to the proper rebounding alignment.

The ball flew, rolled or bounced past me several times, but I never did get to touch it. I was far too dazed to go after it myself, and my teammates would have been more likely to pass it to a spectator. Amazingly, I did vicariously experience some of the thrill of competition and enjoyed watching the action from my on-court vantage point. Unfortunately, I would not get this opportunity often unless I learned to play this game.

I began attending our weekly practices at the YWCA (no, the W is not a typo) and gradually showed enough improvement that when I was assigned to play with a team during a scrimmage, they no longer audibly groaned at their misfortune. Because our coach, Mr. Anderson, took me to and from the Y, and the senior league practice took place after ours—I had to remain for both sessions. I used the additional time to continue my personal workouts when the seniors were running half-court drills, and then carefully analyzed the flow of the action when they played full-court simulated games.

Basketball was becoming addictive to me. I loved the sounds of the gymnasium. There was a muffled resonance of each individual noise, the sharp squeaks of the rubber-soled shoes on the wooden floor, the groans of physical extension, the quick verbal exchanges and communication between players, and the shouts of encouragement and vocal displays of the spectators. Each sound was discernible, as if the action took place in a giant echo chamber.

I enjoyed the five-on-five scrimmages when the score was insignificant and improving one's game was the objective. And it was fun to divide into teams of "shirts and skins" and to feel the almost instant bonding that occurred with players who were briefly placed on the same practice squad. I appreciated the camaraderie and teamwork, and the fact that you could earn another boy's respect through your performance on the basketball floor. The measure of that respect was determined not only by your natural ability, but by your effort and desire.

I slowly developed into an integral member of our team and honed my skills until I became a fairly respectable player. In my final year of eligibility, I was a contributing starter on a roster that featured the coach's son, Randy King. Randy was the indisputable star and the heartthrob of all the adolescent girls in our church. They sighed and swooned at the mention of his name, while the other players simply stood in awe. It was no disgrace to play second-fiddle to a virtuoso. In the dog-eat-dog world of church-league basketball—Tim Simer had arrived.

At Pierce Elementary, I started participating in playground games with my peers and watched intently when fifth and sixth-graders took over the court. There was a boy one year older than I, who stood out as the best basketball player in school. He was soft-spoken, didn't flaunt his abilities and displayed a quiet confidence without appearing arrogant. At first I thought his name was Oscar, because that's what they called him on the court. I later discovered that his real name was Steve Osso, and that they called him Oscar because of the Hall of Fame basketball player, Oscar Robertson. "The Big O" was a local legend who had starred at the University of Cincinnati, and was with the Cincinnati Royals before the NBA franchise eventually moved to Kansas City. Robertson was the idol of nearly every boy in Southwestern Ohio and the player most mimicked on the schoolyard blacktop. I made up my mind then that I wanted to be like Steve Osso—to have other kids look up to me because of my abilities, yet show what a good guy I was through my actions. Basketball, I decided, would become my way of gaining acceptance.

By the following year, I had become the best player in Mrs. Eversole's fifth-grade class. It was announced by our gym teacher, Mr. Van Ness, that there would be a two-week intramural basketball tournament to be played during our afternoon lunch period. The students would organize their own teams and submit a roster of eligible players.

Ken Simmons, the most popular boy in our class and a some-time-nemesis of mine, talked to me about combining forces to organize a team. We made some painstaking decisions about who would be invited to join our ranks, talked privately to our candidates, and organized a secret meeting in the towel closet in the boys' locker room. The meeting was short, but significant. Ken Simmons was elected captain, and because nobody knew the proper term for the second-in-command, I was elected co-captain.

The name of our team was the Voodoos. Our official uniforms were our black gym trunks, along with ribbed sleeveless undershirts that bore our team insignia boldly scripted upon our chests. The insignia was drawn on the fabric with a black permanent ink, felt-tip marker—and was a giant V, with a smaller D enclosed within the V's borders.

I am certain that there was much hoopla and discussion among faculty members when we entered the gym that first lunch hour with the letters VD emblazoned on our shirts. No one ever explained the unfortunate double meaning to us, and our ignorance was not unusual in the 1960s. Luckily no one had the courage or the time to give us an extended lecture on the appropriateness of our logo, so we wore our uniforms proudly, believing the name Voodoo struck fear in our opponents. Little did we know that those initials on our T-shirts were far more frightening.

There were about five teams fielded from the two fifth-grade classes, and as the tournament progressed, two teams rose to the top: the Voodoos and a team from Mrs. Feist's class, which was captained by Steve Broyles. Steve was my closest competition in basketball talent, and each of us probably wondered who was better. When the two teams met in the finals, I had been unable to sleep the night before and felt the pressure of game day throughout the morning.

The actual encounter was not nearly as exciting as the anticipation, though, as we won the game handily and were crowned the champions of the fifth grade. I rode a nearly two-week high, and our classmates shared in our moment of glory because we had bested Mrs. Feist's finest. The team should have presented our teacher, Mrs. Eversole, with an honorary Voodoo jersey. It would have been a tribute that she would never have forgotten.

* * *

The next year Pierce fielded a school team scheduled to play four games against other local grade schools. We emerged victorious three times, our only loss coming on our home floor against a larger crosstown school. That game would be my first exposure to what I believed to be unfair officiating.

The referee was the physical education teacher of the other school, and we had beaten them soundly when we had played them on their own court. I had scored over twenty points in the contest, and that fact had obviously not been forgotten. I was in foul trouble from the opening whistle, spending much of the first half on the bench and fouling out just after halftime. Four of the fouls were of the phantom variety, apparently only witnessed by this instructor/referee. It was the only time I have cried publicly since I was a little boy.

The day was devastating to me, not only because we lost and I didn't get a chance to complete the game, but because it was the first time I had ever seen a grown-up cheat. It was my initial firsthand encounter with this darker side of adult human behavior, and the memory still saddens me each time I recall it.

* * *

I had tasted success as a basketball player and liked its flavor. I relished wearing a uniform and standing before my bedroom mirror in a variety of bubblegum-card poses. It was fun to announce mock game situations, while pantomiming last-second shots that drew nothing but net, as I always emerged the hero. And I took satisfaction in performing before crowds and being recognized in school by people who didn't already know me. I even enjoyed the foot blisters, turned ankles, and scrapes and bruises that made me feel like a tough-as-nails athlete. These injuries provided me a legitimate reason to limp or to wear an impressive ace bandage or lesser first-aid accessory.

* * *

There was a tryout held at Pierce School for the Lindenwald Bills—a team that played in the Keystone League at the Hamilton Boys Club. The league was open to boys in grades 6–9 throughout the Hamilton/Fairfield area. Lindenwald was my neighborhood of residence, and the team was called the Bills because it was coached and sponsored by Bill Smith, who owned Smith Refrigeration. Quite a few kids tried out, but only two grade-schoolers were selected. Steve Broyles and I became the only sixth-grade members of the Bills, and although we didn't play much—it was a gratifying season.

We found ourselves in a league of older boys, many of whom were bigger and better than we were. Our skills improved along with our level of competition. I was able to earn the respect of junior high teammates, which helped my stature when I started attending school with them the following year. And the game situations exposed me to a wide assortment of boys of differing races and from other neighborhoods. My street skills slowly improved, and I was toughened up for the broad range of experiences I would confront as my world continued to expand.

I played one additional season with the Bills and was on my junior-high team the other two years (which carries its own set of tales and recollections). When I began my final stint in the Keystone League, I entered the first practice as the star of the team. The players whom I had worshipped as a sixth-grader had graduated, and suddenly I was thrust into the role of a floor leader.

The highlight of that season was an open-invitation Christmas holiday tournament. We were one of the best teams in the league and had been faring well in the tourney—having survived a few close calls to advance to the finals against the host Boys Club team. The night of the championship I had the game of my life, scoring twenty-eight points as we captured the title and took home individual trophies for our efforts.

As I walked out of the Boys Club that evening, I was no longer the frightened child who had stood at the mid-court stripe at the Hamilton Central YMCA, afraid to take a decisive step for fear it would be a wrong one. And although I had received some recognition as a basketball player, I knew I would never be a Steve Osso. Steve had a rare, first-rate talent for the game, and our personalities were vastly different.

I had worked hard to become a good basketball player and had just played a dream game. Those who played against me respected my abilities, and some younger kids even looked up to me. But all of these circumstances had not transformed me into any of the stars whom I had always strived to emulate. I felt an unusual sense of self-assuredness. Maybe I could never be Steve Osso. But I was finally having some success being myself. I now felt that maybe I could live with that.

7

The Tootsie Roll Man

It was the late fall of 1963, and Randy King and I both were nearly out of space on our church bulletins—having involved ourselves in a marathon session of hangman, connect-the-dots and tic-tac-toe. The worship service had been a particularly long one. There had been a baptism, and although these ceremonies were grand spectacles, they were also quite time consuming.

The baptistry was located behind the altar, which was centered at the rear of the raised stage area of the sanctuary. There were three rows of choir pews parallel to the side walls on each side of the stage and an ornate enclosed wooden lectern in front of each set of choir pews. The baptistry was behind red velvet curtains that were usually drawn, but opened just prior to the immersion—perhaps for theatrical emphasis. My father wore a white robe when performing baptisms, the only time he put on vestments of any kind. Although the baptistry was sunken, I was also certain that he had worn his black rubber wading boots which normally hung on the door leading from the church office to the font. The baptistry had always fascinated me, and I would semi-regularly sneak peeks at this sacred area when I knew I would not be caught.

The woman who had been baptized was not someone familiar to me, but it was still an inspirational experience. Since I had received instruction in pastor's class, I now carefully observed the unusual passivity that people demonstrated when being baptized. They were instructed to let their bodies go limp and allow the pastor to guide their total immersion into the water—while maintaining full assurance that he would return them to a standing position so that they might breathe again. It was a symbolic act of faith and was obviously somewhat difficult to do—considering the mini-struggles and splashing that sometimes occurred during the somber ceremony. That Sunday's baptism had caused Randy and me to put down

46

our pencils, as the drama of the moment dictated that we offer our undivided attention.

Before the end of the service, though, we had returned to our games—enduring a particularly lengthy communion prayer by Ed Grathwohl and some not-so-brief remarks by our Sunday school superintendent, Carl Maupin. By the time the benediction had arrived, the telltale squirmies had infested our youthful legs.

Finally our church shackles were removed, as my father closed the worship with the same four words that he used to end all services that he presided over: "Now, everybody, shake hands!" The organ then joyously erupted into a brief postlude—as if venting elation that its work day had reached a conclusion. For the rest of us, Sunday School would follow, as this morning seemed to have embraced the concept of having everlasting life.

The adults began mingling immediately, turning to those surrounding them and spilling out conversation that had remained bottled up during the service. People extended hands and hugs, smiled and laughed, exchanged family updates and painstakingly described physical ailments.

Children young enough to get by with it began stretching their legs by speed-walking and playing a thinly disguised form of tag—as they pursued each other through and around the aisles of pews. They came as perilously close to playing as the situation permitted. I commenced a weekly chore my father had delegated to me, as I began a trip up and down each row—returning hymnals to the racks mounted on the back of each pew. It was a prestigious assignment for a ten-year-old, and one that I appreciated, because it made me feel important to help my father in his role as minister.

I was occasionally slowed down by people who stopped to say hello and to shake my hand, a skill that I had recently mastered and eagerly fine-tuned whenever someone extended a palm to me. As I reached the end of the back aisle, I spotted a smiling gentleman whom I always looked forward to seeing. It was the Tootsie Roll Man.

The Tootsie Roll Man's real name was Herman Dulli. He was a roly-poly gentleman in his early sixties, with a deeply etched face and chipmunk cheeks. His face was nearly a caricature—as if he had stepped from a Dick Tracy comic strip. When outdoors, Mr. Dulli often sported a fedora—and he smoked a cigar whenever it was socially acceptable. He had a neatly trimmed salt-and-pepper moustache, and when not smiling and viewed from a distance, he looked to be a rather serious and grim character. But as he drew near, and the kindliness of his tired eyes became visible—his tenderness overwhelmed you. His eyes were always very liquid, and upon spending time with him, it seemed that much of life had touched him. No other person I have ever met so completely personified the phrase, "a twinkle in his eye."

He stood before me that day with a spontaneous grin on his face and a Tootsie Roll in his hand. Each Sunday, he would seek out every child in attendance and offer them one of the palatable morsels. Those who did not know his name referred to him simply as the Tootsie Roll Man, and the nickname stuck.

It was almost as much fun to receive the candy from this jovial man as it was to eat the treat on the trip home. He was so at ease with children and seemed so genuinely interested in each boy or girl he talked to, that one would have believed that he was heading the Midwestern United States operations for Santa Claus. Our conversation that day was brief, but delicious. His chubby chin bobbed while he listened intently, and his eyes crinkled to telegraph his teasing. As he turned and left, I found myself smiling. He often had that effect on people.

The reader may be surprised to discover that adults, too, held Herman Dulli in reverence. He was happily married to a kindly and thoughtful woman named Lucille who taught the Coterian adult Sunday school class. And the Tootsie Roll Man was sharp as a tack—as wise as any of the elders and deacons who blew their hot air at congregational meetings. Mr. Dulli was quite simply devoted to children. He absolutely loved to be around them. Adults and children alike knew it—and adored him for it.

The '60s were an ideal decade for a Tootsie Roll Man. No suspicions simmered—no eyebrows were raised. Reasonable distrust has since squelched such uninhibited giving. If Johnny Appleseed were alive today, people would be certain of a catch or angle. But people accepted Herman Dulli for what he was—and felt graced by his presence.

*   *   *

The Tootsie Roll Man was not my personal mentor. He belonged to everybody. There were almost always children around him, so my admiration grew not only from personal experiences, but from watching how other children reacted to him. He could be a most convincing adult, but slid back to childhood with an ease that sometimes made me forget that he resided inside that thickset, old body. Mr. Dulli didn't just remember what it was like to be young—his spirit could still take him there.

At church suppers he would entertain me by turning my placemat into a collection of word games, brain teasers and clever written tricks that I could perform for my friends. He is singularly responsible for teaching me to wiggle my ears, a talent that has often dazzled my chums and forever embarrassed my wife. Even on days that I wanted nothing to do with the world, I made an exception for the Tootsie Roll Man. He could engage me in conversation without intruding—for it was never necessary to communicate on his level. Instead, he always managed effortlessly to adjust to mine.

Mr. Dulli remembered when I had just played a baseball game, knew when my school events were coming up, and scratched my itch to talk about the Reds. He loved to sneak up from behind or suddenly appear as I turned a corner. The Tootsie Roll Man must have known that he seemed almost unreal, like a character created in a child's mind. He was a dashing old sprite who had leapt from a storybook—always clenching a hefty cigar or a Tootsie Roll in one of his ever-giving hands.

*   *   *

I recall one evening that he took me to Movie Night at the YMCA. He did extensive volunteer work at the Y and coordinated an evening of cinematic entertainment, where boys could pay a minuscule admission price to view a feature film. There were about ten boys in attendance, and we were well into *Moby Dick,* when Mr. Dulli briefly left the room. Four of the attendees engaged in a major paper-wad battle, and when he returned to the scene, evidence of the skirmish lay strewn across the floor. It was the only time I ever saw Mr. Dulli angry, and I was probably visibly upset by it. He shut down the projector and made eye contact with each of us before he asked us what had happened.

My face flushed, and I stared down at my feet—torn between my loyalties to Mr. Dulli and the cardinal rule against snitching on your own kind. He then reworded the question, this time directing his attention squarely at me. I had no choice; I pointed out the combatants, and sensed that there was relief rather than anger among the other innocents. After all, they had been spared having to make the choice that I had made. You just couldn't lie to the Tootsie Roll Man.

*   *   *

Herman Dulli died suddenly and unexpectedly when I was twelve

49

years old. There was a lightlessness in the church on the first Sunday after he had passed away. The pews were full, but the church seemed empty—the jolt of his death felt like a repeating camera-flash in my brain. I attended his wake and paid my respects at his coffin. It was the first time I had ever looked into an open casket.

It was immediately obvious to me that I was looking only upon the shell that had contained the man. The twinkle in his eye was Herman Dulli; the natural kindness that motivated so many of his actions was what made children forget that they were buddies with a dapper gentleman in his sixties. I sensed then that in life the Tootsie Roll Man had truly been baptized with the spirit of love. The spirit had engulfed and infiltrated him, drenching him in a gentleness that drew people of all ages toward him. I will never forget his death and the harsh void that it left in our church community. Wounds heal, but his brand of magic can never be duplicated.

A refrigerated drinking fountain for the church rec-hall was purchased from the funds collected in Herman Dulli's memory. A plaque was placed on it as a tribute to the man. It seemed appropriate that he would continue to offer an easement to people even after he had gone.

*   *   *

As an adult, I have given much thought to what makes a man as compassionate and remarkable as Herman Dulli. And I find myself continually returning to the image of baptism that I had pondered at his wake. It seemed that sometime in his life he had reached a point of passivity and had allowed himself to be baptized in spirit. Pure love then dictated so many of his actions. In death, it was no longer necessary to breathe the oxygen of this world again. At that moment he could become completely immersed. He had no longer only been touched by God; he was now embraced by him.

And unfortunately, at least for the time being, those of us he left behind will have to find somewhere else to get our Tootsie Rolls.

8

Mr. Baseball

It was a cool and overcast afternoon in the early summer of 1964, and I was making a quick but thorough final inspection of myself in my new baseball uniform. On this special day, the team photo was to be taken, and the mirror confirmed that everything was in order. The new cap looked as if it had been properly broken in—the bend in the bill curled to perfection. I had spent several evenings massaging the visor into this work of art: a natural arc with a pronounced, yet subtle downturn. I had thus avoided the two looks worn by the rank amateur: the sharp angular squared bend of a stiff new cap, or worse yet, the dreaded cap with no bend at all. This look, of course, screamed to the world that the cap had been snatched directly from a sporting goods store shelf, and that the novice wearer was clearly un-schooled in diamond decorum.

The letter "O" that had been ironed onto my hat conformed exactly with those of the team's veteran sixth graders. The perfectly centered emblem could either be interpreted as a numerical rating of my baseball abil-ity, or a designation of my affiliation with the American Legion Post 138 Orioles. There was no doubt of the Legion's association with our team, however. The huge round sponsorship patch that we sported seemed as big as a basketball and barely fit on the right side of the front of my uniform.

The elastic that kept my glasses on my head appeared properly hidden under my short-cropped hair. The strap had been adjusted loosely enough to avoid the Mickey Mouse look I developed when an over-tight band forced my oversized ears forward. My color-coordinated stirrup socks were stretched to the maximum, which was the look of the day. I lacked the rubber cleats and red long-sleeved undershirt of my wealthier teammates, but I rationalized that I was a hard-nosed, meat-and-potatoes ballplayer who didn't need such fluff.

It was the official opening day of the Lindenwald Little League, and I was experiencing all of the jitters associated with the debut of a budding superstar. I was ecstatic that I had been drafted by the Orioles and had spent the early spring practicing hour after hour with my best friend Mike. We wasted entire days hurling a tennis ball against the front steps of my house, while fielding the subsequent carom. The concept was an excellent one as long as the ball took a forward trajectory. But unfortunately it sometimes hit a stair edge and screamed backward toward the house or hurtled into our aluminum screen door. Whenever this unfortunate incident occurred, the door was flung open by my mother, who usually began her first sentence with, "If this happens again, I'll . . ."

The year before, Mike and I had tried out unsuccessfully and had been relegated to the Farm League. On the farm, T-shirts were the uniforms, and the umpire was often also the coach of the opposing team. We had starred in the league, but of course, the Farm League was nothing compared to "The Show." Mike was now in the seventh grade and hence had reached Little League retirement age, a fact that didn't seem to distress him. He had never had much of a taste for organized ball and had participated the year before primarily because I had nagged him into it. So as the new season approached, I had been on my own and had gone unescorted to the Hamilton Sports Center to get a permission slip and official tryout number. The number was stenciled onto a piece of white square cloth that fastened to a player's shirt with four miniature safety pins. That piece of cloth found an immediate home on my bedroom nightstand, as I envisioned myself as a fifth-grade phenom that would make managers' jaws drop as they fought furiously over the right to draft me.

My actual performance during the tryouts had been a little less than scintillating. My strongest attribute was that I did nothing incredibly wrong. I was immediately panic-stricken when it was announced that drafted players would receive personal notification from their managers by phone over the weekend. That Saturday was one of the most agonizing I would ever live through. Until I received my call late that afternoon, I used all of my young guile and limited bargaining power to keep family members from tying up the draft hotline. After my new manager Mr. Schmitz phoned me, I instantly high-tailed it to Mike's house. I nearly dragged him from his front door, spilling over with all the particulars. We then strutted proudly around the neighborhood for several hours, hoping to see as many comrades as possible to nonchalantly tell them the news. I was now an Oriole.

Being a Little League underclassman meant getting the chance to play with older idols who under other circumstances wouldn't give you the time of day. There was Steve Schmitz, the manager's son, who successfully maintained his tough-guy image throughout the summer. This perception was enhanced by the fact that he was the starting catcher and clearly the biggest kid on the team. Rick Adams was an impish, but non-bullying sixth grader whom I had known from Vacation Bible School and Cub Scouts. He ceaselessly teased all of us, particularly his younger brother Dale—who was a bowling ball with legs. Ron Trester was a good-natured freckled stringbean who was less rigid about associating with the younger players and correspondingly closer to us in athletic ability.

And finally there was Denny Townsend. Denny was the best athlete on our team and the player I most looked up to. He had a natural air of confidence and a razor-sharp sense of humor. Although friendly to all of us, he maintained the distance and deference that any self-respecting sixth grader demanded. He was wiry but graceful, with dark features and an eternal tan. Denny knew everybody—and everybody liked him.

I got along with most of the players my own age, although I had only gone to school with Mike Banks. Banks was an elementary-school slick-haired Don Juan who was more of an acquaintance than a buddy. The girls all liked him, so many of the guys didn't. Two other teammates, Mike Leck and Tim Roberts, would remain pretty good friends of mine until we all graduated from high school. Mike Leck was an intriguing character. He, like me, was an earnest and basically good kid whose sense of humor became increasingly apparent as you got to know him. As the years passed and life took its toll on his naivete, he became one of the funniest people that I have ever known. He was fair-haired and forever playful—and usually wore a hard-core crew cut and smiling eyes. Tim Roberts was simply the kind of guy you liked to have around. He was a cherub-faced kid who didn't stand out in a crowd. He just made the crowd more tolerable.

Joe Vogt and Kevin Pendergast went to Catholic school, so they initially were less familiar to me. Joe was a truly nice guy, an outstanding athlete, and always had an incredible wad of gum in his mouth. He was to become the star of the team the following season and won the instant respect of all of the Orioles. He almost immediately befriended me, which helped elevate my standing with other team members and made my road up the Little League social ladder much easier. Kevin Pendergast was also a good player, but was a little more showy about it than Joe. He had mastered the mannerisms of big league players and used them as often as he got the opportunity. He was a decent sort, although never really a close friend of mine.

The younger players were only warm bodies to fill out the rosters, and their faces are no longer clear in my mind. They were the low men on the totem pole and wisely often segregated themselves rather than absorb the grief that would come with attempting to achieve a degree of respectability. I do recall Greg Bean, a coach's son, who was both talented and clever enough to cross over into our elite pack of men-children. There was a clear hierarchy, and each player found his role and had an impact on the team's overall personality.

Our manager, Mr. Schmitz, was a man's man—a disciplinarian who was respected by the team and taught me much of what I knew about baseball. Mr. Schmitz seemed a large imposing figure, with a trim physique and a dusting of gray in his hair. He was a police detective by trade and was a fair and honest man.

This opening day was particularly unique because it was also the first day of organized Little League baseball at Joyce Park, a newly dedicated multi-purpose park that sported three Little League playing fields and several practice diamonds. It was a far cry from the primitive confines of Riverview Park, where I had played out my illustrious farm league career. Riverview lacked bathroom facilities, which kept crowds down and prompted players to make spirited sprints that had nothing to do with the game, or baseball for that matter.

The new park used the name of Joe Nuxhall liberally. Nuxhall was a fifteen-year-old from Hamilton when he broke into the big leagues during World War II and became the youngest player in the history of major league baseball. He was and is an icon in Hamilton and had been a frequent motivational speaker at many church dinners and youth gatherings that I attended.

On that sunless summer day we had gathered in uniform for the first time. We had our team photo taken, then squirmed impatiently while a recorded rendition of the national anthem blared over the loudspeaker. We then stood and sometimes sat while the adults indulged themselves with an endless opening ceremony. There were loads of proud parents with instamatic cameras and snow-cone-toting younger brothers and sisters. We saw friends and friends of friends in their new uniforms, walking team by team around the park in a cavalcade of bright colors. The parade featured a wide variety of girths and heights and an impressive array of macho adolescent saunters.

Each team played two innings in an exhibition contest on that day. I don't remember much of what happened, so we must have been outscored. I do recall an outstanding grab by our catcher on a pop-up and vividly recollect hitting a ball thrown at a considerable velocity with the handle part of my bat. My hands were numb for several minutes, and I felt a great exhilaration that I had been properly initiated.

*   *   *

It went on to be a grand summer of education about baseball and about life. I learned what it was like to be a part of a unit that included both weak links and strong leaders—and how it is necessary to coordinate talent and non-talent to perform together effectively. I discovered how it felt to be accepted as a male and struggled to become comfortable with both my strengths and weaknesses.

There were the highs of making a good play or mastering proper infield chatter and the lows of making the last out or watching it rain cats and dogs on game days. I was exposed to the positive influences of Mr. Schmitz, Denny Townsend and Joe Vogt, among countless others. And I also coped with the negatives of ornery kids and overbearing parents, who sometimes did things that I simply could not understand.

The American Legion Post 138 Orioles finished in second place that year and were eliminated in the Hamilton/Fairfield tournament by a team that included a son of the great Joe Nuxhall. But in the end most of us were winners. We came out of that summer a little tougher, a little smarter and a little more mature. And some of us even learned a little bit about baseball.

9

A Night at Crosley Field

People had already begun congregating in the parking lot at the Butler County AAA office on High Street, many wearing white baseball caps with a distinctly recognizable scarlet "C" emblazoned above the red bill. Our family had arrived a bit early, so my father could assist the coordinators of this church field trip. A bus was chartered to take us that evening to Crosley Field to see the Cincinnati Reds play the Chicago Cubs—and it was scheduled to arrive in only a few minutes. Church members periodically pulled into the parking lot, and as each new group of faces emerged from their cars, there was a good-natured banter between the newcomers and those already gathered. This usually brought smiles all around and continually increased the initiated welcoming committee for the next arrival.

I had looked forward to this summer evening in 1964 since the first time my father had announced the outing from the pulpit. This game was particularly significant because my father was a lifelong Cubs fan, a peculiar form of insanity that I fortunately had not inherited. He took a considerable ribbing for his allegiance and had remained loyal in spite of the fact he had nearly been swallowed up by the local Red wave. I, on the other hand, had become an almost immediate Reds convert. Moving from the Cleveland area had taken me out of American League jurisdiction, and since my exposure was now almost exclusively to the senior circuit, the shift had been a natural one.

*   *   *

Being a Reds fan made me feel camaraderie with both young and old that day. Baseball was one adult topic of discussion that I could relate to, and in most cases, sound downright intelligent about. And even the very young, who knew little about the game, worshiped stars like Frank Robinson and Vada Pinson and were antsy to climb aboard the bus so that they

56

might make the pilgrimage to pay homage to their superheroes. I, too, waited impatiently—yearning to get on the road, but hoping that one of my church compadres would arrive to share my excitement.

The crowd waiting for the bus had become substantial, and people had begun parking their cars on the street because the immediate lot was full. I spotted a beige Pontiac Bonneville inching its way into a tight spot nearly a half block away, and knew that this meant that Cecil and Doty King had arrived. They were prominent members of the congregation, and their presence would probably further energize the multitude. I peered into the car, looking for their two sons, Jimmy and Randy. Jimmy was considerably older than I and was nowhere to be found, but Randy, who was only a year my senior, was exiting the back seat. I breathed a sigh of relief, since this meant that I would not be forced to sit with my sisters, or worse yet, an adult who felt obligated to entertain me. Randy and I were pals, but our relationship was based more on the fact that we were approximately the same age than from any genuine kinship.

Randy always looked like he had stepped out of a Robert Hall catalogue. He was dark and quite good-looking, with jet-black hair and a confidence that managed to intensify my own self-consciousness. All the girls including my older sister scribbled his name on every paperback book and three-ring binder that they owned, and the other boys fell all over themselves trying to be his friend. Initially, Randy had politely tolerated me because I was the minister's son, but our relationship continued due to the fact that we shared common interests, and because the pool of potential church chums was an extremely shallow one.

Randy spotted me as he crossed the parking lot and gave me "the nod," which was much more masculine than a traditional wave. He immediately made his way over to me, and we began a detached analysis of that night's game, displaying brilliant gems of baseball knowledge whenever possible. I'm sure he was nearly as elated about going as I was, but we tried to repress our enthusiasm in each other's presence.

Eventually, the bus pulled into the lot amid mock cheers, and the faces of Red rooters of all ages lit up with the anticipation of our journey. As a file of people climbed aboard, there was a spriteliness in their step, and even the elderly who required assistance boarding exhibited a little added hop in their get-a-long. Randy and I found a choice spot at the rear of the bus that gave us access to both side and rear windows. As we heard the rumbling bus engine slip into gear, it rang out to us like the bell to Pavlov's dog, signaling an upcoming feast for our young senses.

The yellow brick road to Crosley Field was Interstate 75-South, which provided a gradual transition from the self-contained world of Hamilton to the overwhelming metropolis known as the Queen City. On previous trips, I had selected the passing of the massive General Electric plant in Evendale as my indicator that I was entering unfamiliar and mysterious terrain. Buildings were generally taller, and there were fewer private residences. Traffic became increasingly congested and billboards more extravagant—with a marked increase in the use of neon.

We rolled along at a considerable clip, staring down at the cars below and getting a rare eye-level view into the cabs of large semis. The bus wound its way into the treacherous Dead Man's Curve, so named by juvenile folklore because of the tall concrete walls on either side of the highway. These walls of death had caused countless horrific car crashes, most of which had been artfully fabricated and then embellished, as the stories snowballed in gruesomeness and bloody gore. We held our breath as we safely evaded the grasp of the grim reaper, and soon could discern skyscrapers and the radiant glow of the big city.

Randy and I stared silently while frequently craning our necks—panning the surroundings as if we were on a tram-tour of a humongous zoo. Although the city was only a short distance from our homes, it felt like a foreign country, as we now rumbled through local neighborhoods where people walking the streets appeared surprisingly comfortable in their surroundings.

The bus finally came to a halt several blocks from the ballpark. As our coach unloaded, one could hear tempters peddling Reds souvenirs while scruffy gentlemen in top hats and tattered tails hawked salted peanuts in the shell. Randy and I willingly surrendered some of our autonomy and stayed within reaching distance of a recognizable adult, trailing along like a pair of overgrown and underexposed ducklings.

We crossed through the turnstiles, and I purchased a scorecard with a picture of the Reds' cartoon mascot on its cover. The mascot had a human body decked out in a classic Reds' uniform, but was cursed with a baseball for a head. He sported a handsome handlebar mustache, though, making him the only spheroid in history who had undergone puberty.

The group located our seats in the grandstand, and Randy and I watched in awe as an usher wiped our thrones clean for us. A parade of food vendors sang out in varying tempos and pitches. Evidently, serving temperature was of tantamount importance, as nearly everything was served either ice-cold or piping-hot. Randy had a wad of dollar bills that he obviously intended to use, and he began sampling the wide choice of food items to be consumed and/or tossed onto the cement floor. I would save my limited funds to purchase an ice-cold lemonade and an ice cream bar. These were slowly savored for several innings, as I sucked down each individual piece of crushed ice and carefully tongued off the last residues of ice cream while avoiding any surface-to-surface contact with the coarse wooden stick. The slightest slip-up in mouth placement could cause the dreaded heebie-jeebies, which were usually accompanied by an embarrassing outbreak of goose bumps.

*   *   *

The field was a brilliant green, and the players, although not recognizable without binoculars, provided a vivid contrast of complementary colors and graceful motion. The Cubs were dressed in their road grays with bright blue caps and accessories. Our Reds wore their white pinstripes with sleeves that were bright red from the shoulder and donned white caps with matching red bills. Everyone who had ever slipped on this uniform was magically transformed into an instant good guy with regional hero status.

I checked my scorecard and could see many of my favorite players running wind sprints in the outfield. There they were: Pete Rose, Chico Cardenas, Tommy Harper, Johnny Edwards, Vada Pinson and my personal idol—Frank Robinson. Among the enemy troops, I spotted the legendary Ernie Banks, Ron Santo and Billy Williams. I was particularly in awe of Banks, a man whom my father always discussed with quiet reverence. I did not need binoculars to recognize him, as it was obvious who he was by his quiet confidence and demeanor.

The almost blinding banks of stadium lights seemed to seal the park off from the starry skies, creating a magnificent lid of night sky and cityscape. The air was crisp, yet thick with the soothing hum of crowd noise. The stadium organist tickled both the keyboard and the fans in attendance with Reds rally themes and corny renditions of popular tunes. As the public-address announcer boomed out the starting lineups, the sensory painting received its final strokes. This was a baseball game.

Many specifics about that night have faded in my memory or blended with countless other extraordinary trips to the ballpark. But several stretches of time have been filed in the archives of my mind. I remember locating the rest room almost immediately and proudly walking there myself on several occasions. This was a monumental breakthrough, because it helped exorcise the demons that had haunted me since I had attended a game as an eight-year-old. A church family named Crothers had extended an invitation for me to attend a game with them, and I was slightly intimidated by the idea of spending the evening as their adopted son. Nature eventually called, and I was too frightened to venture out alone and too embarrassed to drag someone away from the game to escort me. My indecision ultimately resulted in an unattractive third option that left me with damp blue jeans and even damper spirits. It is a memory I would love to forget.

I also recall being mesmerized as I watched Ernie Banks and Frank Robinson ply their craft on the same ball field. Robinson did not have his finest evening at the plate, striking out several times. He was incessantly hounded by Steve Anderson, a verbose baseball critic who doubled as a Garfield High School student. I normally looked up to Steve, but was enraged at his lambasting of my hero and didn't speak to him for several weeks afterwards. I seriously doubt that he ever noticed.

Frank Robinson looked magnificent in his uniform, though, and he carried himself like a proud thoroughbred, policing left field with grace and agility. I worshiped him. Months later, my father would take me to the grand opening of a B.F. Goodrich store in Hamilton where Robinson was making a personal appearance, and he truly went out of his way to be congenial. It was one of the biggest thrills of my childhood, and he retains exalted status on my list of personal heroes.

When I first witnessed Ernie Banks trot onto the diamond, it was an almost religious experience, as my father had forever filled my head with tales of his miraculous feats. I had now shared something that Dad was passionate about, and I reveled in the connection that it created. When we spoke of Ernie Banks from that moment hence, I could rubber-stamp my father's effusive endorsements because I had seen him play.

The only other powerful recollection that I retain of the evening was a foul ball that floated in our direction and was snatched by Les Brate, a middle-aged real-estate agent, who was promptly awarded the then-customary, honorary Reds contract. He let me examine the ball and because he had been sitting so near to me, it provided me with an "almost" story that I recited for several years.

*   *   *

After the game, we returned en masse to the bus—dodging empty and half-empty beverage cups and walking quickly past a group of men who had over-imbibed. As we crammed back onto the bus, people were abuzz with analysis of the game and the grandstand goings-on. The overhead lights on the bus ceiling were illuminated and created an eerie dual world, as I stared at our reflections in the window glass, but could also see through the mirrored image onto the hectic and unfamiliar city streets. We waited for a few stragglers, and then the inside lights were dimmed. We set off for home, retracing our path through the now less-active surroundings. Cincinnati seemed almost peaceful, as if it had gone to bed, leaving on a multitude of night lights.

As the minutes elapsed, the conversation dwindled until there were only a few whispers as we approached the Hamilton city limits. Young children slept, and everyone appeared drowsy, as they were gently rocked by the contours of the pavement. The score and the game specifics would soon be forgotten, but the experience would linger in our minds. There would be lively conversation among the attendees at church on Sunday.

*   *   *

I haven't lived in Ohio since 1977, but I will forever be a loyal Reds fan. They have grown to represent my upbringing and hometown to me, and when they experience success, I can vicariously share in the community's joy. I have been an appreciative eyewitness to many monumental moments in Reds' history. I was there for the glory days of "The Big Red Machine," when Pete Rose, Joe Morgan, Tony Perez, Johnny Bench and company ruled baseball. And I stood among the celebrants at Cincinnati's Fountain Square after the Reds had won the 1976 World Series against the New York Yankees. I cheered Tony Perez at Riverfront Stadium when he made his first appearance after his unfortunate trade to Montreal. And I saw Pete Rose tie the all-time hit record at Wrigley Field in Chicago and break it in Cincinnati against Eric Show and the San Diego Padres. Most recently, I was on hand as Danny Jackson won his twentieth game against the Cubs in 1989, and I now attend Reds' games whenever they come to the Windy City.

*   *   *

Baseball has always been my favorite sport. It lives in its proud history and traditions, and breathes the outdoor air from the reluctant emergence of early spring to the foreboding frigidity of early October. Its heart beats a consistent precise rhythm that clearly defines victory from defeat, fair from foul, and ball from strike. Its fans give the sport its muscle, and regional pride sets its essence into motion. The Reds are my team because Hamilton is my town. My devotion to the Reds helps me define who I am, not only to those with whom I interact, but sometimes even to myself.

Each time I sit in my living room in Chicago and watch the Reds play, or read the line score, or see their game results flash on my television set, I am uplifted. I realize that the real world is still in motion beyond my walls and windows, but I can also see the distinct reflections of old dear friends and precious family members who will always surround and protect me. And I'm going home. I'm going home.

10

The Christmas Story

It was the final week of school prior to Christmas vacation in 1964, and the tiny gymnasium was jammed with proud parents and tired-eyed faculty members. On this evening, hordes of brightly costumed elementary school students were presenting their annual holiday extravaganza—a musical revue with the unlikely title of "Santa Claus Conquers the Martians."

The production utilized a flimsy thread of a plot in which Santa is captured and held hostage by space aliens. I performed the coveted role of Billy—one of six children who plot to rescue Saint Nick after they are visited by concerned citizens from most of the planets in our solar system. Each planet's inhabitants were represented by a different grade at Pierce School, and every delegation sang a rousing musical number en masse before being scooted off the stage. My recollections of the show itself are vague, but I do recall memorizing about ten lines. And I distinctly remember watching several hundred life forms parade across the proscenium, adorned in costumes made with reams of colorful netting, and lots and lots of aluminum foil.

My beloved Jill Wolsefer was also cast as one of the starring six who emancipate Santa, and she had commanded nearly all of my attention. I had relished the opportunity to gaze at her during rehearsals, and the high emotion of the season had made my love for her even more dramatic.

Jill had jumped the gun on the old stage adage and had quite literally broken her leg very early into rehearsals. Her performance appeared unaffected by the temporary disability. She hobbled about on her crutches like Tiny Tim—all the while smiling courageously—which only served to accentuate her already breathtakingly beautiful dimples. I studied her every movement throughout the evening and pondered the effect that the theatrical lighting had on her angelic face. This pleasant diversion nearly made me forget my own stage fright. I found it both exciting and torturous to adore her so much.

As each class filed onto the stage to perform their musical number, I saw many children gleefully playing it up to their parents and the audience. Other more timid souls seemed mired in a nightmare that would be retold years later in traumatic therapy sessions. One would have surmised from observing this show that all space creatures walked in single file, shuffled their feet when standing and were prone to cry quite easily. It was either a very good or very bad experience for each of us; there was little middle ground.

The performance was a smashing success, primarily because practically everyone who saw the show was also in it—or was a boastful relative of one of the performers. As the gymnasium slowly emptied and the audience trickled into the lobby, extraterrestrials mingled comfortably with earthmen in an impressive display of intergalactic peace. Cameras flashed, and proud teachers and parents gazed lovingly upon children whom they had clad in gaudy and outlandish costumes. They had subjected these antennaed innocents to public humiliation, for no better reason than to gush about how adorable they looked. Many spacemen had already begun to peel off as many unnecessary clothing items as possible, as they attempted to regain some degree of dignity.

A gathering of younger children stood staring hypnotically at the school Christmas tree—a large silver aluminum model that was the rage of the day. Aimed upon it was a colored light wheel that variously transformed it from yellow to blue, then green, and finally red, before repeating the cycle. The changes in color were mesmerizing, and each gave the tree a different mood and personality. Beneath the tree were canned goods wrapped in white tissue paper that students had donated to aid the needy. Many were decorated with artistically tied ribbons, and the large mound that had been collected seemed a rich bounty of gifts for those less fortunate. I felt a convivial warmth fill the room as parents and teachers chattered and chuckled, while children squirmed impatiently, flustered by adult adoration. I was certain that Jill had glanced in my direction several times, as I uncharacteristically stood near my family.

The week had been a hectic one. I had conscientiously prepared for my Thespian debut and had also performed in two shows with the Pierce choir. Our choir had entertained at a student assembly and a special evening concert at the historically reconstructed log cabin near the Soldiers Monument. The monument was located on the river, in the heart of downtown Hamilton. These two city landmarks were the town's half-hearted attempt to satisfy city visitors starved to indulge in almost any form of sightseeing. That fateful evening continued to haunt me and remained on my mind even during this opening (and closing) night celebration. I winced as I recalled my log-cabin catastrophe.

*   *   *

It had been a nippy evening, and few people had attended the festivities. Only a collection of dedicated parents and a few curious downtown shoppers were there to witness the debacle. I had been asked to sing an a cappella solo of "Oh Holy Night," a task that I had fretted about for several weeks. The log cabin had only recently been dedicated, and I imagined that half of Hamilton would be there. People would be spilling over into the streets, yet would listen silently and intently to every note as if they were attending an evening at the opera. Naturally the sparse turnout had disappointed me, but I was swept up in the moment of my first public solo.

The choir sang several holiday standards, and then there was a petrifying extended silence. Our music teacher, Mrs. Farst, slowly reached into her pocket and pulled out her pitch pipe. She looked at me intently, nodded her head, and blew a single note that signaled that my moment had arrived.

The words, "Oh, Holy," had just slipped from my mouth when a cold sweat swept over me as I realized the song had been pitched too high. There was no way to inconspicuously start over and no place to hide. The next two minutes seemed to drag on until New Year's Eve, as I reached for notes as high as the moon, and stared like a frightened deer at a host of faces contorted in pain. They grimaced not only because they suffered for me, but because they were forced to endure the shrill and plaintive wails that emanated from my mouth.

Almost surprisingly, the song eventually concluded. The hushed quiet that followed a smattering of applause was similar to the silence one would hear after the merciful shooting of a lame horse. My parents and even my sisters were properly supportive after the fiasco. But I wore my embarrassment like a scarlet letter until it became close enough to Christmas Day that I could become completely distracted. I can state unequivocally that it was in no way a "night divine."

*   *   *

The torment of that moment lingered, even as I stood in the crowded lobby during this proud post performance celebration of our "Santa Star Wars." I was certain that when my back was turned, parents sadly shook

65

their heads and pitied the poor boy who had howled like a wounded wolf at their children's choir concert.

My eyes and mind wandered as the lobby gradually began to empty, and families bundled up to face down the bitter December weather. The room's picture windows had steamed up, as the outside doors accommodated the departing traffic. A mighty burst of shivery air chilled the panes each time the heavy doors were forced open. Frost formed over the glass, and the color wheel aimed at the tree cast a corresponding reflected glow on the icy windows. The moment was a Christmas memory; an instant uncoupled from the continuity of time—its emotional power apparent even as it was occurring. The scene branded itself into my memory. And it forever evokes not only a visual recollection, but all the feelings and sensory stimulations that originally accompanied it.

My mother's voice returned my focus to the present, as she suggested that it was time that we leave. I took a final furtive glance at Jill to pay her proper homage, threw on my coat and gloves, and departed for the numbing walk home.

*   *   *

The remaining two days of school passed quickly, my concentration being squarely centered on preparations for the upcoming holiday. The final afternoon of class was devoted to an in-room Christmas party, with several mothers bringing in freshly baked cookies. We made merry throughout the day, nibbling on sugary snacks, while sipping Kool-Aid and singing our favorite Christmas carols. It was a loosely structured, rousing good time, made more enjoyable because such behavior was usually strictly forbidden. I left the building that day with a sunny spirit, dimmed only by the fact that I would not see Jill until the new year.

There was much to be done at the Simers' to get ready for the holiday. First and foremost, a tree had to be selected. This popular chore was traditionally done at the vacant lot next to Miller's Drive-in Root Beer Stand on Central Avenue. Our entire family would pile into the car and take the five-minute drive to Miller's. The Studebaker Lark doors would then simultaneously fling open, and my sisters and I would scurry off in different directions. Anyone who spotted a tree that deserved consideration as a keeper bellowed out to one of our parents, so that they could make an official inspection. If we had made a strong case regarding the tree's virtues to our elder judges and the tree had passed the initial once-over, a lot attendant was called into action. The attendant, usually outfitted in lumberjack attire, then sauntered over and held the tree upright, so we could carefully inspect it from all angles. Although it was difficult to reach a consensus opinion, eventually a candidate emerged as an indisputable Simer tree. We never left disappointed and sometimes took home a jewel in the rough—aware of its imperfections, but overwhelmed by its unmistakable character.

The house was filled with our favorite Christmas decorations. Our small ceramic cherubs sat together on a miniature wooden bench, always with their noses in the air and their lips poutingly puckered. If they were placed on opposite ends of the bench and posed with heads facing in opposite directions, it appeared as if they had just had a tiff. However, when the cherubs were placed snugly together and turned toward each other, their puckered lips touched, and they seemed in the throes of a lovers' kiss.

The candle on the mantelpiece was covered by an elongated pentagon of translucent colored plastic, with all five faces framed in a lightweight metal. Each side was a different color plastic, so that the candle seemed to be housed within five stained glass windows. When the candle was lit, the heat caused the pentagon to spin and created a carousel of vivid hues. The steady flicker of the single flame gave each petite window that revolved into view a life of its own.

Our nativity scene was hand-constructed of natural wood, with figurines of several stable animals, the shepherds and wise men, Mary and Joseph, and the baby Jesus. A kindly angel was suspended from the front beam of the manger. Behind the angel and at the highest point of the rear of the structure, a hole had been cut out of the wood backing. The opening was large enough to insert a single white Christmas light that cast a subtle moon glow when the house lights were low.

These keepsakes, along with many other trinkets, snow domes, and wall and table decorations were boxed up in January, and brought out again the following December. They were friends who visited us for several weeks each year and became important contributors to our family history and Christmas tradition.

Decorating the tree was a task that required an entire evening. My father would meticulously fiddle with the light placement until his neck flushed a deep red, and he uttered words not befitting a man of the cloth. My mother tried to keep the peace between my dad and his evergreen adversary, while orchestrating our positioning of the ornaments and tinsel. We were to put on tinsel one strand at a time, but it was far too tempting to toss wads of the silver spaghetti everywhere. The strings of lights that wound around the tree held standard bulbs. Emphasis was to be placed on the natural beauty of the conifer, rather than the glitz and glitter of lavish decorations. Atop the tree was a star with a depiction of Christ at its center. The star was illuminated by a single white bulb, affixed to its backing on a wire spring. When this finishing touch had been precisely positioned at the tree's pinnacle, our labor of love had been completed. We then turned off all other house lights, lit candles and sang Christmas carols while sitting in a semicircle around the manger scene. We would go to our bedrooms that evening united as a family and recharged with enough goodwill that some would even carry over through the year's conclusion.

Sometime before Christmas Eve it was a Simer tradition (sans my father) to decorate Christmas cookies. The kitchen table was covered with old newspapers, and each child was given a stretch of rolled dough and an assortment of holiday cookie cutters. We would squeeze as many shapes into our dough allotment as was possible and then cautiously peel off the excess. My mother then snatched up the floured treasures and transferred them to a cookie tray that would be slid onto the next available oven rack. Shortly thereafter, they re-emerged freshly baked and accompanied by an unmistakable mouth-watering aroma. These blank canvasses were then painted, using several different colors of decorating pastes, a collection of sprinkles, cinnamon buttons and the ever-popular teeth-breaking silver beads. Usually someone would become discontented with their decorating skills and threaten to quit, and there were the typical artistic differences one would expect from master chefs, but eventually our work was completed.

The cookies were practically inedible with all the goodies piled on top of them, and there was an alarming number of three-legged reindeer and headless Santas. But each of us would save our masterpiece for Kris Kringle, with the remainder being placed on a giant serving plate. These were then savored with the same appreciation that adults afforded fine wine, for we shared intimate knowledge of the great effort that went into making them.

The holiday season would have been incomplete without the annual High Street Christian Church Christmas program, held on a weekend evening in our church basement. Almost every child and teenager participated in the program, with a talented few showcased by solo recitations and songs. Although I felt the added pressure of being the minister's son, it really made little difference whether any of us made a respectable showing or laid an egg. The attendees were always delighted by our efforts and seemed to sigh lovingly and quite audibly at everything we said or did.

After our modest presentation, Seborn Wilhoit, a spirited and talented musician who also happened to be sightless, pounded out Christmas carols on the piano while everyone sang along. Seborn played with great panache and zeal, and had the uncanny ability of uplifting one's spirit while lowering their inhibitions. Year after year, the congregation belted out the familiar first verse of each carol, then continued more tentatively with each additional stanza. They would listen carefully for anyone who sang these verses with confidence, then cautiously attempt to mimic them until they could cut loose on the next chorus. The result was a lot of yuletide gibberish, but the tradition was unshakable. The sing-along concluded with a rousing rendition of "Jingle Bells," which was preceded by a special surprise announcement. If we sang the tune with all the enthusiasm we could muster, there was a chance that Santa himself would appear.

After repeating the chorus at least three times, sleigh bells could be heard in the hallway behind the stage. Moments later a person dressed in a well-worn Santa suit emerged from the hall entranceway. Whispers traveled among the older children in the audience, as they tried to guess who the obvious impostor was. This church volunteer was easier to determine than most, because he was actually a she. Jean Falk, a rotund and animated woman, was a natural Santa except for her unmistakable vocal register. It was fun to pretend, however, and all the children lined up near the stage to visit with Santa or Jean, depending on the youngster's age and perceptiveness. Each child would climb the stairs to the corner of the rec-hall stage and confide their Christmas wish list to the jolly old elf herself. As they departed, they received a small cardboard box of candy with a handle made of heavy shoestring yarn. The contents were either hard or rock hard and often made better weapons than foodstuff. If extra candy remained after Santa's line had dissipated, my father would make sure that I received an additional box. It was definitely one of the lesser benefits of being a preacher's kid.

After Santa had jingled his way off the stage, the older youth gathered with their Sunday school class leaders. Caroling crews were then organized to visit the homes of shut-in church members. I had only recently reached an age that I could join in on this adventure and enjoyed rubbing elbows with kids who had a grade or two on me—as well as some bonafide teenagers. Each group would load into a leader's car and visit a designated list of houses. Of course, each person vied to go with their closest friends and/or the most attractive members of the opposite sex. To sit in a chilly car next to a girl who was my age or older was a newly discovered and pleasurable sensation not normally associated with the holiday spirit.

The caroling was fulfilling. As we entered each residence or nursing home, it felt as if we breathed life into the room. Most of us had only an indirect association with these shut-ins, so we could comfortably distance ourselves from their predicaments. As we walked out of the staleness of their homes and into the brisk night air, they disappeared from our lives, and we were once again insulated. Only over time would we grow to realize that their lives also continued.

After completing our designated stops, our youth leader drove us around the immediate vicinity to view some of the more impressively lit homes. We laughed, exchanged stories and ooohed and aaahed at the most ingenious and handsome displays. We slowly worked our way back to the church, where we sipped hot chocolate, ate Dunkin' Donuts and bathed in the gratification of goodwill toward men.

Another holiday event of significance that took place at the church was the Christmas Eve candlelight service. Held in a darkened sanctuary, a small unlit white candle was given to each attendee. Each candle had been inserted through a circular piece of cardboard, so that the circle fit snugly around the candle's base and collected the excess wax that dripped from a burning wick. The service was brief and much quieter than most. At its conclusion, a group of elders came forward to ignite their wicks from a single candle that burned in the front of the sanctuary. They then lit the candle of the first person in each row, and the flame was passed along until everyone's candle had been lit. The symbolism was obvious even to an eleven-year-old boy. And the flickering rows of individual flames cast these people in a light that made them appear as tranquil and serene as I would ever see them. The event always helped set my mood for the remainder of the evening and the following day.

Christmas Eve at the Simer home was a time for both preparation and worship. As soon as we arrived home, a television tray had to be set up where Santa could take five. His tray was immaculately set with our masterpiece cookies, a Pepsi-Cola along with instructions on how to obtain ice—and a carrot for Rudolph. At this juncture of our lives, only my youngest sister, Laurie, viewed this as a legitimate effort, but we still willingly acted out our parts and enjoyed the tradition on its own merit. The food and drink would mysteriously be missing the next morning—replaced by an empty dish and beverage glass, a half-eaten carrot, and a gracious thank-you note from Mr. Claus.

After tying up any loose ends, we held our family Christmas Eve service—a collection of scriptures and hymns in booklet form. The compilation had been prepared for Standard Oil employees, but had somehow been mysteriously pirated through connections my mother never spoke of. The living room was dark except for the light cast by the Christmas tree, our holiday candles and the single white bulb that accentuated the manger scene. Invariably one of the weary younger Simers would pout during the service, but I think we all relished this opportunity to be together. The moment was our final reminder of the true meaning of the holiday season.

We willingly went to bed early, though it was nearly impossible to sleep. I experienced a strange combination of great anticipation and inner peace, as I heard my parents scurrying about downstairs and realized how much they must care for us to spend all these hours in preparation. I nodded off occasionally, sleeping lightly and uncomfortably, until I woke up enough to remember what night it was. Then my brain would click back on, I would fantasize about the magical day ahead of me, and it would be fifteen or twenty minutes before I slept again.

Finally, when it became light enough to legitimately awaken our mother and father, we coaxed them from the comfort of their bed. My sisters and I lined up at the top of the stairs and awaited an official command from the designated parent/starter. "Ready . . . Set . . . Go!" The upstairs hall was a blur of arms, legs and flannel pajamas, as we shot down the stairs and into the living room.

Before us lay a mountain of presents beneath the tree and four brimming stockings on the mantelpiece. In front of each stocking was a dining room chair, where our most significant presents were showcased unwrapped on the padded seat. I had received a beautiful ebony black, six-transistor Admiral radio with a genuine leather case. The distinct smell of the newly unpacked, hard plastic casing convinced me that this was the finest radio that I could have received. Meanwhile, each of my sisters was squealing about her own chairful of riches. We noisily exchanged gift information while we emptied our stockings, and carefully examined everything that Santa had laid out for us.

After the initial commotion had subsided, we each found a comfortable spot near the tree. There we opened our more practical gifts and the inexpensive presents that my sisters and I had purchased for each other and our parents. I had taken care of most of my gift buying at Tri-County, the largest and most impressive shopping center in the area. During the holiday season they usually employed the most convincing Santa and featured a spectacular all-you-could-drink lemonade fountain in Pogue's toy department. Everyone seemed to enjoy the gifts I had bought them, or at least exhibited enough grace to protect my feelings.

We frittered away the remaining morning hours, reveling in our new toys and sneaking handfuls of candy from the table of fruitcakes, nuts and various sweets that Santa had left us. My best friend Mike and I carved out some time together to eye each other's new prized possessions. And he commenced his onslaught on our remaining hand-decorated cookies, exhibiting an addiction that none of the rest of us shared. Our time together was brief but significant, and we soon reluctantly parted ways. After all, as our parents insisted—this was a family day.

By mid-afternoon, the six Simers would load into the car and visit the homes of several church families. Each of us had selected one present that we were permitted to bring, and the Simer sleigh would hopscotch to a number of stops, some more entertaining than others. We all eagerly anticipated our visit to Red and Eva Lemon's spacious old home. They were nearly family and had two grown daughters, along with a reliable history of keeping Christmas well. The Lemons owned an elaborate train set that they assembled each year around their always-towering and bushy tree. I would remain stationed there for hours, blowing the engine whistle, billowing smoke from the smokestack, and directing a hardworking mechanical man to load and unload magnetic milk canisters onto a metal loading dock from a refrigerator car. When it was time to leave, my parents would nearly have to drag me away from my borrowed toy, and we would then exchange genuine and predictable holiday farewells before our journey home. The remainder of the day was spent admiring our overabundance of loot, which we quite intentionally spread across our entire living room floor.

*　　*　　*

It was a wonderful time of the year and a wonderful year to be a child. The season presented us invaluable family time, a strong connection with our community and the opportunity to learn the joy of giving. It provided reliable traditions, fellowship and religious inspiration. And it filled my senses with dazzling lights and unforgettable smells and sounds that still trigger a child's tenderness in my heart.

I have neglected to mention that my birthday falls on Christmas Eve. The date is so incorporated into my holiday experience that it was and is only an extension of my celebration. Christmas is my time of year, and in a strange way I am convinced that the season belongs to me. It is a celebration of life and the beginning of my life. It is a season of love and a time to remember and cherish the people I love. Christmas is about Christ, and it brings me in touch with powerful feelings about my faith and my God.

I try to regain the spirit of the Christmas of 1964 during each holiday season. And anytime I can touch that child within me, I have reached the essence of who I really am. These December remembrances evoke sensations and emotions that make the past as real as the present. They are Christmas memories, united with our souls.

11

The Farm

Our new two-toned red-and-cream Volkswagen bus was crammed with travel-weary Simers as we approached the junction of what appeared to be a T intersection. There was a small road sign with a two-headed arrow painted upon it, indicating that our only available alternatives were a right or left turn. We were in the heart of Southern Illinois farm country, and the blazing heat of the late afternoon sun steamed the surrounding vegetation and sent its fragrant vapors drifting skyward. They infiltrated the open car windows and filled the vehicle with an unmistakably sweet scent that seeped into the fractures that life had placed in my heart. I never realized how desperately my spirit had needed these aromas until I breathed them once again.

When we reached the end of the pavement and our moment of decision, we opted for a third alternative and defiantly continued past the cautionary road sign and down a single-lane dirt road. An uncontrolled growth of foliage spilled over into our path, and branches were snapped back by the momentum of the vehicle. I could reach outside my car window and snatch up overgrown weeds and wildflowers. The lush jungle extended into the clearing like suspended hovering waves—ominously positioned to wash back into the temporary man-made parting of a vast sea of green. Behind us we left a billowing trail of road dust—the wheels making becalming music as small patches of gravel were pinched and spit by the tire tread. My sisters and I edged forward in our seats, our five senses reinforcing that a full year of fantasies had once again been transformed into three-dimensional and tactile reality. It was the dog days of summer in 1965, and we were visiting my grandparents' farm on a week-long vacation that was, simply put, the annual highlight of our young lives.

My grandparents did not live on this farm. In fact, no one did. They owned a home in a residential area of Robinson, a lazy downstate community whose chief claim to fame was the Marathon Oil refinery and Heath

English Toffee. The farm, as we called it, was a large tract of land owned by my grandparents. The fields were cultivated both by my grandfather and a subcontractor, who worked a designated portion of the acreage.

Amid rows of planted corn, string beans, melons and various other crops was an extended plot that contained a two-room cabin—situated only a few yards from the dirt road. There were three ponds—the largest with an extended picnic area—and a tire-worn path that connected this recreational expanse to the grounds surrounding the dwelling. As we approached the end of the dirt road, we came upon a clearing that exposed a stretch of tilled fields. Adjoining these fields was a fenced-in and mowed grassy yard that corralled the cozy homestead and a variety of fir and shade trees. The trees tended to insulate the area from the nearby farmland, giving it a feel of sheltered seclusion. There were no houses or other buildings within sight, and the bordering carefully landscaped croplands were the only indication of recent human intervention.

We came to a halt in front of a white wood-plank entrance gate and lifted and swung it open. It felt as if the pearly gates had been unbolted, and on the other side of the fence I could see my grandparents slowly advancing toward us. The looks on their faces convinced me that they had hugging on their minds. The VW bus rolled across the gateline making our return to Shangri-la official, and we parked the bus near the gray shingled cabin. Car doors fanned open, and we slowly piled out and began stretching our inactive muscles.

My grandmother, a fairly tall, robust, full-figured woman, stretched out her arms and made her way down the line of grandchildren who bashfully stood before her. Her hugs felt as I imagined a grandmother's hugs were supposed to feel—forceful and nurturing. My grandfather followed closely behind her, drawing us close with his powerful sun-weathered arms. He wore his traditional short-sleeved button-down plaid shirt and a cap with a visor. Although not particularly large, he seemed quite imposing to me, with the look of a man who had worked with his muscles and his hands. The face of Roy William Henry Rees was intense, but there was a purity in his expression that hinted at his compassion and decency. Whenever he opened his mouth, his keen humor and virtually endless collection of puns, witticisms and silly songs held me mesmerized. As I buried my face into his shoulder, I felt the roughness of his day-old beard and inhaled his familiar and pleasant odor. His clothes smelled as if they breathed the outdoor air, and there was the unmistakable scent of Mennen Skin Bracer—the aftershave he nearly always wore.

My grandmother was cackling at something my mother had just said. Elsie Rees was a strong-willed and disciplined woman with determined eyes and wire-rimmed glasses that did nothing to soften her fiery appearance. When she smiled or laughed, her eyelids dropped into slits, and she seemed a bit more accessible. She cooked and baked with seemingly effortless proficiency, and her house was always perfectly ordered as most of her life seemed to be. She was certain of her beliefs, confident of her role in her family and community, and resistant to anything that disturbed the rigid structure of her daily routine. Both Grandma and Granddad (as I called them) led lives that were representative of many hardworking patriots in rural America. They were honest people who provided positive influences on our young lives.

After briefly listening to the adults catch up on current goings-on, the younger set sneaked off to fulfill several nearly sacred rituals. These rites would proclaim to the Rees Farm that we had returned as we had promised we would, when we had last been forced to say good-bye. Located about fifteen yards from the cabin was an old hand-operated iron pump that drew water from a natural well. Our presence would not be fully recognized until its handle had been pumped vigorously enough that it squeaked out a sound resembling a donkey's bray, and water flowed freely from its spigot. A cobalt-blue metal cup hung from a hook on the base of the pump. The cup was reverently removed so that we might partake in a communion of sorts, as we each took a sip of the naturally cool water.

Just a few feet from the pump was a dinner bell mounted on a tall iron pole. Both the bell and the pump were regularly repainted a shiny silver and looked as if they had held vigilance over the homestead since the beginning of time. In the tranquility of the country, its peal could be heard anywhere on the property. The bell nearly danced on its axis in joyous celebration, as we all tugged mercilessly on the connecting chain and notified the resident wildlife that like the migrating birds—the Simers had returned. Laurie and Becky buried their bottoms on two nearby tree swings, where we each would eventually spend time in quiet meditation.

My grandmother had climbed the two stair steps to the cabin and was about to open the front door. This was our sign to drop anything that we were engaged in and explore the inner recesses of our favorite vacation haunt. As usual, my grandparents had lovingly readied the cabin for our habitation. The propane tank had been replaced, so that we could operate the small gas stove and refrigerator. Lamps had been filled with kerosene, and the beds and cots had been made up with freshly pressed sheets. The small kitchen cabinets above the stove had been filled with grocery necessities, and the Servel gas refrigerator was humming and stocked with perishable goods. A cookie jar on the kitchen table was full of sandwich-cremes, and there was an abundant supply of dishes and silverware.

The cabin had the odor of a structure that had remained closed for a lengthy period and had recently been aired out. The smell was neither stale nor breezy and was a welcome scent distinctly associated with these two rooms. In the front room there was a long table for serving and storage, a meal table that could be expanded by raising the leaves, and a wood-burning furnace. Against the far wall was a bed where I slept and a shelf near the ceiling where my grandmother stored crayons, dominoes and a few small toys to while away the afternoon hours.

In the back room there was a double bed where my parents slept and a cot for each of my three sisters. This sleeping room also contained an ancient dark-wood mirrored vanity and a small bookcase which held many religious titles. On the rear wall, a second door offered a stairless exit to the great outdoors. The cabin was illuminated by the sunlight that spilled through the screen doors and back windows during the day, and the glow of four kerosene lamps in the evening.

There was no running water or electricity. When nature called, it meant a trip to the "House of the Three Bears"—the much more delicate nickname we used to describe the outhouse. There was a trio of holes carved into the long wooden bench, each precision-cut to conform to a different-sized derriere. A visit to the Three Bears was never a highlight of our trip, and a reluctance to visit sometimes led to a subsequent bout of constipation. A nighttime sojourn was a particularly harrowing experience. It was just a portable kerosene lantern and me in the darkest of night—with only my imagination to keep me company. Any living creature that I had ever seen at the farm could be lurking within the confines of the outhouse door, and some mighty private body parts would be exposed. I was never able to complete my business more quickly and efficiently.

I had taken a seat at the kitchen table and watched the traffic entering and leaving the cabin. The large spring on the door-hinge groaned each time someone walked in or departed, and the wooden door then slapped itself shut—the large screen somewhat lessening the volume of the impact. The wooden floors creaked as people moved about. Footsteps would suddenly become muffled, and shoes squeaked when they trod across the brittle old sheets of linoleum on the kitchen floor. Outside I could hear familiar voices and occasional laughs, and I remember thinking that there was surely not a more peaceful location anywhere.

It was now quite late in the afternoon, and there were discussions of a picnic by "the lake"—the largest of the ponds. It had been so named because it was impossible to convince an impressionable child that a body of water deep enough for a rowboat to float on was not at the very least a lake. After unpacking the last of our items, we collectively drifted down the dirt path that took us past a producing cornfield and toward a picnic area near the water. I rode in my grandfather's Ford Fairlane and was enticed by the tempting aroma of chicken à la king drifting from my grandmother's picnic basket. Other members of the family opted for the approximately one-block hike, which took them past an old natural-wood barn with a rust-ridden tin roof. They arrived lakeside shortly after we did.

The pond appeared placid in the light breeze, and the surrounding area seemed identical in appearance to my last visit. The waters were up, and the raised eastern banks clearly suggested an elevated water level. Behind these banks was a patch of woods that provided an ideal backdrop to the picture-postcard setting. The grasses around the pond had received a recent mowing, and the trimmings filled the air with the sweet fragrance of summer. On the south shore, a short pier reached out into the water, and a green wooden rowboat lay overturned by the water's edge. Near the boat and about ten feet into the water was a tire-sized circular concrete overflow designed to help alleviate flooding. The north and west banks were lined with clusters of cattails, and when looking north beyond the lake, there was a long stretch of grassy fields mowed only a short distance beyond the water. South of the pond were the sizeable picnic grounds complete with three tables, a large brick barbecue and several metal lawn chairs.

As I made my way onto the pier, I could see a bullfrog sitting motionless in the muddy greenery at the rim of the water and two dragonflies darting in tandem when not hovering precariously near the water's surface. There was still the faint odor of algae—although due to recent rains the smell was not as pungent as it sometimes was. The crickets hummed their shrill yet tranquil song. Clearly although humans were rarely there to witness it, the farm was always vibrantly alive.

We devoured dinner while watching the sunset by the lake, and as usual, my grandmother's offerings were delectable. Besides the chicken à la king, there were home-grown vegetables and homemade preserves, wheat and white breads and deviled eggs. For dessert we had persimmon pudding—which was tasty by itself or soaked in milk. There was much updating to do, and we patiently listened to a few hours of dreary grown-up talk while politely answering questions that were directed to us.

Occasionally we would sneak off, hop into the rowboat and take a brief trip around the pond. Laurie, being the youngest, was a willing passenger aboard an endless number of guided scenic tours. The dark waters would swirl when the oars were dipped in, and they offered only faint resistance when the paddles were pushed through their murky depths. Whenever we drifted too near the shore, the oars would bring up a tangle of weeds that disappeared when they were immersed in deeper waters. The conversation being carried on at the picnic table traveled so efficiently across the nearly still waters, that if we sat silently in the boat—we could hear exchanges never intended for our ears.

It was now early evening. The dusk had blanketed the horizon when my grandparents began gathering their belongings. Although they would be driving back to town, the cabin would remain our residence for the week. The fish had begun jumping, and their brief leaps into alien environments created circular ripples that swelled in diameter until their force eventually dissipated. Occasionally a turtle's head would rise to the surface to investigate our intrusion, but would soon resubmerge as he opted for his less-complicated underwater world.

The fast approaching darkness dictated that we either light a lantern or conclude our evening's visit, and we opted for the latter. Our family began the short walk back to the cabin, but the four Simer children sprinted away from the pack—attempting to arrive before the Fairlane did. As we veered off the path and angled back to the cabin, we raced past the House of the Three Bears and could see a pair of trailing headlights grow in intensity and size as they rapidly closed distance. We won the race against our unaware opponents and were standing by the steps when my grandfather parked his idling car and approached with door key in hand.

My sisters and I entered the dark front room and watched as he lifted the clear glass chimney, adjusted the wick and lit the kerosene lamp nearest the entrance. The match's glow spotlighted my grandfather's face before the steady flame of the lamp returned life to the setting. With the aid of a mirror that the lantern had been placed near, the entire room was charged with a soothing light. As other lamps were ignited, the cabin felt increasingly insulated from the mysterious sounds and haunting darkness that lurked outside its confines. My grandfather promised to pay us a visit the next morning and bring some nightcrawlers for fishing. Tomorrow evening a number of relatives would gather for a much larger get-together. It would be a relaxing, but active day.

After my grandparents departed, the family remained awake for nearly an hour discussing the trip, our grandparents and any minor differences that we had noticed at the farm. We never wanted anything to change and wished that the farm could remain frozen in time—free from the evolution that occurs with all other earthly things. The cabin seemed a dreamlit oasis and invited us to wrap ourselves in our blankets and feel the assurance of being loved and cared for. We changed into our bed clothes, and the lamps were dimmed to a blue flicker. The sounds of the night would prompt me to grasp my pillow and pull it to my chest, while feeling the perfumed crisp pillowcase against my face. Within minutes, I would fall into a peaceful slumber.

*   *   *

The call of the bobwhite, whippoorwill and a chorus of songbirds woke me up before anyone was stirring in the next room. The morning air beckoned me, and the two-room cabin could not house my boyish enthusiasm to begin the new day. I silently nudged the cabin door open and stepped out into the dewy grass. The blades tickled my toes, and I felt the damp chill on the soles of my feet.

I wandered over to a metal-braced hammock located only steps away and delicately positioned myself on the cool and clammy canvas—where I remained for several minutes. There I simply watched and listened, while mindlessly twisting the frills on the hammock's periphery. Hushed conversation could soon be heard from inside the cabin, so I returned—more noisily this time—hoping to stir up enough commotion to hasten the morning's beginning.

My mother was first to shed her covers, and she soon was scooting around the front room, the flow of her nightgown shadowing every sudden movement. Within minutes she lured four heavy-eyed zombies from their non-eternal rest with irresistible wake-up bait. A heavy metal spoon rattled reveille—from a mixing bowl filled with Bisquick pancake mix. Soon, batter bubbled and bacon sizzled in the iron skillet, and the kitchen table was surrounded by five impatient flapjack fans who partook of the tempting smells as if they were the first course to the morning's meal. Breakfast was tasty, and only the large tea kettle boiling on the stove top (indicating dish duty) impeded my total enjoyment of the sunrise fare.

The dishwashing passed quickly, and I dried the last plate just in time to witness the spectacle of my father shaving. I was too old to admit it, but watching him wield his razor in the great outdoors was a show I did not want to miss. He stood near the pump at a rustic weather-worn green table with a tree-trunk base and a small woodboard top. On it sat a white metal basin filled with steaming water, an Old Spice shaving mug with brush, along with various other toiletries.

To my father, shaving was an art form. Preparing the lather with great verve, he gently whisked it onto his face as if doing a Mary Kay demonstration. He was meticulous with his straight-edged razor, rinsing his equipment frequently and showing creative flair with a gentle twist and flick of the wrist after every stroke. Few words were exchanged while I watched him, but he seemed to be sharing a manly ritual with me. After finishing, he vigorously toweled down his cheeks and carefully rinsed his shaving tools, readying them for the next day's performance. His face appeared squeaky clean and had a smoothness that he would literally grow out of in a few short hours.

I drew a fresh basin of pump water so that I might take a sponge bath. The water was underground cool and felt even more chilly when my skin was slapped by the light breeze. I very quickly dabbed my private areas and gingerly wiped myself clean, while cringing at each contact with the cold, drenched washcloth. I then brushed my teeth with baking soda, a treat reserved only for vacations at the farm. Determining that I was clean enough to pass a casual inspection, I returned to the cabin where I built intricate domino houses and waited for everyone else to wash up.

My grandfather arrived as the last basin of rinse water was being dumped behind a temporary clothesline. He wore a matching blue-denim jacket and pants and carried a white cardboard carton filled with nightcrawlers in a fine mulch. He had a hankering for a morning cup of java, so he relaxed at the kitchen table and shared some instant with my parents. I quietly eavesdropped, as I lay flat on my back in bed and counted the nails hammered into the fiberboard ceiling.

I found myself almost in awe of my grandfather. He was a handyman, a comedian and a philosopher—and was as masculine as any man I had ever met. The current topic of conversation had tickled him. His laughter sounded like a guttural giggle and resonated as powerfully as did his deep-bass speaking voice. He laughed well and often.

After patiently waiting for this adult drivel to wind down, my younger sisters finally began pleading that we make our morning visit to the lake. Although I remained interested in my elders' conversation, I was antsy to get there myself. Mom and Dad were unusually tolerant of our intrusion and quite easily relented. So we slipped into our bathing suits and collected outside the cabin for a mass exodus to our all-day lakeside retreat.

The younger Simers ran full-tilt down the lane, our shoeless feet slapping against the grass-bare portions of the path. After rushing to the water's edge, we stood poised at the pond's rim—waiting to spot one of our lagging parents before entering the water. The Fairlane arrived before my parents did, as my grandfather flipped open his trunk and removed two old inflated tire inner tubes that had been patched and repatched.

My mother sat at a shaded picnic table and read, while Laurie and Becky snatched the coal-black inner tubes and heaved them into the water. They bounced as they hit the surface and drifted several feet before floating nearly motionless, gently rolling with the water's subtle movement. The calm was quickly disturbed by two charging human retrievers barreling full-tilt into the pond, their legs churning vigorously until the density and depth of the water drove them face-first into a cushioned, but very wet fall.

Emily and I trailed behind, taking the transition in temperature more gradually. As we crept forward, the level inched ever higher. The water near the surface had been warmed by the morning sun, while the pond bottom contained chilly pockets that had somehow evaded its reach. Small portions of the floor were still covered liberally with sand, the aftermath of a project my grandfather had undertaken several years before. The shallow end on the south side of the pond had at one time been completely surfaced with sand for his six grandchildren's aquatic pleasures. But the years had caused the floor to resettle, and Mother Nature had resurfaced much of the area. The clay would temporarily stain our feet an almost orange-brown by week's end.

Emily was now leading an underwater somersault drill as all three of my sisters launched themselves from the miry floor and submerged simultaneously. Then only their legs and feet popped into sight mid-flip before their faces eventually reappeared. They gasped for air and giggled as pond water dripped from their faces.

I latched onto an inner tube and leapt upon it, my posterior fitting snugly in the center, while my legs dangled over the tube's sides. I rode my miniature raft until the rubber surface baked dry and became hot to the touch. Then I simply turned the inflated craft over and repositioned myself on the slick, cool, water-darkened flip side. I alternately stared into the sky at the cottony cumulus clouds or at the trees that seemed to tower over the water's banks.

Except for sneak attacks by several demonic horseflies, my nearly half-hour meandering journey was pacific. The remainder of the morning was spent teasing my sisters or stretched out on the pier examining the grain of its painted wooden surface. The sun imperceptibly panned its spotlight until it shone directly overhead and signaled that it was time for a lunchtime intermission.

We reluctantly trudged out of the waters and toweled off, wiping our feet on some long grasses as if they were a door mat. A faint breeze caused us to shiver, and our prunelike fingers revealed the lengthy period we had spent in the water. My mother had already returned to the cabin, but had left the new Sears Silvertone FM/AM portable transistor radio on a nearby picnic table. The radio was our sole daily connection to the civilized world. It blared with solid-state, hi-fidelity clarity as Gary Lewis asked us the important musical question, "Who's gonna buy this diamond ring?" The radio was a daytime night-light, reassuring us that the world had not ended—we merely had temporarily escaped from it. We sat hovered around the radio, singing along whenever we all knew the same lyrics and bickering whenever there was more than one version of them. A persistent breeze rustled the trees' leaves, and it stroked our cheeks while making our wet bathing suits feel colder than the water ever was.

The piercing clang of the dinner bell soon proclaimed that lunch was being served. We quickly returned to home-base where my mother had prepared some Chef Boyardee spaghetti that was now being served alfresco. The morning swim had left us ravenous, and we wolfed down the steamy noodles as if they were the finest in Italian cuisine. Canned spaghetti, which we normally would have only tolerated, never tasted so good.

My granddad, who had spent the morning doing some mowing, was now preparing to leave. We looked on as he emerged from the barn and padlocked the door, but not before removing four bamboo fishing poles—already equipped with hooks and bobbers. I began to fidget with anticipation. Fishing was my favorite pastime on the farm, and although I now viewed using a cane pole as kid's stuff, I was neither knowledgeable enough nor did I have sufficient tackle to prepare my new rod and reel. I had not been assigned kitchen duty, so I selected the longest and sturdiest pole, removed the live bait carton from the refrigerator and strolled down the trail feeling like Tom Sawyer en route to an afternoon of fishing on the mighty Mississippi.

When I had reached the lake, I walked counterclockwise to the east water's edge and selected the ideal location about three-quarters of the way down the narrow embankment. I pulled a single worm from the large living knot within the carton and artistically wound a segment of it onto my hook, convinced that the presentation often made the meal even more enticing. I stepped as close to the bank's edge as was possible, leaned over and used the bobber like a swinging pendulum before depositing it a considerable distance into the now rippling water. The pond was stocked with bass and bluegill, but bluegill were the primary prey when cane-pole fishing.

The bobber was my favorite type—with an egg-shaped base balanced in the water by two narrow pointed spikes on either side of the oblong core. It was painted predominantly white, with a horizontal stripe in the center, and the spikes' tips finished in royal blue. When the water was still enough, and the line was properly weighted, it sat with a spike upright—the water level lining up with the center stripe of the bobber. A nibble would cause the bobber to thrash about teasingly, then quickly bounce back to its upright position—like a child's inflatable sand-weighted punching balloon after a kayo blow. A full-fledged assault on the nightcrawler morsel would send the flotation device plunging—burying it beneath the pond's surface and pleading with the angler to nab the greedy culprit.

Landing the fish was exhilarating, removing the hook not nearly as enjoyable. I was now far too grown-up to appear affected, though, and I even faithfully came to the aid of my sisters whenever they found a fish on their line. After the messy surgery was completed, the prize was carried with both hands to a live-box located next to the pier, where the captives spent their final hours.

I came up empty during my solo expedition, and when my sisters deserted their fishing posts and began frolicking in the water like a trio of hyperactive sea lions, the shouts and splashes provided me a legitimate excuse for my lack of success. Even then, I enjoyed watching the bobber roll in the water. When the ripples eventually drifted the bait too close to the shore, it gave me a reason to examine my annelid artwork before sending it back on its self-sacrificial mission. The afternoon had been ideally lazy, although my sisters and I had hooked only two bluegill—one of which was sent back with instructions to fatten up so that he might be recaptured at a later date.

It was now deep into the day, and my father had finished the reading that he had been so engrossed in most of the afternoon. The time seemed ideal to ask him to string my new Pflueger rod and reel, and he grudgingly obliged. He was calmer than usual and managed to complete the task with a minimal amount of aggravation.

I put on the hookless practice lure and repeatedly sent it soaring across an expanse of open grasses, being careful not to inadvertently lasso a tree or a sister who happened by. Eventually I developed a reasonable degree of accuracy and distance and decided that the rod would be put to its first test after dinner.

Within the hour, people would begin arriving for the evening get-together. My recently developed quirk of caring about my appearance demanded that I freshen up and change into a pair of clean shorts and T-shirt. When I entered the cabin, the rest of the family had remained lounging by the lake. The setting sun peered through the windows of the back room, and I sank onto the edge of my parents' mattress, acutely aware of how similar the moment was to many dreams that I had experienced. The farm often invaded my sleep—demanding that I recognize its existence and flushing my soul with a unique serenity and sense of belonging.

I slowly made my way out the door and to the pump, wiped myself down with a damp washcloth and wetted and combed my hair. Returning to the cabin, I pulled an acceptable clothing ensemble from a neatly packed suitcase and slipped into a fresh T-shirt and fringed jean cutoffs. Although no one else was present, I did not feel alone. I felt enveloped by the sun and breeze that teased my skin—while nature's murmur perked my ears with its clarity. Almost prayerfully, I made the return walk to the lake to rejoin my clan.

Laurie and Becky were still in the lake, motoring their inner tubes through the water using vigorous hand and leg locomotion. Emily and both of my parents sat at a table, poring over various reading materials—so I elected to take the rowboat out for a brief private junket. As I pushed off, the boat slid across the soggy high grasses, leaving a V indentation in the mud that was quickly overridden with seeping waters. Taking a long step into the craft, it suddenly ceased to drag the surface and began to glide as if airborne. I walked cautiously to the oarsman's seat. As I shifted my weight, the waters spanked the boat's sides, creating an almost tympanic irregular rhythm that did not cease until I settled into a more stable seated position.

I maneuvered to the center of the pond and then simply drifted, staring into the sky and feeling the now restrained but substantial power of the water's movement. After it gently rocked me too near the shore, I paddled back to my original location and began a repeat journey. As I gazed at the western horizon, I saw billowing dust rising from the northwest landscape. These stirrings meant that a car was grinding through the gravel in our direction. Within minutes, my grandparents' Fairlane rolled up, and we were soon exchanging greetings and unloading grocery bags, dishes and a thermos onto an adjoining table. Several vinyl-strip lawn chairs were set up, and just as we were poised to settle in—another road cloud rose in the distance. I imagined the dust was an Indian smoke signal—foretelling the arrival of additional relatives.

Before I knew it, Uncle Jim and Aunt Lorna were flinging open the front doors of a Ford Mustang, while my cousins, JoLynn and Susie, bolted from the car and tore in our direction. Genuine smiles and sincere embraces abounded, and even more food and drink were unloaded. My grandmother carefully spread her tablecloths, and the immediate vicinity began to smell and look like a full-fledged picnic. Additional chairs were unfolded and though absorbed in conversation, ultimately we all found seats and formed an almost-perfect semicircle. Everyone was talking, and almost no one was listening—but it didn't seem to make any difference.

Gradually the high-intensity gabfest slowed to a handleable pace, and the younger set began to wander. Susie and Emily paired off as they usually did—since they were nearly the same age. I trailed them much of the time, but tried to keep it from being obvious. Susie was blonde and vivacious—fun to tease and quite capable of good-natured retaliation. JoLynn was considerably older than the rest of us, trapped in that nebulous zone between youth and adulthood. She was a striking strawberry-blonde high-school student, and I would have been smitten with her if she were not my cousin. JoLynn alternated her time between the older folk and her younger cousins—and was perfectly capable of blending into both worlds.

My amphibious little sisters had returned to the water, and Emily and Susie were divulging intimate romantic secrets while I chauffeured them via boat around the pond. Their conversation had just snatched my undivided attention when the dust again began to fly. Another car was approaching, and we knew that it must be Uncle Kenny and Aunt Norma. Neither were actually relatives of the Simers. Aunt Norma was Lorna's sister, and her husband Kenny was the best friend of my mother's brother, Uncle Jim. I proclaimed their arrival by shouting across the pond like a town crier.

Everyone hustled back to the picnic area, so that by the time they arrived, we were all limbering our arms for some serious hugging. Aunt Norma spread her arms even as she approached us—ready to squeeze the stuffing out of the first child whom she encountered. Norma was a stocky and spunky woman who wore her heart on her sleeve, and she bubbled over with love and a zest for life. I found her to be a remarkable woman. Kenny was a tall, quiet man with a cool demeanor and subtle sharp wit. His wife usually commanded center stage, while he appeared most comfortable when no one noticed him.

After Aunt Norma had made her rounds, we collected ourselves and each drifted to our area of specific interest. Uncle Kenny and Uncle Jim grabbed their tackle boxes and headed to the west shore to do some fly fishing. My dad and I took our rods and reels to the east bank to try our luck with surface lures. Laurie and Becky stood near us with cane poles in hand, and Emily and Susie headed back in the direction of the cabin with instructions to return within the half hour. Everyone had been doused with mosquito repellent and appeared relaxed and settled in for the evening. Voices and laughter echoed across the water from all directions, and this sweet music soothed my spirit like a mother's lullaby.

I watched intently as my Uncle Jim dragged on his cigarette while manipulating his fly rod with the effortless flair of a master. He was my idol—an honest intelligent man with a heavily-lined concerned face. His voice was deep and distinctive, with an accent that affirmed his southern Illinois upbringing. Uncle Jim was adept at all traditionally masculine endeavors, yet was amazingly softhearted and approachable.

My casting was improving by the minute. But because I had not had a single strike, the event now evolved into target practice as I attempted to drop my lure into specific locations. However, the welcome announcement that dinner was on the table caused me to reel in my line at a speed no sea creature could duplicate. I raced back to the tables, propped my rod against a tall tree and sat down to a feast fit for a king.

The tables were filled with casserole dishes and relish plates, a large

Jello salad, breads and two home-baked pies. Our main course was Grandma's homemade noodles—a scrumptious mixture of her melt-in-your-mouth thick pasta and petite pieces of tender chicken. Before we could dig in, my grandmother said those five words I had heard before countless meals: "Dad, would you say grace?" We bowed our heads and Granddad offered a brief prayer.

When the magic word "Amen" was uttered, fourteen heads raised nearly in unison and the dish merry-go-round commenced. Plates were heaped with varying combinations of goodies, while those individuals either ignorant or unconcerned about rules of etiquette ceased talking and made better use of their mouths. Between bites, there were still several conversations being conducted at a time. I could participate in any of them or exercise my child's prerogative of being seen and not heard—and merely listen.

Individual voices became barely distinguishable, as laughter regularly erupted from all ends of the table. Everyone seemed particularly animated, as if each person was meeting with a dear friend that he or she had not seen for years. The enthusiastic chatter brought a smile to my face, and I felt the satisfaction of being a member of this family. Each person was so absorbed in the food and fellowship that they were unaware that I was looking at them so adoringly.

After dinner, Grandma sliced her pies, and I captured a particularly healthy slice of her famous mince meat—made with actual bits of beef. I closed my eyes and took a bite, sliding it back and forth in my mouth so that I would still taste it long after I had finished eating.

As people completed their dessert, they began to peel off and return to their recreational activities. Emily and Susie took Becky and Laurie to go bluegill fishing. Dad and I rubbed our lower legs with Pine Sol, because we would be walking through the taller grasses on our way to the North Pond. The ever-lurking chiggers—those disgusting little bugs that burrow into the skin—seemed to steer clear of Pine Sol. The North Pond was stocked for bass fishing, so we toted our tackle boxes past the lake and through a field of unmowed grass. After a three-minute walk, we arrived at the tiny pond.

We cast for about a half-hour with no success, but it made absolutely no difference. I had been blessed with some private time with my father—a rare occasion indeed. The crickets were plentiful in the high grasses, and they performed their night song in a series of fades and crescendos. The sun had set, and the grey blue twilight created a world of shaded shapes and hazy definition.

Sound superseded sight, and the light grew so dim that there was a sense of relief each time a lure was cast, and we heard it hit the water. Occasionally as we shifted positions, we heard the loud splash of a startled frog escaping the thunder of our approaching steps. Darkness became an insurmountable obstacle as the horizon dimmed, and an ocean of stars came into focus. It was time to head back. As we climbed the final incline in the rolling grasses, we could see the lake and our party on the other side. A Coleman lantern had been lit, and a fire blazed with a circle of chairs and people gathered around it. The images of light shimmered on the pond surface, and their boisterous happy voices seemed to be a call of the wild that said welcome.

We found seats near the fire, and I pulled mine close enough that the drifting smoke sometimes burned my eyes. The creased embers of the larger logs cast a flickering glow that made them appear as if they were breathing. Multicolor flames swallowed newly added wood, and my grandfather conducted the light show, using his poker like a performance baton, as he orchestrated the location and intensity of the flames. The wood crackled, whistled and occasionally popped when isolated sparks were launched from the flames like miniature skyrockets.

We spent the next hour or so singing hymns and silly children's camp songs. The fire's glow cast a flattering light on everyone's faces, as it smoothed the skin and made eyes glisten. I looked at my Aunt Lorna, who always seemed to be smiling, as she gently rocked in her chair while she sang. She was naturally pretty with silky fair skin and an obvious deep pride in her husband and daughters. Uncle Jim leaned back in his seat with eyes cast skyward, his eyeglasses mirroring the movement of the flames. Aunt Norma's broad face was rife with emotion as she dramatically mouthed the lyrics of each hymn that we sang. Granddad's big bass voice rumbled as he provided the music the depth that it deserved.

Each family member was so precious, their voices so calming, that I felt that I never wanted to leave this circle. But the evening had to end, and eventually Granddad allowed the fire to burn down and then separated the logs. I sought out people to say my good-byes. It was a particularly wonderful night, because they would all be returning later in the week. The vacation was only beginning. The sky was thick with stars and was a spectacular sight, as the lantern was extinguished and the firelight became a crimson dust. We all hopped into autos, and I rode back with Uncle Jim—seated next to JoLynn and smiling like a Cheshire cat.

Lanterns had already been lit when I arrived at the cabin. The gate leaving paradise had been opened. Hand waves were exchanged, and horns beeped their fond farewells as a procession of cars exited. Then there was silence. It was the kind of silence that makes you immediately take notice—a stillness that screams out to you that you are indeed alone.

We quickly broke the spell and talked briefly, while my dad savored his regular evening Pepsi-Cola. We had convinced him to play his harmonica, so we stretched out in the back room and listened to the sweet sounds of his silver-plated Hohner. My eyes became heavy as I listened to "The Old Rugged Cross," and I think that we all sensed that the day was now complete. I gave each of my parents a surprisingly enthusiastic hug before I crawled into bed. I still smelled of insect repellent, and my fingers provided aromatic evidence that I had handled fish. My father dimmed the lamp, and I curled up and thanked God that the farm existed and had such a profound effect on me. I would express this gratitude regularly for the remainder of my life.

*   *   *

My grandfather used to throw on a straw hat and hop aboard a tractor coupled to a small wooden flat bed loaded with Simer children. We'd bounce through the heart of the woods, past the South Pond and into the crop fields on a deluxe scenic tour of the Rees grounds.

When I was in the fifth grade, I fired my first pistol when Dad and I shot at oil cans behind the old barn. I was taken by the impressive look of the weapon, although the recoil nearly knocked me off my feet.

Our beagle Rover endlessly chased rabbits at the farm each year until we lost him when I was about ten. When he was unleashed and allowed to roam free, he would run like the wind in no particular direction—wearing a silly dog grin on his face. I felt that way about the farm too, sometimes.

On rainy vacation days, we would listen to the patter of rain on the cabin roof while we worked crossword puzzles, read and played card games. When it came to shelter from the elements, nothing was cozier than a tin-roofed cabin.

Saturday night meant a trip to my grandparents' to bathe or shower. We would remain in civilization for the evening, and attend their church the next morning. Grandma's bed sheets smelled cleaner than any I have ever laid my body on.

One year my father caught a five-pound bass in the dead of night when the two of us went out on a private fishing excursion. I was boastfully proud of him.

These are the small moments that give the farm its enormous heart. They are the vivid recollections that I have lived over and over and over again.

*   *   *

My grandfather and grandmother have both passed away. Norma and Kenny are gone, as is my Uncle Jim, who wrote a lengthy reply to a letter I had written him shortly before he died. Aunt Lorna remains in Robinson and still owns the farm. Susie and her husband are currently living in southwestern Ohio, and JoLynn is thriving in Champagne/Urbana. It has been years since I have seen Robinson, Illinois.

*   *   *

I have a recurring dream. I am suspended airborne, gracefully gliding over the farm. I float past the cabin, across the corn fields and hover over the lake. The entire family is gathered again—sometimes at the dinner table, sometimes around the campfire, but always locked in at a particular age that I choose to remember them. I realize then that the moment is mine—that the people and the farm belong to me, and no one can ever take them away. Sometimes I wake up while still in flight. Other times I descend and share a moment with my loved ones or just breathe the sweet air that helps to sustain me.

I have traveled to many places and plan to see many more before my life on this earth has ended. But my frequent cerebral nighttime visits to Rees Farm only reaffirm what I have always known. For my money, it will forever be the most beautiful spot on this planet.

12

The Drive-in

The Simer family had nearly completed an early Friday dinner, and I sensed that something was unusual. One glaring peculiarity was that we were all sitting at the kitchen table together—a true rarity for our family during the summer of 1965. My father often worked late into the evening, and my sister Emily had blossomed into a junior-high-school socialite who often couldn't find time in her busy schedule for meals. Usually I could be found at a Little League practice, or with my derriere securely adhered to the seat of my two-wheeler—as I pedaled vigorously throughout the neighborhood as a member of Mike Engel's two-man bicycle gang. And my sisters Becky and Laurie always had several alternate dining options available at various neighbors' homes.

My mother and father seemed unusually upbeat, and my sisters and I were monitoring the situation closely—searching for any clue to explain their mysteriously pleasant behavior. Our answer was not long in coming. It was ceremoniously announced that we were going to the Valley Drive-in Movie Theater, and quite suddenly the evening exploded and took on a life of its own. The drive-in was our favorite family activity and ranked only behind Christmas Day, vacations at my grandparents' cabin and the annual church weekend retreat as the most monumental events in our young lives. However, there were specific rituals associated with a scheduled trip to the drive-in, and our time had been limited somewhat by this uncharacteristically late notification. We quickly sprang into action.

Any neighborhood child old enough to converse in the English language and unfortunate enough to be caught outside their home had to be told of our stroke of luck. Those considered best or nearly best friends who were confined behind closed doors should either be quickly visited or contacted by phone. Drumming up a degree of envy was essential. The evening newspaper theater advertisements must also be located—not to find out what was playing, but instead to affirm that this was indeed an official entertainment event. My mother feverishly packed a picnic basket containing specific required snacks and filled our scotch-plaid thermos with the Kool-Aid flavor du jour. Finally the four youngest Simers had to change into their favorite sleeping clothes. This long-standing tradition probably began so we didn't need to change for bed when we got home, but continued because it was so avant-garde to wear pajamas in a car.

Just before dusk as the crickets tuned for their evening's symphony, we piled into the station wagon, battled for advantageous positioning, and set off for the Valley Drive-in. The Valley was outside the city limits and very near the town of Seven Mile. The village was so named, interestingly enough, because it was located approximately seven miles from Hamilton. The Valley had a reasonably nice children's playground, but it paled in comparison to the Acme Drive-in's—which had a corkscrew slide so impressive that it was a thrill even to view it from the highway. A schoolyard conversation on Monday might center more on what drive-in a child had attended than on what movies he had seen.

We pulled into the entrance drive and listened to the quiet crackle of churning gravel beneath the tires as we proceeded to the ticket booth. Once there, we paid our admission to a lone employee stationed inside. I was convinced that this should someday be my first job. Early evenings would be spent in a cozy, well-lit shelter with AM radio blaring. Then at twilight's arrival, I would take in countless movies while serving steaming cheeseburgers and jumbo hot dogs in between features.

The drive-in lot was already a sea of cars. My father artfully maneuvered past the island oasis known as the concession stand and into a well-centered location that we hoped against hope would have a functioning speaker. As he untangled and stretched out the long black electrical cord and mounted the speaker on the car window, the tinny sound of a Beach Boys' tune signaled that his mission had been accomplished. We were now miraculously tapped into all the sounds that brought the films to life and privy to all-important projection-booth announcements. For the next several hours, our car would be our haven. We had food and drink. If it rained, we would hear the steady patter on the car roof, but would be protected and warm. Every family member was close enough to reach out and touch. There was no greater sense of security.

My youngest sister Laurie abruptly broke my serene mood. She shot from the car and made a beeline toward a flock of children and a tall swing set that appeared to have a seat vacancy. Laurie was a scrappy six-year-old with unruly red hair and piercing blue eyes. She was considerably younger

93

than the rest of us, and because of the age discrepancy had become fiercely independent. In general, she had coped well with my endless teasing and her sisters' occasional indifference and remained sweet, yet strong. Although she maintained a grand enthusiasm and zest for life, her spirit was sometimes regrettably broken by the dark side of her adolescent siblings. I watched her from the car as she tugged on the chain links of the swing and aggressively leaned into her dance with gravity. She seemed completely unaware that she was the only playground participant dressed for bed. I envied her innocent defiance.

Emily was staring vacantly out the car window and seemed oblivious to the world. She was the oldest of us and was undergoing a physical metamorphosis that saw her slowly exiting her prepubescent geek stage and into the uncharted realms of young womanhood. This was confusing not only to her, but to the rest of us, who were also witnessing this wonder of nature for the first time.

Suddenly, but not surprisingly, Emily erupted into song—bellowing out the Beatles' "Michelle," but using alternate lyrics that she had recently composed. "Michelle, my belle. Why don't you go to a place . . . where it is nice . . . and warm?" She had a lovely singing voice, which we all heard more often than we cared to. And this new improved version of "Michelle" had been repeated countless times throughout that day.

My older sister was extremely creative and comfortably outgoing—rich with talent and blessed and cursed with an overflow of love to offer. She was about my height at the time and a bit blonder, with delicate skin and clear hazel eyes that nearly stung when making contact. Emily was my best female friend and had been since my birth. We almost never fought, and I often felt as if our bond was older than our years.

Becky pleaded with our mother to silence the fifth Beatle, a tactic designed more to irritate Emily than to achieve her stated desire. Becky was two years younger than I and often compensated for her exclusion by becoming her siblings' nemesis. She was an attractive child—towheaded with characteristic blue eyes—but she often wore a grim scowl. Although keenly intelligent and diversely talented, she felt constant pressure to measure up to her older brother and sister. Becky could be gentle when she wanted to be, but her true tenderness would only gradually surface over the years. I recognized her as both friend and foe and determined her current status by analyzing her recent disposition and making a quick read of the situation at hand.

My mother, acting as diplomat, attempted to smooth over the situa-

94

tion without taking any action. She was relaxed and happy that evening, which meant that she was at her most beautiful. Mona Simer's brown eyes were deep and overpowering, but were well-framed by her dark chestnut hair and subdued by her smooth English complexion. There was a softness about her that always soothed the child in me, and which I later learned sometimes left her too vulnerable to pain. Her relationship with my father had been strained for quite a while, and this always left her spirit slightly wounded. Her predicament often left me feeling sad, without quite understanding the reason why.

My father seemed delighted by the goings-on and was enjoying my mother so much that he had become slightly flirtatious. This was a rarity that did not go unnoticed, as we all now peered at their every move. Scott Simer was a small man with dark wavy hair that had receded noticeably—and thoughtful, but resentful green eyes. He had been afflicted with scoliosis during his adolescence, which left him with a pronounced curvature of the spine and accounted for his diminutive stature. His demeanor was intense, and he was quite outspoken about his beliefs and convictions. Known as an outstanding speaker, he was blessed with an incisive quick wit, but seemed discontented by his situation and often was distant with his children.

This was a magical evening, however, and we could see that he had been amused by something my mother had said. The back of his head was bobbing up and down as his body shook with laughter, a reassuring sight from our backseat vantage point. It seemed a telltale sign that the night would be a peaceful one.

In just a matter of minutes the pseudo-conflict between Emily and Becky was conveniently resolved by the stark and impressive dimming of the lot lights. Suddenly the glory of the night ruled, as our ears became acutely aware of the sounds of evening. The sky immediately came into focus, and the projected images on the giant screen became clearer and brighter by the minute. The balmy breeze of the summer night felt like a cool washcloth on our faces, and the tinny sounds of the movie were perfectly complemented by the clicking crickets and soothing echos of other speakers in other cars.

Laurie had reluctantly returned from playland, and soon the car was humming with activity. Dixie cups were filled with ice-cold cherry Kool-Aid, and assorted sandwiches were dealt. The car, if viewed from a distance, must have appeared to house an octopus, as arms reached over seats in all directions. Ritz crackers crunched, there was an occasional unintentional slurp and the words, "Be quiet!" were uttered from children and adults alike.

I remember little about the first-run film, "It's a Mad, Mad, Mad, Mad World," and nothing at all about the second. I was much more impressed by the snack-bar teasers between features that convinced me that the concession stand had the most marvelous carry-out food available anywhere. Money had always prevented us from eating there, so many years elapsed before I had to confront the huge disappointment of paid drive-in dining.

I was incredibly enticed that evening, however, and the urgency of a concession-stand fix was amplified by the exciting on-screen countdown to the next feature. This served as a convenient gauge to time a last-minute dash to the bathroom. And it also afforded me the opportunity to walk through the refreshment center so that I might hobnob with the upper-crust who dined there.

Ever the observer, I captured many mental pictures of all that surrounded me on that precious night. It struck me as I glanced at Emily that we would not be children in the back of a Studebaker much longer. I was nearly twelve at the time and growing up quickly. Although I coveted the fast lane of junior high school, I already mourned my childhood. In some ways it was hard to let go—particularly on a night like this one, when the elixir of snappy summer air implored you to be a kid again.

$$*\qquad*\qquad*$$

After the movies we drove home and quietly pulled into the driveway of the parsonage. Three drowsy Simer children gradually emerged from the Lark. Laurie had fallen asleep, and my mother wrapped her in her arms and gently carried her through the back door. I recalled when I was her age and would feign sleep, so that my feet would not touch down until they were lowered onto my mattress. Those days were over now; time would no longer stand still for me.

I walked slowly toward the house, cradling the memories of the moment close to my heart. I was much more sensitive than the world would allow me to be.

13

The Coterian Retreat

The arrival of September was a dismal occurrence in the life of a boy entering the sixth grade. It signaled the last gasps of summer vacation and the commencement of yet another school year. But for me, it also heralded the advent of an annual custom that rivaled Christmas as the most-anticipated event on my calendar. Each fall the Coterian Sunday school class at High Street Christian Church would gather for a weekend family retreat at Camp Luella May— a local Girl Scout camp made available for group rentals at summer's end.

The Coterian Retreat was a forty-eight-hour departure from bland predictability and life's daily routine. During that weekend, boy/girl relationships developed at the speed of time-lapse photography, and a torrid juvenile romance could evolve to full blossom and quick fade before camp broke on Sunday. The retreat was always over too soon, yet it lasted forever. Vivid recollections of past retreats could always be recaptured at a moment's notice. They were among my most poignant memories and were at the ready when life seemed to get the better of me.

The Coterians were the more colorful of the two adult Sunday school classes. The campers were an odd hodgepodge of straight-laced stick-in-the-muds and creative cutups who, when intermingled, became a pretty entertaining and entertained assemblage. Their combined chemistry brought out their best good humor, as the mischief-makers had an almost intoxicating effect on their more milquetoast counterparts.

For the youthful offspring of class members, the retreat meant a weekend of adventure and potential puppy love. It represented two full days of bunk-filled cabins and roaring fires—of sleeping bags and late-night gabfests. And it provided us the opportunity to isolate ourselves from the tiresome adults, while being reassured in the knowledge that they remained within shouting distance.

Preparations began at the month's beginning, though the retreat was usually scheduled late in September or early in October. Our Sunday church services became a rumor mill of who was coming and who wasn't—and which kids were bringing friends to make the juvenile contingent even larger and the mix more interesting. The weekend usually coincided with the premiere of the new television season, so parents had to be coerced to lug enough black-and-white portables to the camp that there would be a set in every cabin inhabited solely by minors. And the organization of the Saturday night variety show commenced, with plenty of stage time available to anyone with a touch of theater in his blood.

*   *   *

In the Simer household, little else was discussed during that month. Emily had even composed a jingle whose concise lyrics consisted solely of the phrase "Coterian Retreat" repeated ad nauseum. We would serenade our parents with it ceaselessly, singing the piece over and over again as if recorded on an audio tape on a continuous loop. The excitement reached a fever pitch on the Thursday night before our Friday departure—an evening designated for packing for our weekend getaway.

On what was a typical autumn Friday afternoon, we all dashed home from school, helped tote suitcases to our Volkswagen bus and headed out of Hamilton to Camp Luella May. Luella May was located near Darrtown, a village whose chief claim to fame was being the hometown of the late Los Angeles Dodger manager, Walter Alston. After traveling a few secluded country lanes and entering the camp on a narrow gravel road—the grounds emerged into view. The most prominent structure was a stained wooden lodge with a substantial dining room and kitchen, along with rest room and shower facilities. The building also housed a recreation hall with a sleeping loft on the second level, where the less rugged of the adults bedded down.

The lodge main entrance faced a number of unheated and graffiti-filled cabins interspersed in a sparsely wooded stretch of gently rolling grasses. On the side of the lodge nearest the camp entrance was a small parking area and a volleyball net with a court area large enough for open invitation games involving anyone who could toddle or walk on two legs. Adjacent to the opposite end of the building, there was a large foot-worn athletic field where we often recruited enough reluctant volunteers to field two respectably stocked teams for a game of first-rate touch football.

As the Volkswagen bus pulled to a halt, the back door slid open, and the four youngest Simers were spring-ejected from their escape hatch. We were launched in the general direction of the lodge, where silvery silhouettes could be seen through the fine aluminum screening of the dining hall windows.

There were two sets of double screen doors on either side of the lodge entrance. As I pulled open the doors nearest the parking lot, I cast my eyes on the familiar dining area—housing four long rows of Formica-topped dinner tables with wooden benches spanning the distance of both sides of each table. Several families had already arrived, and women were unpacking casserole dishes and foil-covered serving pans from grocery sacks and picnic baskets. Two foursomes were seated at separate tables, each person eyeing a fan of playing cards. They were engaged in a friendly game of Pitch, the most popular card game in Southwestern Ohio.

Most of the adults took the time to address me, many still calling me Timmy. It was a little boy's nickname that I no longer considered acceptable except when used by church members, relatives, or teammates at a sporting event. After awkwardly and bashfully responding to each greeting while devouring the attention, I did a quick inspection of the dining room—hoping to find no changes since my last visit.

Against the side wall nearest the parking lot was a large trough filled with a variety of sodas buried in a sea of ice and frigid water. A soup bowl perched on the ledge near the trough already contained a small handful of change from early imbibers. At the rear of the dining area was an extended open serving counter that fronted the camp kitchen. Here several women were scurrying about on a floor elevated about three feet from ground level. They were reheating entrees and side dishes while digging out serving spoons, hot pads and spatulas as they readied for the evening's covered-dish feast. Between the counter and the side wall was another screen door that led into the rec-room. If one ventured through this door and opted to make an immediate hard right, he would confront the entrance that led into the kitchen.

Between the serving counter and the rec-room entrance was a large refrigerator/freezer chest packed with individual cartons of milk, ice cream sandwiches, Eskimo Pies, and vanilla dessert cups with attached coarse wooden spoons. An empty wicker basket on top of one of the compartment doors dropped a not-so-subtle hint that the treats were not complimentary. The freezer was refrigerated by chunks of dry ice, that baffling scientific marvel that kids just can't stay away from. Suspended from the ceiling against both side walls were evenly spaced strips of fly paper, their raw carnage offering proof positive that they had successfully achieved their intended purpose.

As I walked in the direction of the rec-room, I heard children's voices through the screen door, along with the metronome-like cadence of an extended Ping-Pong volley. I climbed the two stairs that led into a spacious room done entirely in wood and natural stone. Once entering, I glanced up at the steep cathedral ceiling and breathed in the history—allowing the moment to trigger memories of past visits. The room smelled of old wood and maintained the odor of the last fire that had blazed in the hearth, as well as the heavy ash that remained below the grate. The fireplace was on the wall nearest the kitchen and was constructed of large flat rocks that had been laid like bricks to create a rugged wilderness appearance. A large stack of logs was at the ready and would be burned freely during our brief stay.

Just beyond the fireplace was a staircase that led to an upstairs sleeping loft. A Ping-Pong table was nestled beneath a much lower ceiling created by the loft floor—its deck supported by several sturdy wooden beams. The rustic atmosphere was accentuated by a scaled-down, hand-carved and painted totem pole mounted on the back wall near the dining room. On the side wall opposite the fireplace was yet another screen door that opened into a small outside porch—where wedged lumber was piled high for the upcoming winter season. My initial tour of the building had not produced evidence of any youth in my age bracket, so I ambled back to the dining area. Once there, I planted myself inconspicuously in a corner and watched for several minutes as a steady flow of people streamed into the room.

Cars had begun to arrive with regularity, and adults and children who now joined the early arrivers had the eager expressions of people who were expecting to have a good time. Hands were pumped, picnic baskets were emptied and small children were unmercifully hugged. Adults who walked by me sometimes affectionately rubbed my head or quickly squeezed my shoulder if only to recognize my presence, and I felt genuine appreciation for their kindness. As casserole lids were lifted, and aluminum foil was rolled back, steam snaked where air and heat collided, and invisible fragrances fanned throughout the room.

The Andersons soon arrived, followed by the Kings, Falks and Faths, along with several other families with children my age. The dining room was now quite full and took on a jovial tavern-like ambience. Soon the intense and steady clink of a single drinking glass quieted the din after which my father delivered grace, while several toddlers and babies chimed in with their own nonsensical prayer addendums. I had joined a small group of my peers, and as we emerged from the buffet line, we found a cluster of empty seats where we could talk shop and decide which of the many cabins we would choose to inhabit.

The "boys' cabin" pecking order soon became obvious. Jon Falk and Jim Fath were several years older than I and were clearly running the show. Randy King had a year's seniority on me and stood next in command, while I easily could have been perceived as the tag-a-long if it were not for Jim Fath's kid brother, Johnny. Jim was not juiced-up about it, but Johnny, who was two years my junior, would be bunking in our cabin. Although I wouldn't have admitted it, I was relieved that he had come. We would branch off whenever we sensed we weren't wanted and could engage in games and activities that only younger boys were allowed to enjoy.

*   *   *

I glanced around our table and was pleased to see several girls who I had hoped would be there. Jon Falk's younger sister Ann was my age and particularly pretty with huge and decidedly brown eyes. She didn't work very hard at being attractive and didn't have to. Ann was salt-of-the-earth and thoroughly uninterested in me. Becky Anderson was my older sister Emily's age and looked like an adolescent Campbell's Soup Kid. I had liked her from the moment we'd met, but fully recognized the insurmountable two-year age difference that came between us.

Donna Werk was both my close buddy and someone I had just recently come to recognize as a female. She was a feisty tomboy with a tender heart and was heavily burdened with playing mother hen to her four younger siblings. Her determined dark eyes divulged both her courage and fragility, and her obvious intelligence usually left her with more questions than answers. Janet Coyle was the Ginger to Donna Werk's Mary Ann. She too, was a seventh-grade older woman—petite and brunette with a seductive mole on her cheek. My feelings for her stemmed more from my boyish fantasies than reality, as she usually made our age difference unpleasantly clear to me. The weekend's players were now seated around me. It was time for the games to begin.

Following dinner, people sought out the activity that best suited them. Several people had drifted to the volleyball net and had begun playfully

101

fisting and swatting the ball back and forth in hopes of baiting a few extra participants. Jock wanna-bes trotted off to the athletic field—where those who were able ran pass patterns, and those who weren't sent spiraling bombs at sprinting human targets or stood doubled over, gasping for air. Some people remained in the dining room, lazily chatting and sipping coffee or huddled in quartets carefully studying the most recent hand of cards that had been dealt them. In the rec-room, a fire had been kindled, and two half-pints stood on either side of the Ping-Pong table swinging their paddles like baseball bats and sending the ball flying in nearly every direction. They spent more time scurrying after errant hits than volleying and were lured to the table only because they perceived it to be a game for people beyond their years.

A lively ten-man touch-football game had commenced, and I had aggressively thrown myself into the middle of it. Five men and several of the older boys were competing against one another and were not pulling any punches. I had grown considerably in stature and strength over the past year and now held my own with several of those playing. In years past, when I was handed the ball I would wildly zigzag the field while defenders would humor me and themselves by pretending unsuccessful attempts to catch me. I came to believe that I was a football prodigy and would sometimes serpentine the turf for more than a minute before ultimately racing for a touchdown. The high school boys jokingly referred to me as "The Snake," a nickname I took quite seriously and bragged about to my classmates.

But on this day there was no snickering, and although I was rarely designated a primary pass receiver, I was competing on an adult level. Our team eventually emerged victorious, and as the exhausted conquerors and physically sore losers dragged into the dining room, most took a direct path to the ice-cold soft drinks.

I had a pocketful of allowance change, so I joined them, soon clutching a wet ice-sprinkled bottle nearly upside down, as my lips funneled the steady stream of chilly soda into my parched throat. I would consume almost a case of soft drinks throughout the weekend with a decided bent toward the red Fanta Cream Soda. Bottled pop was a once-a-week treat in our household, so this was a rare opportunity to guzzle what I normally slowly savored.

*   *   *

Dusk had shaded the surrounding woods in grays, and the overhead fluorescent bulbs now eclipsed the slight light that the sun spilled over the horizon. After I had given my gullet a refreshing ice bath, I hauled my duffle and sleeping bag toward our darkened cabin. A television set provided the room's only light, and I saw intermittent flashes as camera angles and scenes changed, or the network went to a commercial break.

The cabin was one of two located closest to the lodge. It was constructed entirely of wood and was square with a roof that formed a slowly rising pyramid comprised of four triangular sets of rafters. All of the cabins were elevated several steps from ground level and had screened windows on three sides with shutters that closed downward from within like vertical trap doors. The room reeked of old wood that had been cut decades before and mattresses that had soaked up a daily dose of warm summer breezes.

Almost as much handiwork had gone into carving all matter of graffiti into the walls, bunks and support beams as had been put into the cabin's construction. There was at least a day's worth of whittled reading material, and one would leave comforted to know that so many people had been in love and would remain that way 4-ever.

The cabin was empty, although sleeping bags had been unrolled on several beds that had already been claimed. I flipped on the light and selected a bunk with an acceptable view of the television set. After shuttering the single window that had remained open, I sat down on the bed and slipped out of my sweaty clothes. It was a brisk evening, and the buttons on my bare mattress seemed to conduct the cold. They took an icy nip into my back when I lay on them and sent sudden shivers down my spine. I quickly bounded up and searched for a suitable wardrobe selection, then ran a comb through my hair and threw on the clothes that I had picked out.

A new show called "The Addams Family" was to debut in only a few minutes, and I had been quite intent on watching it. I reclined in my bed, threw a small blanket over my legs, curled up and fixed my eyes on the small screen so that I would be able to intelligently discuss the new comedy at school on Monday. About five minutes into the show, the front door groaned and then snapped shut as Johnny Fath walked in. Knowing the dire importance of fall preview week, he remained as silent as if he were entering a library. He found a seat on another bunk, and within minutes he too was staring hypnotically at the screen.

At least two discriminating young critics liked what they saw during that half hour. Johnny and I were particularly enamored with a supporting character named Lurch, a towering, nearly silent butler whose vocabulary seemed limited to gravelly bass groans and the soon-to-be-immortalized phrase, "You rang?"

After the show concluded, we shut off the television and went back to the lodge to check out the early-evening activity. In the still silence of nighttime, the lodge seemed to be a living, breathing entity. Laughter echoed from the dining room, while the faint sounds of a rec-room piano rang out with the melodic strains of a familiar hymn.

As we pulled the front door open, we walked past a group of card sharks amid a marathon partners session. We each selected an ice cream treat and entered the recreation hall where Seborn Wilhoit was tickling the keys of an ancient upright piano located near the loft staircase. A fire was blazing on the hearth, and several people were seated around it, holding well-worn paperback hymnals while they sang along. Their faces glowed as the flames danced in their eyes, and the natural warmth of the fire seemed to melt whatever tension remained in their faces.

Seborn, who was unsighted, displayed his emotions with his hands more than his face, as he stretched out his fingers and massaged the keyboard while occasionally breaking into an almost twitchy grin. Many of the younger children sat or stood pressed against their parents, as they leaned on their mothers' everlasting arms and listened to old church standards as if they were lullabies.

I glanced across the room and saw my sister Emily sitting with Donna Werk. Many of our chums were either prowling the grounds or gossiping in the girls' cabin, but I had little desire to join them. I enjoyed seeing those present in these more casual surroundings. The weekend provided me the opportunity to recognize church members as real people who led full lives on days other than Sundays. With those individuals I already felt connected to, the retreat seemed like an extended reunion among old friends.

Sebourn was taking requests, and I summoned up the courage to ask him to play "The Old Rugged Cross." It was my father's favorite hymn and one I associated with significant family moments at my grandparents' farm. We had sung the song around the campfire or in the quiet of their cabin while my father accompanied us on his harmonica. Now my church family sang it with me, and their sincere voices along with the power and resonance of the off-key piano saturated the cavernous hall with a penetrating warmth that the crackling fire could not replicate.

The songfest lasted about an hour, with a steady flow of people coming and going. As the outdoor temperature dipped, the gathering drifted ever closer to the hearth. And even after the music ceased, many people remained—enticed by the beckoning roaring fire and comfortable companionship. Donna Werk, Emily and I had positioned ourselves on a long wooden bench directly in front of the grate. The wavering blaze stirred the embers' glow while extending its dexterous reach to unconsumed logs. Time wrapped itself in flames and smoke, and until yawns became contagious and mothers carried out small children like snoozing kittens, we were unaware that another hour had passed. We eventually arose and headed back to join our sleepmates. A wet frost had formed on the grass, and condensation was kicked up as we shuffled toward the brightly lit adjoining cabins.

*   *   *

Our camp companions were congregated in the girls' bunkhouse and had stretched out on upper and lower bunks, most either bundled in blankets or wrapped in their sleeping bags. We exercised our jaws until the grounds were silent, and you could feel the heartbeat of the great outdoors. Flirtations were cautious and probing. Becky Anderson and my sister Emily were both enamored with Randy King, as was nearly every other female who had ever laid eyes upon him. He would have been easy to despise if he hadn't been such a nice guy.

There would be no budding romances on this evening, however, and soon respectability demanded that we call it an evening. We gathered up our belongings and reluctantly headed back to our cabin. Johnny was already buried in blankets in his bunk, so we took this irresistible opportunity to awaken him. Good-natured barbs were exchanged, and everyone except Johnny and Jim went to bed friends. They feuded as brothers are supposed to and continued to grumble at each other until we all became too drowsy to listen. We soon fell asleep, confident that all would be forgotten with the new morning.

*   *   *

I woke up quite early, and except for Johnny, who had already left the premises—everyone's head was still buried in his pillow. I trudged through the thick wet grasses and soon picked up the scent of frying bacon wafting from the screen doors of the dining room. The flag pole near the lodge was proudly flying a pair of men's cotton briefs—a cabin prank that no one ever confessed to. The lodge front room was empty, but several people were congregated in the kitchen. Other early risers were near the fire in the rec-room with breakfast plates in their laps. The building was filled with the odor of sizzling bacon and of coffee brewing in a Bunnmaster. Becky Anderson's mother, Waneta, greeted me and asked me how I would like my eggs cooked. I humbly placed my order and soon held a platter heaped with bacon, wheat toast and two eggs sunny-side-up.

I sat down next to Johnny Fath, who leaned back in his chair with arms crossed and feet propped on a bench he had placed in front of him. Johnny was a dark blond with the fleshy face of a young boy. He was quite bold and not easily intimidated, having been regularly manhandled by his older brother. We talked while I ate, and it was decided we would make a trip to the nearby river later in the afternoon.

Soon our cabin mates straggled in, rubbing their eyes and following their noses in the direction of the popping skillets. The girls arrived shortly thereafter, animatedly chattering and giggling as if they had never taken the time to sleep. I sighed deeply as I geared up for the busy day ahead of me. We would try to pack a year's worth of memories into the next thirty-six hours.

*   *   *

It was a typical afternoon and evening at the Coterian Retreat. There were so many things to do, and the day was so full that there was little time for preplanning or reflection. The best way to enjoy the weekend was to immerse yourself in it and allow it to offer its unique spontaneity. There was a "let's play!" attitude among adults and children alike. If you weren't afraid to take a few chances, there were bound to be some pleasant surprises.

That morning and afternoon, I played Ping-Pong until my wrist was sore, taking on all comers and being defeated by most of them. Donna Werk was my favorite opponent, although the games proved secondary to her company. By the end of the day, we briefly held hands instead of paddles, in a fleeting but monumental moment of juvenile romance.

Johnny Fath and I played tennis, or at least stood flailing rackets on opposite ends of the court. I trusted he knew the game, because I certainly didn't—nor did it make a whit of difference, considering there was no one there to dispute our imaginative rules. And an older and much-improved version of "The Snake" dominated the gridiron that afternoon, as I intercepted a pass and took a very unsnakelike direct course to the goal line for a touchdown.

106

Johnny and I also made our trip to the river where we captured about fifteen crayfish that we brought back in a large washtub. We held them in captivity just long enough to receive our proper recognition and a few gasps of horror. Our captured crustaceans were then humanely returned to the scene of the kidnapping, to tell the tale of their harrowing experience.

There were a few pensive moments at lunch when I sat silently observing the adults whom I admired most. It was amazing how much they resembled kids when they were having fun and unaware that anyone was watching them. And after lunch, there was a huge water balloon fight that proved a bit chilly in the early autumn air.

There was even a lengthy volleyball game when I gawked admiringly at Janet Coyle, Becky Anderson and Ann Falk. Each was fashionably dressed in properly faded sweatshirts and snug jeans, and their faces flushed irresistibly in the heat of the competition. Of course, I was only able to spend so much time studying them, because they were not returning any of my glances. It was hell to be thought of merely as Emily's younger brother.

Sandwiched between these entertainments, I found the time to drown myself in soda pop and scarf down several ice cream bars. At the conclusion of the afternoon, I was both dog-tired and filled to the gills. When dinner was announced, I dished up only a token amount of spaghetti, being careful not to eat enough to spoil my appetite for additional late-night frozen treats.

At dinner the conversation was more subdued. People talked about their shared experiences, but there were more lapses in the discussion as everyone had begun to feel more at ease and familiar. A unique bond came with living together, and everyone had at least somewhat lowered the guard that they fiercely maintained the remainder of the year.

*   *   *

Immediately following dinner, the excitement built as preparations began for the evening variety show. In the recreation room, folding chairs and benches were arranged in rows, and performers slipped into inelaborate costumes. Many people who had been unable to stay the entire weekend had driven out for the evening and would remain for the worship service the following morning. As newcomers arrived and weekend campers leisurely drifted in, the hall became the focal point, and soon nearly every available chair was filled. A fire burned brightly, and the high enthusiasm of the audience assured the production would be a boffo crowd pleaser.

I wish that I could recall the show more clearly, but after seeing more than a dozen of these revues they have all seemed to blur together. Suffice it to say that there were several silly skits, a few songs and lots and lots of genuine laughter. The evening offered a moment at center stage for a cast of starstruck adults in ill-fitting costumes—although they looked and behaved much more like overgrown grade-schoolers.

I stepped out briefly during the show, walking out onto the side porch and then around the back of the building to the athletic field. I had no concrete reason to leave, but it simply seemed as if things were happening too quickly, and I had not had the time to realize exactly where I was. It had become chilly, and goose bumps rose on my bare arms. Laughter and music echoed from the lodge into the hushed darkness and seemed a stark contrast to the isolation that I experienced as I listened to the clarity of my own footsteps. The grounds were hauntingly beautiful, and the lodge's illumination against the blackened shapes of surrounding structures made it appear to be an oasis is a world of shadows.

It was at that moment that I fully appreciated where I was. My early-autumn Christmas had arrived, and I had already begun receiving my presents. I filled my lungs with the invigorating air and listened as my feet returned me to the lodge. I was in the midst of a weekend retreat at a Girl Scout camp, but when I opened the front screen door, I knew I had come home.

The show ended nearly twenty minutes later, and as the theater was converted back into a recreation hall, I extended my congratulations to a few cast members and knocked off two more ice cream sandwiches before heading back to our quarters. We gathered in the girls' cabin for a brief discussion about the evening's entertainment. Flirtations were still subtle, and it appeared that because Randy King was considered the only real prize, the competition had been temporarily postponed. Donna and I had scared each other with our earlier hand-holding and felt more comfortable resting or sleeping on our romantic laurels. When everyone had reluctantly resigned themselves to the fact that nothing was going to happen, we said our good-byes. My cabinmates and I returned to our private men's club where I listened to Jim and Jon talk about life as a teenager. It seemed a distant dream to me. I could not imagine my body being that large or dating females who more closely resembled young women than girls. People nodded off one by one until Randy and I, who were most affected by the conversation, were the only ones still noticeably attentive.

Randy was only a year older than I but was maturing more quickly. He was much cooler and more confident than I was and made me want to somehow accelerate the aging process. Luckily my zest for childhood served to retard my transformation into a man, and I still sometimes feel that I have never completely grown up. I finally drifted to sleep envisioning romantic encounters with nearly every female in the cabin next door. Coping with one's hormones was troublesome business.

*   *   *

Sunday morning meant buttermilk and buckwheat pancakes cooked on a griddle by a typically cheerful and chuckling Don Anderson. The rec-hall was then rearranged for an early worship service, as the mood became quiet and contemplative. My father would conduct the service at the church, but nearly as many people attended this more informal gathering. It was an emotional highlight of the weekend, and in the peaceful tranquility of the wildwood, the worship held particular significance. Those who had spent the weekend together felt a unique affinity for one another, as the intimacy we shared drew emotions to the surface and tears to my eyes. These were my favorite people and collectively were nearly as important to me as my own family. As the gathering concluded the service by singing "Blessed Be the Tie That Binds," I looked into their moist eyes and wished my arms were long enough to surround them all and draw them to me. I realized then that perhaps the lodge and the retreat had already done that for me. It had brought all of these individuals together and allowed me to hug them with my heart.

After the worship service, there was a noisy baked ham luncheon in the dining room. At the meal's conclusion, people packed their belongings, loaded their cars, said their emotional and sometimes weepy farewells and reluctantly headed back to the humdrum routine. We were refreshed and relaxed and felt a wholeness that comes from being a part of something substantial. The retreat was the last that we would attend while my family was still together and thriving. It is a weekend I will never forget.

*   *   *

If you refer to a dictionary and look up the word *coterie,* the definition

109

will read something to the effect of "an intimate group of persons with a unifying common interest and purpose." As I now reflect on my childhood experiences, I see Hamilton and my fond recollections of youth as my coterian retreat. When things are happening too quickly, or I lose myself in my work or predicaments, I sometimes find myself stumbling about in what feels like total darkness. Right and wrong look like a foggy gray, and life's most excruciating decisions only point to my isolation.

But when things seem to be at their worst, I usually discover a faint light in the recesses of my mind. My memories of hope and friendship, of support and identity still thrive in a brilliantly illuminated stained wood lodge. And there is a wealth of music, laughter and love that emanates within. It is my coterian retreat calling to me, beckoning its weary son to come home.

14

LeSourdsville Lake

When I was in elementary school, there was really only one amusement park that kids from Hamilton attended with any regularity. After all, Coney Island was in Cincinnati, and that was worlds away. But if you drove straight out of town on Route 4, LeSourdsville Lake Amusement Park was only a fifteen-minute jaunt down the highway—and a day in these environs provided an adventure you would talk about for days to come. LeSourdsville was a place you would connive, scheme or wangle to go to.

When you set foot in the park, you entered a recurring dream that had often invaded your waking and sleeping hours. The park was alive with all the electricity of a live stage performance and created the impression that the festival atmosphere had been created for your personal enjoyment. It was as if the rides, the refreshment areas, the arcade games and even the other patrons had miraculously dropped from heaven for the entertainment of the group of people you had arrived with.

The dream that was LeSourdsville Lake Amusement Park now lives only in the minds of the thousands of adults and children turned adults, who once walked its hallowed grounds. With the opening of Kings Island, a multi-million-dollar venture in nearby Mason, LeSourdsville became a dinosaur—a relic of another time and a quite different way of life. Although a park still operates in the location where LeSourdsville Lake thrived, America's passion for privately owned local amusement parks has been dying a slow death. An entertainment venue that consists primarily of carnival-type rides, a midway and an old-fashioned penny arcade has little place in today's world of high technology and corporate domination. It has no place, that is, except in our memories.

In our mind's eye, that which we have revered and then lost still flourishes. Although our recollections are not always crystal-clear and dates and faces seem to blur, the feelings that the memories stir within our souls are as real as they were in the 1960s. LeSourdsville Lake often reopens its gates to my recall, and I feel it tug at my heartstrings as it did when I was a child.

*   *   *

My return on this occasion is as a twelve-year-old. Our sixth-grade class was taking its end-of-year field trip, and my friends John Timmer and Bozo Allen were there to share this intoxicating adventure with me. As we entered the main gate, we resisted the allure of a series of enticing edibles and instead drank in the sensory circus that lay before us. We walked past the tempting sweet aroma of French waffles sprinkled with powdered sugar and a walk-up window where they were selling the then-quite-popular fresh saltwater taffy. Butted up against the window was a taffy-pulling machine that twisted and turned a giant ribbon of the stretchy candy, creating an almost hypnotic rhythm of motion.

It was a balmy day in May, and the temperature was rising quickly, as the still air baked in the bright morning sun. The unseasonably hot weather had provided an excuse for people to drag their shorts out of mothballs, and a sea of ghostly pale legs provided evidence that it was spring in the Midwest. Nearly every booth or ride we walked past possessed large mounted speakers which were blaring out rock music, playing pre-recorded messages or amplifying a barker's pitch to test your skills and win a prize.

John Timmer was rangy, with brown hair and freckles, and had been my friend since he moved to Hamilton in the fourth grade. John was a hard-nosed kid with a sweet streak, and we shared an interest in a wide variety of sports, all of which he played with considerable skill. He lived down the street from me on Griesmer Avenue and possessed the most impressive collection of *Playboys* of any boy I knew. Juan "Bozo" Allen was a good-natured, affable sort who always had a grin plastered on his face. He was gentle and easy-going and had a permanently playful look that typified his personality. Bozo was a close friend of John's and an occasional running buddy of mine. We banded together on that day at the school's request. Our class was roaming the park in groups of three because our teacher, Mrs. Engel, ascribed to the theory of safety in numbers.

Our game plan included an immediate trip to the roller coaster and an attempt to "spontaneously" meet up with either Jill Wolsefer or John's love, Karen Weber. We had no idea what we would do if we saw either of them, but hoped that a spark would ignite a touch of elementary-school romance. I was hoping to get a special smile from Jill or perhaps to share a

112

ride car with her. In my wildest dreams, I envisioned holding her hand or building the courage to sneak my arm around her shoulder. But being an average sixth-grade boy, I was obligated to make the roller coaster my top priority—and we were now high-stepping it in that direction.

The LeSourdsville roller coaster was the most frightening that I have ever ridden. It was not the steepest or the longest, nor did it make a 360-degree loop. But it was just rickety enough and had just enough play in the lap bar that when your car departed, there was a hint of doubt that you would return in one piece. The line to get on was always a long one, but the ride's wild popularity only added to its allure and mystique.

While we waited nervously, we heard the standard narrations about young innocents who had allegedly been bucked by this unbroken bronco on rails. I don't think anyone really believed these grim fairy tales, but the creative yarn-spinning was a little like telling ghost stories at a sleepover. The steady flow of the line gave us an opportunity to girl-gawk, and the unusually warm weather offered an early preview of the bare skin of summer. As we neared the boarding dock, our attention diverted to the arriving and departing cars. Newly loaded cars were regularly exploding forward, while returning terror trains screeched to a body-jarring stop.

Many brave or foolish souls departed and arrived with hands held high in the air, apparently demonstrating their desire to complete the journey without the security of a vise grip on the safety bar. Most of those participating in this silly exercise would immediately hold on for dear life when they negotiated that first frighteningly steep descent, then re-raise their arms before returning to the platform. Those silly enough to finish the ride hands-free proved nothing but a lack of good sense. Only someone who actually was catapulted completely from the car without ever attempting to save himself would exhibit true courage, and he probably wouldn't live to accept his just accolades. I had decided years before that I was quite willing to make use of any safety feature that the park provided to me.

When we finally reached the ride's departure point, we drew comfort from seeing the scores of people now waiting behind us, and as we climbed aboard, we sensed that we were now a focus of attention. I jammed my eyeglasses into a front pocket of my pants and watched with hazy vision as the attendant pushed down on and then checked my lap bar. As usual, the bar was not firmly locked into place. It instead exhibited just enough limited mobility that I could imagine slithering through its grasp and being launched nearly airborne, my hands still clinging to the bar as I completed the ride resembling a human streamer—with legs flapping in the breeze.

My time for worry ended abruptly as we suddenly jerked forward, and our coaster was off, approaching the foreboding first ascension where a powerful rail chain took us into tow. We began creeping ever so slowly to the first hill's apex, the gateway to an unknown stretch of track that lay on the other side of this steel mountain. The cars squeaked and groaned, squealed and clanked as they crept to the peak of the slope, then spilled over until gravity flexed its mighty muscle.

The cars plummeted downhill, and with each subsequent dip and ascent, my posterior levitated from the seat. It hovered ominously on a cushion of air and remained there until Newton's law commanded a return to its resting place. We whizzed past a jungle of metal beams, many appearing to be positioned in the direct path of my panic-stricken face. At the last instant we would veer out of harm's way only to instantaneously confront another potential decapitation.

The whirlwind excursion ended too quickly, and as we slowed to approach the end of the rail line, hands shot back into the air, and there was a jubilant cheer from the returning survivors. When the coaster finally screamed to a back-snapping stop, we climbed out of the car and strutted off, exhibiting a little more swagger to our gait.

Our adrenaline was running high, so we proceeded to ride a representative sampling of our old reliable favorites, dizzying ourselves on the Scrambler and Tilt-A-Whirl, and then spending several minutes suspended upside down as we were voluntarily tortured on the Rock-O-Planes. By the time we had completed these brain-churning shock treatments, we staggered in the direction of the penny arcade—my favorite spot at the amusement park.

The penny arcade was a large one-room building that was always hopping with a primarily adolescent clientele. Its inner walls reverberated with clangs, bells, buzzers, pinball ditties and other curious noises, all emanating from an abundant variety of electronic games that were vying to feed their insatiable appetites for pocket change. The extended open room housed a wide array of arcade games, from the most modern pinball machines to coin-operated relics of days gone by.

Centered near the front door in a glass-enclosed booth was a mannequin of an old gypsy woman, with only her upper body visible. In front of her, there appeared to be a small table with a deck of cards fanned on its surface. When she had been slipped the proper coinage, the madame performed a spiritual reading that would dazzle and amaze. The gypsy miraculously came to life—slowly pivoting her head from side to side as if reading your destiny in the cards. Her arm would slide back and forth over the deck, as she patiently waited for the unearthly to speak to her. After several seconds, the arm came to rest, her finger pointing at the playing card that held your fate. Her sage prognostication would then magically materialize from a thin slot below. The fortune was predictably vague, but there was something undeniably mystical about the old girl.

Another personal favorite was located against a side wall near the rear of the arcade. A full-sized mechanical gunslinger stood there—decked out in full cowboy regalia. Located about fifteen feet from this ornery varmint was an iron pole which holstered a replica Colt .45 attached to a very unwestern electrical cord. If you deposited your imaginary horse and a few quarters at the hitching post, the immediate area was transformed into a showdown in Dodge City. His grizzly pre-recorded voice spit out a few fightin' words before he challenged you to a showdown. It was widely known that his Achilles' heel was a large silver button located at heart level. After he had barked out the commands, "Ready! Draw!!" his right arm would elevate, and a bright red light flashed from the end of his pistol barrel. If the red light had flashed before you returned fire, you were a goner. But if you had a lightning-quick trigger finger and aimed directly at that silver shirt button, he would howl in pain as if he had just stubbed his toe, claim you were just lucky and implore you to go at it again. This wrangler had more lives than Legs Diamond; no matter how many times you shot him, he was still standing tall and pleading for one more chance to seek his revenge.

The penny arcade offered a myriad of ways to remove the jingle from your step. There was a punching bag that measured your masculinity, a love thermometer that evaluated your passion quotient and a vibrating foot massager to soothe your tired tootsies. The walls were lined with pinball machines, most in use by young wizards who had mastered the art of stylish body English. Each machine sent its pinballs on a wild and noisy ride, and along with the steady slaps of the replay levers and the background chorus of competing mechanical amusements, the room was filled with sweet music seductive to the ears of young arcade aficionados. The din was as comforting to them as the levered whir of slot machines would be to avid casino gamblers.

On the wall opposite the quarter-eating cowpoke were numerous ski-ball lanes where keglers were rolling baseball-sized rubber balls up miniature alleys toward three-dimensional targets. The ball would travel an approximately ten-foot slightly elevated ramp, become airborne and then land in a raised circular archery-like target area. It would then fall into one of the concentric circles, disappear into a hole, and the corresponding points scored would be registered on a tote board above the lane. The closer to the center of the target that the ball landed, the more points the contestant received. A game consisted of around ten balls, and if your total score was high enough, a loud bell would sound, and an attendant would rush over to award you a coupon redeemable for prizes.

On the back wall of the arcade was a prize display area, where you could salivate over beautiful premiums that you needed to win a number of games to obtain. Or if you preferred, you could redeem your coupons immediately for something that would next be displayed in your wastebasket at home. Since my funds were limited, as was my talent at ski-ball, I avoided the temptation to play. But I could not resist a longing look at the monstrous stuffed animals, clock radios, sports equipment, watches and other dream goodies that beckoned me to blow the remainder of my allowance. I immediately recognized an ID bracelet in an enclosed glass case that was identical to the one I had won for Jill Wolsefer the year before. The bracelet had probably long since broken, but it had been the closest thing to "going together" that I then understood. Jill and I had found it quite difficult to go steady in elementary school, though—since we never did "go" anywhere together, let alone do it on a steady basis.

My attention was diverted by John and Bozo, who were now imploring me to continue our park exploration. I temporarily bade the room farewell, certain that I would be returning several times during the long upcoming summer.

*   *   *

It was decided that our next destination would be the park's frontier town, which could be reached via a scaled-down railroad system. So we hopped aboard the Iron Horse train and chugged our way to what was called Tombstone Territory. On the way we were told that we crossed through hostile Indian country, but we salvaged our scalps and arrived at our destination with nary a scratch. We were fortunate that these Indians must have been only passively hostile.

We disembarked at a surprisingly small watering hole that consisted of a few Western-type structures, most of which could be looked at and not entered. We stopped in at the saloon, but since the territory was dry, we settled for a tall icy glass of sarsaparilla. After our whistles were wetted, we threw open the saloon doors and strolled through the heart of town.

On the main drag we spotted a peacock strutting the street and, believe it or not, a piano-playing chicken. The chicken resided in a small glass house and when change was inserted into the coin slot of his dwelling, a ration of corn kernels would spray onto a tiny toy piano. The chicken would peck at the corn and inadvertently strike an arbitrary series of piano keys. I felt sorry for the bird, who resided in very tight quarters during his recitals—but I suppose it is always preferable to be eating rather than be eaten.

We stopped into another unpadlocked building where a middle-aged woman in a large bonnet and full-length pioneer dress showed us a multi-media presentation on the travel of covered wagons across the western frontier. After absorbing as much knowledge as we could tolerate on a recreational field trip, we skedaddled and hopped on the next train back to civilization. Even then, Tombstone Territory seemed like a good idea that had come up a few dollars short and had the appearance of a deserted Western set from an episode of "The Twilight Zone."

*   *   *

Our intention had been to hit the midway next, but while in transit we spotted a group of recognizable faces outside of the Haunted House, and my fluttering stomach told me that Jill Wolsefer was among them. I drifted in her direction and tried my best to maintain a semi-intelligent exchange with the people who had clustered around her. Speaking directly to her seemed out of the question. My heart was pounding so hard that I could feel my pulse in my ears, and I was far too fidgety to engage in any prolonged eye contact. The idle conversation continued for several minutes as I tried to shout over an irritating little voice in my brain that insisted I ask Jill to go on this ride with me.

Several of those gathered joined a line of people who were waiting to be seated in the snug ride-cars built for two. The cars entered the building at regular intervals as they pushed open the swinging double doors that took them into darkened privacy and several minutes of unsupervised bliss. Buoyed by the power of love, I turned quickly and instinctively toward Jill and asked her if she was going to go through the Haunted House. We both knew that I was really asking her to join me on the ride. Her beautiful dimples gave me her answer before a word was spoken.

We walked deliberately toward the line and stood silently side by side until we climbed into our awaiting carriage—and crossed into a new world of romantic intimacy and human touch. I would love to report that I kissed her while in our brief seclusion or at least fulfilled my fantasy of holding her hand or putting my arm around her waist. Unfortunately, I was not that bold. But I did sit leaned against her with our bodies touching and felt her warmth nearly burn a hole into my side. I experienced the tugging magnetism of her accessibility and a desire to get even closer to her that I could not then completely understand.

I remember almost nothing about the actual ride. My sole recollection was Jill pressed next to me, and for those few minutes even the air around us no longer existed. Only the brilliant flash of reemerging daylight transported our car and my mentality back to the sixth grade and into the Land of LeSourdsville. When we emerged from the vehicle, we abruptly parted company. I was still stunned by the strange feelings that stirred within me.

For the next half hour or so I could only manage to go through the motions and wait for my head to clear. I'm fairly confident we rode the flying scooters that took a circular wire-suspended flight that could be made much more exciting by expertly navigating the scooter's rudder. And I'm sure we hopped into the Dodgem cars as I attempted to jolt myself back into reality by colliding with nearly everything in sight.

Time had now become a consideration, so we rushed back to the roller coaster, where we made at least two more laps around the treacherous track and became a little giddy from the daredevil experience. Our final stop was the midway—potentially the most dangerous attraction the park had to offer. Scoping our options and computing our odds, we initially avoided the taunts of pitchmen and ignored near-wins by others who had been lured into this seductive spider web that LeSourdsville preferred to call games of chance. And I successfully steered well clear of a small building where people were seated playing a tic-tac-toe ball game known as Fascination. Those in the air-conditioned room competed against each other, as each contestant rolled balls toward a grid of twenty-five holes. The object of the game was to put a ball into five holes in a row—either vertically, horizontally or diagonally. The first person to obtain tic-tac-toe was awarded a coupon redeemable at the Fascination prize counter. A miked voice boomed out a lilting lure as the building's sound system trolled the avenue. My ears perked as he spoke his rehearsed Fascination pitch in a stylized cadence:

118

"It's easy to play . . . it's easy to win . . . so come right in . . . Let's all play . . . Fascination!"

My strength of spirit was short-lived. After John won a large stuffed animal from a shocked booth operator, I succumbed to my gambling spirit and made two unsuccessful attempts to win another of my favorite games—a simulated greyhound race. The contest involved flipping a lever that sent a small rubber ball enclosed in a glass box into one of two holes. Each hole represented a different distance that your greyhound would travel. The racing greyhounds were mounted on a large upslanted board that spanned nearly half the booth. Each dog had been placed on his own individualized track and had a contestant controlling his movement. The greyhounds advanced a measured distance toward the finish line after each completed flip of the lever.

The barker, who had enticed enough passersby into his game to justify the race, also broadcast the approximately two-minute sprint over a speaker system. A loud bell sounded when the winner crossed the finish line. The bell prompted players to immediately look up and scan the booth counter, so that they might sneak a peek at the hound-jockey that had defeated them. That moment was probably more gratifying than any prize the winner might receive. A single victory would result in a premium that was almost worth keeping, or you could opt for a coupon that could be applied toward a more spectacular reward. Naturally, this second option required that you return to LeSourdsville—a decision that would provide fuel for your summer dream machine. But after my bitter defeats, I had no options but to wallow in last-minute self-gratification. We surrendered to the only appetite that the park had not yet satisfied—stuffing our mouths with hot dogs and potato chips and sucking Coca-Cola from jumbo wax-covered paper cups.

*   *   *

It was a fitting ending to a near-perfect day. The park, like the barkers, always managed to lure you in. Although appearances indicated a poor return on investments, bragging rights obtained for having been there and a gratifying thrill-ride hangover headache always made the trip seem like a gold mine. We exited the turnstiles and climbed onto a yellow school bus that was soon crammed with sunburned classmates wearing souvenir hats and lugging piles of worthless junk. I was flat broke, and my stomach was a little queasy—and the feeling was marvelous. That day at LeSourdsville was particularly special because it represented the last social event of my days as an elementary school student. I was walking the tightrope between childhood and adolescence, and those brief moments in the Haunted House with Jill Wolsefer may have sent me irreconcilably tumbling in the direction of my teenhood.

Yes, LeSourdsville Lake is still quite alive in my mind's eye. My subconscious has soaked in its flavor like a sponge, and I can wring out its soothing reflections from a memory that never seems to run dry. It was a fantasyland at a time when we all could escape more easily and had far less frightening things to escape from. The sights, sounds and smells of a Lesourdsville Lake still reside within all of our minds. But we must first allow ourselves to be drawn in. So turn back the clock and join the game. . . . Come right in. It's easy to win. So let's all play. . . .

15

The First Day of Junior High

The wonderful summer of 1966 had ended, and I was walking to my first day of school—taking a route that crossed through territory that was not intimately familiar to me. The summer vacation had been a particularly memorable one. I had ended my stint in elementary school, thus taking an immediate psychological vault toward young adulthood. It had been fun to speak of the seventh grade as a distant dream, and the early summer months had provided me that cushion. But now the dream had become a reality. Whether I was ready for it or not, I had suddenly and officially been transformed into a budding teenager, and I had to begin acting like one.

I had spent the last three months nosing around for information on sixth-grade graduates of other elementary schools who would be attending our junior high. I found out the names of movers and shakers, associated those names with faces and attempted to make personal connections whenever possible. My sister Emily and my best friend Mike Engel, who would both be ninth-graders, had briefed me on the social hierarchy of George Washington Junior High School. They listed who was popular and who wasn't, which teachers to seek out and which ones to stay away from and what abuses I could expect as a rookie teenager.

It was going to be a difficult transition. I had climbed to the top in elementary school, only to realize that I had conquered but a foothill of a much more imposing mountain. The situation was worsened by the fact that I looked so much like a seventh-grader. Except for a blessed few, seventh-grade males were an alien race of mutant geeks. We had disproportionate bodies, awkward and gawky mannerisms, and cracking voices that were constant reminders that we were trapped in an adolescent twilight zone. Ours was an uncomely metamorphosis. Although I knew that I now appeared to be a caterpillar, I hoped that people would somehow see the butterfly within.

As I reluctantly walked through unexplored neighborhoods that morning, I caught a glimpse of the bi-level brick school building. I felt the uneasy irony of walking toward something that I instinctively feared. When I reached the sheltered walkway that led to the main lobby, I saw some of my more fortunate friends being dropped off by parent chauffeurs. We nervously exchanged pleasantries, then I opened the lobby door and contemplated the new world that lay before me. This situation was the antithesis of the old adage about the month of March. I entered that day as a lamb and would exit three years later more closely resembling a young lion.

*   *   *

The school lobby and halls were bubbling with activity as upperclassmen gathered in clusters and watched unnerved neophytes wander the building in panicked confusion. The tenderfoots' eyes were riveted on the numbers posted near each portal that they passed. They all hoped to find matches to the room designations listed on their class schedules, which they now held in front of them like bingo cards. I had attended the junior high orientation day at the end of the summer, when we had visited the building and listened to long-winded speeches. We had learned the school fight song, toured the halls and received our locker assignments. But there weren't so many distractions at that grandiose event. This was no fire drill—it was the real thing.

I quickly found my locker and remained there for several minutes, hanging onto its door, as if anchoring myself safely away from the hazards that were rushing by me. I felt some sense of relief when Ken Simmons, my friend and sixth-grade classmate, walked up to the locker next to mine. We compared schedules and found out that he would be in my homeroom, a double bonus for me because he had also been the most popular boy at our old school. To be seen with him could only enhance my image.

Our feeling of being lowly seventh-graders was intensified by the physical maturity of the oversized bruisers we now dodged in the halls. And the halls themselves seemed so large that Ken and I felt scaled down to the size of munchkins, as a bevy of provocative Dorothys sashayed past us. The most depressing thought of all was that we would be competing with ninth-grade whiskered beasts for the attention of these females, a competition that would have been laughable if not for the fact that our romantic futures hung in the balance.

Ken and I located our homeroom quite easily since it was situated only two doors from our lockers. We gingerly made our way through the masses, as if negotiating a path through a live minefield. When we entered this safe haven, we saw a huddled assemblage of our species, licking the wounds that they had suffered in their new hostile surroundings.

Our homeroom teacher was Mrs. Clark, a scowling, aged art teacher with weathered skin and tightly-drawn graying hair. She wore a sky-blue smock that seemed far too cheery for such a dark and gloomy character. I don't think I saw her smile once that entire year, and it appeared that decades of frowning had cemented such a grimace on her kisser that an up-turned lip would have defied the laws of gravity. She was, to put it mildly, not a pleasant woman.

Perhaps I am somewhat prejudiced because art was not one of my best subjects, a fact that Mrs. Clark made painfully clear to me. But I do know that whatever respect she garnered was earned through fear of her considerable wrath and her generous distribution of detentions, more commonly known as D.T.s. Detention meant an extension of one's school day, along with a notation on your permanent record. I never saw my permanent record and honestly doubt that any of my employers or pastors of churches that I have attended have seen it either. But I suppose that when I die, it will be forwarded to some higher authority or buried in a time capsule to warn future generations in the event I attempt a return to this planet.

Mrs. Clark gave us an uninterested recitation of vital information, as well as the rules of her homeroom. These rules included a stern warning that she would confiscate any material we were caught reading that she deemed unacceptable. I was later to find out that this included my copy of Salinger's *The Catcher in the Rye,* which became an addition to her personal collection that very year. She distributed a stack of mimeographed sheets, and we listened to principal Phillips drone a few announcements on the intercom. The bell then sounded, and we were off to face round one of our junior-high experience. I felt as if the day had nowhere to go but up.

*   *   *

Amazingly, I was on time to all of my classes. It turned out that the seventh grade was divided into seven sections of students, and section placement was based on I.Q. and past performance. None of us was thick-headed enough to be unaware of what the section designations meant, even though no one ever officially explained them to us. And be-

123

cause of this section system, I kept seeing the same students in most of my classes.

I was already completely enthralled with two girls whom I noticed throughout the day. Janalee Alf was very tall, with long, straight brown hair that stretched down to her waist. She had already mastered eyelash-batting even at this tender age and made my heart race whenever she so much as glanced in my direction. Janalee had a model's face and blue eyes the likes of which I had never encountered.

Vicky Helcher had a head start in the puberty game and augmented these prominent attributes with dark eyes and Brooke Shields brows, an amazingly sultry Demi Moore voice and a stellar personality. It did not take long for the upperclassmen to take notice, so I immediately recognized the futility of my crush—but she fit nicely atop the pedestal on which I had placed her. I maintained a pleasant friendship with Vicky and appreciated her beauty from afar, as one would fine (and very erotic) art.

My elementary school sweetheart, Jill Wolsefer, was in another section—so my affections waned very gradually until she eventually transferred to Catholic School. I was, as I entered this new school year, a free and lonely man.

*   *   *

A group of boys from Hayes Elementary school interested me most as potential new friends. Ray Sharp, an olive-skinned Adonis, was the ringleader. All the girls thought he was adorable, and he did too. Ray called the shots and obviously enjoyed the gig.

Jeff Harrison, a lanky, style-conscious dresser with dark curly hair, was certainly not the looker that Ray Sharp was. But he had a comedian's flair and just enough sarcasm to give his humor an irresistible edge. I loved to listen to his mind work.

Jimmy Howell was the cute and shy type that women would call cuddly. His deerlike eyes were hidden behind dark-framed glasses, and he had a swimmer's build and a gentle demeanor. He was the consummate nice guy and didn't have an enemy in the world.

Mickey Turner was the member of this crew who accepted me most readily. I had played some basketball with him, and we became immediate friends. He was smallish with red-brown hair and freckles and was more of a free spirit than the others. Mickey didn't give in easily to peer pressure and all but insisted that I be accepted by the rest of the group.

I wasn't exactly welcomed with open arms; it was a tight-knit circle that had developed over several years. But these guys seemed to have everything going for them. They were smart, they had the attention of all the cute girls, and they were more financially comfortable than I was. I admired their closeness and wanted to be one of them.

It seemed that my friends from Pierce Elementary had fallen through the cracks. They were nowhere to be seen. Either I no longer had classes with them, or I lost track of them because of the sheer numbers of students in our grade. As that first day wore on, it became evident that there was now a new order. All four elementary schools had melded together, and new alliances were developing. This political world of social cliques was definitely too complex for mere grade-schoolers.

*   *   *

My first lunch was a truly memorable adventure. The cafeteria was off the main lobby and was swarming with people when I walked in with several other Pierce alumni. The room had the overpowering odor of warm, wet plastic, as a student cafeteria-worker piled clean and still-damp brown lunch trays at the front of a long line of hungry students. The dining room echoed with the sounds of clanking dishes and trays, the bell-like tinkles of loose silverware and the buzz of enthusiastic conversation. As one neared the cafeteria servers, there were no distinguishable food fragrances. Whatever food smell there was combined the various odors of warm bread, dairy products and some nondescript meat—all overwhelmed by the smell of a pungent disinfectant. This aroma did not vary from day to day, so the lettered, felt menu board on the food line was the only clue to the daily bill-of-fare.

The menu was much more diverse than the one offered at Pierce. The special changed each day, but they always offered hamburgers, hot dogs, pizza—and my personal favorite, cornbread drenched in butter. The daily selections also included Ding Dongs, Ho Hos, Twinkies, etc., and a full line of non-sweet snack items. It was a smorgasbord of inexpensive junk food.

Stunning eighth and ninth-grade goddesses regularly passed by, providing lively lunchtime banter or no-cost sexual fantasies. It was remarkable to see all of these students in a room at the same time and difficult to imagine that this would ever seem commonplace to me. That afternoon, I realized how completely different my school life would be. I had taken a giant step toward becoming a full-fledged teenager.

After our meal, we sat on risers in the huge gymnasium and waited for the bell to ring. Outside the gym was a concession area where students were stationed selling George Washington Junior High School notebooks and book covers, and various other school supplies. The main lobby and cafeteria were a virtual circus of activity, and the nonstop bustle was a post-meal feast for the eyes.

*   *   *

Several teachers I encountered that day stood out in my mind and became influential to me over the school year. My math teacher, Mr. Sandbach, was the most feared of all my instructors. He was a sturdy, blond gentleman with a crew cut and glasses and had a noticeable limp for which he used a cane. This, of course, only served to enhance his dictator's image. Mr. Sandbach was a strict disciplinarian who assigned a voluminous amount of homework and expected its completion.

His classroom methodology always kept us on our toes, since each student was expected to participate on demand. If a pupil didn't grasp a concept, it was embarrassingly evident. And if a class cutup took the course or its teacher lightly, the dullard would pay for his indiscretion with a tender posterior—since Mr. Sandbach made frequent use of his much-feared and aerodynamically crafted paddle. Rumor had it that this wooden original traveled through the air at an accelerated rate of speed, since it somehow defied the effects of wind resistance.

If Mr. Sandbach kept you after school, you worked on his assigned homework while there. Tutors were available to answer questions and to help with specific math problems. He was not one of the best-liked teachers in school, and his tactics were sometimes questionable, but I learned a lot in his class.

*   *   *

Mrs. Erwin was the U.S. history teacher—an impeccably dressed and meticulous, full-figured woman. She was a true lady in her late forties with dark brown hair, glasses and tasteful makeup. The clarity of her presentation was always excellent, and her class period was so well-organized and orchestrated that you felt an obligation to be an attentive audience. She, too, assigned considerable homework and also taught us how to outline the material that we read. From that point forth, all assigned history reading had to be outlined and submitted the following day. This exercise proved invaluable in later years, as it taught me to seek out the important passages of my scholarly reading.

To be honest, the impact of this course was also augmented by the fact that I sat next to Vicky Helcher, who could never have dropped enough pencils to suit me. The teaming of Mrs. Erwin and Vicky made history my favorite subject throughout that school year.

* * *

Mr. Cooper was the free-thinking, young, liberal reading teacher who stirred the hearts of idealistic seventh-grade schoolgirls. He had dark brown hair, a chiseled face and was built like he had played some college sports. His class was dynamic, with heated discussions and debates over such hot topics as the Vietnam War and contemporary civil-rights issues. It was a prerequisite that each pupil subscribe to either *Newsweek* or *Time* magazine while taking the course, and we were regularly exposed to the Sunday *New York Times*.

This class was filled with only the brightest students and included Janalee Alf, whom I was constantly trying to impress with my incisive wit and awesome intellect. She began glancing over at me occasionally, which usually caused me to blush or to unintentionally swallow quite audibly. It was embarrassing that she affected me so strongly.

Mr. Cooper would also become my seventh-grade basketball coach. Although our relationship was never a close one, I admired his fire. He left Washington the following year, and I often wonder whether he remained in the teaching profession.

* * *

I am proud to report that I survived my first day at George Washington. As I left that day, I tossed the books I would not need into my locker, slammed the metal door and secured my new Master combination lock. As it clicked shut, I felt an exhilarating rush, as I was reminded again that I was really in junior high school. The halls had partially cleared, so as I departed the building, I threw back my shoulders and walked a little taller. At least for the moment, I was confident that I could endure my accelerated journey toward adulthood.

There were so many important events that occurred during that school year. It was a monumental year for romance as Jill Wolsefer, my elementary-school angel, faded from my life and took with her the tame and uncomplicated world of elementary school crushes.

I had my first junior-high relationship with a girl named Pam Ball, a shy and tiny blonde with a captivating smile. We officially "liked" each other in the junior high sense of the word, though we almost never spoke. She proudly wore my oversized Spirit Shirt on Spirit Day, an occasion when students brought in old white dress-shirts on which they had written encouraging and clever motivational phrases for our football team. These included old standard favorites such as, "Go, Eagles, Go!" and "We're Number 1!" The shirts were then passed around to friends to autograph like yearbooks or awarded to girlfriends to represent sincere commitment. I still recall how wonderful it felt to see Pam in mine.

I even had a brief fling with Janalee Alf—until she discovered that I was totally inept at relating to the opposite sex. But we passed notes for several weeks, and I fought back a wide smile whenever one of those folded triangles was secretly passed to me. It was a reaffirmation that our "like" was still alive.

This was the school year that I attended my first party where a game of spin-the-bottle was the primary source of entertainment. I was told that Ann Baney had labeled me a sloppy kisser, which led to occasional private rehearsals on my hand and a few passionate sessions with the bathroom mirror.

It was also a time of adolescent pride. I began to shave once a week and established my teenhood by using my first acne medication. I discovered English Leather cologne and began to pay attention to the clothes I wore. And I became an accepted member of the close-knit group of boys that I so wanted to be a part of.

*   *   *

There comes a juncture in a young man's life when it seems necessary to actively begin growing up. It happens because of societal and peer pressures or because his body and/or mind tells him that it is time. But it happens. When that moment arrives, it is as if the hourglass is turned—and time begins. From that point forth, that individual begins to scale the competitive ladder of adulthood. Achievement and measuring up become all important, and the sands of time begin to flow more rapidly with each passing day.

When I reflect on my memories of seventh grade, I remember the excitement of beginning. I did not know what lay ahead or what my final destination would be, but I knew that each day would be filled with stimulating new challenges. As I became more aware of the responsibilities of growing up, time began to elapse—almost imperceptibly at first. And as a middle-aged adult, I now yearn for a way to slow its movement.

Perhaps if we perceived our days on this earth with the same enthusiasm we held for them in our youth, our lives would no longer seem like a timed race to an abstract goal called success. There are subtle to significant variations in each day that offer the potential to make it extraordinary. And there are roads that beckon us that are travelable—yet untried. Life's episodes always offer fresh twists and circumstances—only our hearts and the way we view the world become stale. If we behold each sunrise as a new beginning, we might be able to see the world through an adolescent's eyes again—and even a noontime meal in a local cafeteria can be a glorious adventure once more. However, for your sake—I hope that nowadays the food smells a lot better.

16

Starting Over

By the time I had completed my first year of junior high in the spring of 1967, it was obvious that the relationship between my mother and father had become hostile. My father spent almost no time with us—and when my parents were together, there was strained silence that was sometimes interrupted by sudden venomous outbursts. In the late evening, their conversations in the living room would often explode into shouting matches that could be heard from my upstairs bedroom.

The cracks in the foundation of their marriage were worsened by accusations of infidelity. Although their dirty laundry was rarely aired in our presence, we still caught wind of its stench. My mother's suspicions were not new, but she was now convinced that my father was involved with her best friend, Pat Burger. To make matters worse, Pat was a church member and married—with three children of her own. Our families socialized together regularly, and their two girls, Karen and Patsy, were close friends of my two oldest sisters. It was an ugly situation filled with mistrust, suspected betrayal, and violent conflicts of emotion.

Whether rumors of the affair were founded or not, they had infested church circles, and had prompted members of the congregation to relate to us with an uneasiness that made me feel as if we'd all done something terribly wrong. I spent most of my time away from home, searching for breathable air that had no tension in it.

I was not surprised when in July, my parents finally took each of us aside and told us that they intended to separate. The breakup had been anticipated, but I couldn't begin to understand its finality and long-range ramifications. My knowledge of divorce was limited to what I had soaked up from television shows, newspaper articles and speculative discussions with friends. Their separation looked and sounded as I imagined it would, but it unfolded like a movie script. I was convinced that the melodrama would play itself out, and stability would then return to my daily routine. In retrospect, all that registered with me every time the divorce was openly discussed were the spoken words. These words did not carry the awesome weight that would soon be placed on my shoulders. Not only was I forced from the security of a childhood nest, but I was being pushed out long before I was ready to fly.

*   *   *

The family structure collapsed like a house of cards as my dad eventually submitted his resignation at our church. And before I could gather my breath, my sisters and I stood in our driveway bidding him good-bye. The feel of my father's embrace just before he left still lingers in my memory. I buried my fingers into the tautness in his arms and back, and he pulled me so close that his breathing seemed a function of my own body. When I finally pulled away, his hands continued to cup my shoulders even after his arms had let go. Embraces between us had always been rare, and the urgency in his fingers prodded feelings within me that were raw to his touch. He was unable to offer a father's support. Instead, I sensed his fear and immediately retreated from it. As our bodies and lives disengaged, profound sadness swept away the simplicity and blind faith that had dominated my childhood.

He reluctantly climbed into our Volkswagen bus and drove off. As he pulled out of the driveway and turned on to Pleasant Avenue, I remember thinking what a large vehicle it was for a man alone. I carried myself bravely for more than a day—then broke down. Locking myself in the closet, I wept for two full hours. The hurt couldn't be cried away.

*   *   *

My mother tried her best, but she was not holding up well to the pressures of supporting four children while an uncontrolled anger burned within her. The perceived double betrayal of both husband and friend was more torment than she could bear, particularly in a new role that called for her to be stronger than she had ever been.

We moved from our roomy home on Pleasant Avenue—to a house one block away near Avenue Pharmacy. Our landlord was the owner of the drugstore, and the house, although a nice one, seemed gloomy and stifling. I spent countless hours in my bedroom—a closed door away from the dark emotions that shuffled through the hallway. My detachment represented a psychological quarantine from anyone who might have been able to help

131

me. The atmosphere pervading the home was unhealthy, yet it was I who had been banished in isolation.

I was thrust into the role of man of the house, a title I neither wanted nor was equipped to handle. I was thirteen, had just survived my first year of junior high school and struggled to cling to any aspect of my life that had not been altered by the divorce. My wounds needed tending, but instead I was called upon as a source of strength for my family. Too many of us were pleading for help, and no one was available to administer aid.

My mother overflowed with rage and cried frequently. I resented my increased responsibilities, and at times, even my mother. Her bitterness and anger had darkened her personality, and often she lacked the stability to take charge. She had taken a job at the public library, but that income along with child support money did not make ends meet. We could not afford an automobile—and necessities like clothes, shoes and eyeglasses either had to wait, or we made do with what we did or did not have. I usually found myself more bitter about what I was deprived of than grateful for what I received.

Soon the much-dreaded news arrived that my father and Pat Burger were to be married. She, too, had filed for and received a divorce. Although their current relationship was a given, the announcement destroyed any ability my mother had left to mask her contempt. Her spirit snapped—its splintering caused as much by the fact that she still cared as by the violation of her trust.

The announcement and the subsequent marriage made my father's visitations even more difficult. He had moved to Chicago and had taken a position as a social worker at a suburban hospital, so I rarely saw him. My trips to Illinois were infrequent, and our encounters in Hamilton were polite, but nervous and awkward. Each time I returned from a visit, my mother behaved as if I had been touched by hands that made me unclean. The towering wall that had been created by the divorce seemed insurmountable. He was my father, though, and I continued efforts to make a connection—and accepted the wrath I would incur for doing so. I didn't know why, but I knew that I needed him in my life.

We continued to attend High Street Christian Church where a new pastor named Joe Copelin had been hired. He was married and had a daughter named Elaine, who became my girlfriend almost immediately. Joe Copelin was a first-rate man and solid citizen—and was more a Christian servant than a minister. His style was decidedly unflashy, but his quiet resolve helped steady a turbulent situation.

It was a dire moment in our church's history. People had lost faith in their leadership, and our family's presence on Sundays was a constant reminder of a tragedy that they would have preferred simply to forget. An inevitable polarization had taken place, as the congregation chose sides and concocted their own scenarios to help it all make sense. Mr. Copelin focused instead on things that he could do something about and stayed above the fray of church politics. In an environment that screamed out for love and compassion, a Good Samaritan had arrived.

*   *   *

Our family's despair hit rock bottom one weekday evening when I came home from basketball practice to a roomful of frightened faces. The piercing sound of tumultuous sobbing could be heard from an upstairs room. Mom had come home from her day's work at the library to discover that my little sister Becky had decided to bake a cake, but had poured the batter into a pan that was too small. The cake had spilled over while baking, and the kitchen and oven were a smoking mess. Apparently this calamity triggered an emotional outburst that had still not ended. It had begun as a reasonably coherent tirade. But once the dam collapsed, frustrations flowed unhindered, and the weeping crescendoed until it resembled eerie gales of hysterical laughter. Months of frustration and pain bled from her, and my sisters had no idea what to say or do to repair the damages.

They decided against seeking immediate medical help—primarily because of the consequences that we might face if she needed to be hospitalized. Contacting our pastor, Mr. Copelin, seemed a good short-term solution. He lived in our old home just down the street, and if professionals had to be called, he could make that decision. My sisters phoned the parsonage, he rushed over immediately and was upstairs trying to calm my mother when I had come home. He instructed my sisters and me to remain downstairs, where we prayed for a silencing of her jagged-edged cries of grief.

My mind worked feverishly as I sat alone on our enclosed front porch, while my sisters awaited word inside. We had each waged battles to maintain our personal sanity since the divorce, sometimes nearly trampling one another to escape our despondency. Self-preservation was no longer the only issue. For the first time, I confronted my ongoing fear that my mother might not be able to psychologically survive this ordeal, and I chastised myself for providing resistance rather than cooperation. Almost by reflex reaction, I could feel myself bracing for another shocking change in my life. But I was also acutely aware of my own fragility—how much I needed to be held and told that things would be all right. Rather than uniting us, the divorce had severed our connections. We had been resisting the redefinition of our family roles, while waiting for some outside influence to save us. I now found myself staring into the ugly face of the divorce and recognized it as an enemy that would not go away.

A terrible hand had been dealt to us. Our world would never return to what it had been, and options had been temporarily limited. We would either struggle to rise to our feet again, or accept defeat and curse our misfortune. There were no guarantees and no quick answers. As hard as we had tried, each of us had failed to cope with the dilemma on our own. The Simers who were a minister's family no longer existed—and my mother wept for all of us. When family members perish, those who remain often gravitate toward one another for consolation. On that day, my father died as a member of our family.

There was soon silence upstairs, and several minutes later Mr. Copelin appeared and informed us that my mother was doing better. He cautioned us to avoid disturbing her and encouraged us to call him if there were any additional problems. The remainder of the evening was spent in somber silence and without incident.

*   *   *

I would like to report that we awoke the next morning, joined together in a family hug and lived the remainder of our lives in peace and harmony. But that just isn't what happened. Instead the changes that occurred evolved slowly, with many pitfalls and relapses.

But in a strange way the drama and emotion of that evening had a cleansing effect on our interrelationships. Each of us felt as if the unbridled outpouring had been our own, and a great deal of personal inner pressure had been released. We remained diverse personalities that sometimes clashed and often succumbed to the petty battles that occur between brothers and sisters—children and parents. But we had discovered a collective strength that often only develops in the most devastating of times. We shouted at each other less and talked more, and each reluctantly took on additional responsibilities. Our family developed an underdog's identity—and found a peculiar comfort in having our backs to the wall. Most

134

importantly, we grew to accept that our immediate family no longer included a father.

Meanwhile the church had become more a means of support than a source of additional heartache. The rumors of the affair had rocked members' sensibilities, and when my father resigned and Pat Burger filed for divorce, people had angrily pointed fingers and then steadfastly stood by their intuitions. The concept of adultery and deception emanating from moral leadership was nearly unthinkable. And the fact that a member of the congregation was also implicated only made the situation more unsettling—and prodded sensitive moral questions that tried members' capacity for compassion and forgiveness. Our continued attendance would not allow them to put the issue aside, however, and over time many people tabled all judgments and simply welcomed us back. We had initially returned as the pastor's broken family, but as the congregation's pain subsided, we were more often viewed as church members who needed love and understanding.

*   *   *

Much of what I have related here is a story of heartache and sadness, incongruous with the positive memories that I carry with me about my days in Hamilton, Ohio. But this story, like the others, is my recollection of events that have had a powerful impact on my life. Genuine tales of hope often do not provide total resolution, and happy endings are in the eyes of the beholder. Often when we are lifted up, it is only so that we have the opportunity to try to walk on our own again—sometimes we are only provided a chance to survive another day.

As I now look back upon the evening that my mother broke down, it seems that it represented the darkest of night. The calm that followed the storm offered a faint glimmer of hope that things would be different. Emotions had been released that we had not allowed ourselves to feel, and their unplanned emancipation had helped clear a path to becoming a family again. Most significantly, we had decided that we were not willing to give up on each other.

Our dogged determination to maintain a relationship with our church family was rewarded by a number of exceptional people who offered us their hearts. These cherished friends lived their Christianity and spoke their faith with deeds rather than words. Their steadfast support allowed our glimmer of hope to swell and distend until we again believed that there

135

could be a new day. These people were earth angels who looked after our family and encompassed us with protection in our time of need. They had no ulterior motives, and their efforts on our behalf can only be interpreted as acts of love. Although the words "too numerous to mention" seem appropriate here, the story would not be an accurate one if I did not include portraits of a few of these special people.

*   *   *

Red and Eva Lemon adopted our family as if we were their personal responsibility. Eva was an attractive, gray-haired ex-schoolteacher with a cotton-soft complexion and an understated elegance. Always willing to offer transportation or help with an errand, she was a frequent baby-sitter for any or all of the Simers. She played the role of a doting aunt, always interested in what was happening to each of us and often there to root us on at school functions and other special events.

Red was a sturdy, outwardly gruff and quiet man. When he did speak or sing, he had an earpleasingly deep bass voice that filled a room—and always seemed to lend a mood of stability. Red's face was full and rugged, and he wore conservative wire-rim glasses that downplayed eyes that gave away his softheartedness. His nickname had obviously been given to him in his younger days, but when combined with his surname, fit the distinctiveness of the man. He displayed his generosity without fanfare and his love without an excess of words.

Many weekend afternoons were spent at their spacious old home in Seven Mile, and their huge back lawn was the site of numerous church picnics and summer get-togethers. It was in their well-tended yard that I looked on longingly as Red and other church men tossed lawn darts and horseshoes, and spoke of things that were exclusively masculine. I hoped that someday I would be a man like Red Lemon.

Every December, Red and/or Eva would take us to choose our Christmas tree. After a final decision was reached, my mother would pay a ridiculously low price to a jovial and obviously well-tipped attendant. Whenever there were costs involved for some church activity, they were anonymously paid—and the Lemons were always prime suspects. I felt their love and genuine caring and slept better at night knowing they were looking out for us.

*   *   *

Don Anderson was a handsome, bald man with mischief in his round face and a highly infectious laugh. His friendly grin and mirthful eyes made him immediately approachable, and he had an uncanny ability to bring a smile to your face. Having always been an outstanding athlete, Don was a coach of mine for both church basketball and softball—and in the Babe Ruth youth baseball league. He steadfastly provided my transportation to practices and games, so that I could participate in organized sports.

Each Sunday after the worship service, he would sneak up behind me, pinch my side or poke my shoulder and then feign innocence when I turned to acknowledge the touch. His straight face would eventually erupt into a broad smile, before he cut loose with a hearty laugh that always made me happy that we shared this silly ritual. He was a powerful masculine influence in my life and brightened the day of anyone with whom he came into contact.

His wife Waneta was heavy-set and pretty, and although not as outgoing as her husband, was an ideal complement to him. She had a lovely alto singing voice, and usually provided the highlight of any worship service in which she sang a solo. Waneta could get teary-eyed at the drop of a hat and was highly intelligent as well as acutely sensitive. She was one of my mother's dearest friends, and there was never a doubt in my mind that Waneta cared deeply about each of us.

The Andersons had three children, two of whom were approximately the same ages as my sisters, Emily and Laurie. Although their eldest son Steve had left the area while I was still quite young, their other two children, Becky and Timmy, were church cronies who also attended the same schools that we did.

Timmy was too young for me to bother with. But Becky was two years older than I and was quite pretty, with a feisty personality. I was consistently frustrated by our huge age disparity, though—since as a child, it seemed that a one-year difference equated to approximately an adult decade. Their entire family was an integral part of our history, both at church and in our day-to-day lives.

*　　*　　*

Pat Wilhoit was a short, but imposing elementary-school special-education teacher with a wry wit and a noticeable southern drawl. She was a born leader and a highly respected teacher, but to us she was also a first-rate friend and child-sitter. A visit to her house was chock full of surprises, as she would involve me in various arts-and-crafts projects. Pat exhibited the patience of Job when we constructed a wooden doll crib for my sister Laurie. We toiled on the project for several weekends, and although she had done the lion's share of the work, I was given exclusive credit.

Pat and Seborn Wilhoit had a well-trained dachshund named Trudy who would play fetch with an old sock whenever someone was willing to hide or heave it. Trudy would continuously wind through the downstairs rooms at an awkward gallop, in search of her cotton-knit prey. She would skid noisily each time she hit the kitchen floor, regain her stride on the surer footing of the carpet and then build up enough speed so that the momentum of her next leg churning slide would carry her across the kitchen once again. Trudy was smart as a whip and far more entertaining than many children I had encountered.

Pat's husband Seborn loved to tease and was an outstanding piano player. He filled in for the church organist during vacations and was always willing to accompany members in a sing-a-long or entertain at recreation-hall gatherings. Seborn was blind, but dealt with his challenge with good humor and a casualness that made it seem just another aspect of his character. Each baseball season he would proudly hand me a Cincinnati Reds schedule that he had picked up at Tom's First Ward Cigar Store. And whenever my name appeared in the Hamilton *Journal-News*, he would approach me with his mouth curled into a tight-lipped grin and tell me that he had seen my name in the paper. The word "handicapped" in no way applied to him.

* * *

Our minister, Mr. Copelin, would often serve as a Simer taxi, offering us transportation whenever he was able. He was a tall barrel-chested man with dark-brown hair that he combed straight back—and a long face and guileless expression. His down-to-earth demeanor seemed so atypical for a pastor. Mr. Copelin wasn't interested in the title of Reverend and preferred that adults address him simply as Joe.

Joe Copelin took me under his wing and quietly and unobtrusively offered me his knowledge and assistance. He didn't try to replace my father—but offered me the companionship of a man. I was paid to mow the lawn and to help him with odd jobs while he worked at the church building on Saturdays. My first razor was a gift from him, and he taught me how to use it. And he went to the trouble of putting up a hoop and backboard in his large driveway that I could use at any time. This gesture was made even though neither he nor his daughter had any use for the game of basketball. Joe Copelin was a much more important part of my life than I allowed myself to realize at the time.

His wife Marian was quite shy, but always kind to me. And his daughter Elaine was almost irresistibly attractive, with penetrating eyes, short red-brown hair and legs that were too shapely to be attached to a thirteen-year-old girl. The Copelins were in Hamilton for only about three years, but their impact on the Simers and High Street Church cannot be measured.

*   *   *

Many other church people had regular and profound effects on our lives. They drove us to and from church services, youth meetings and doctors' appointments. And they acted as baby-sitters, repair people, cooks and philanthropists. Their names and their deeds are alive in my memory, and they brighten my spirit whenever I recall their kindnesses. They were just everyday, ordinary people—but they did extraordinary things. And as so often happens with honorable and generous individuals, they probably remain unaware of the great significance of their actions. When people like these enter our lives, we are truly blessed.

*   *   *

There were many difficult times our family had yet to face. We own emotional scars that have never completely healed and pain that we still carry with us and continually attempt to exorcise. Each member of our family made mistakes, and we sometimes hurt each other. We limped out of the experience—but many ordeals and years have since transpired—and we are still walking.

My parents' divorce was devastating. Each time I recall the events leading up to it, I hear the echoes of fury in my mother's voice—and feel the emptiness of life without my father. When I see photographs of my family before our parents' separation, I want to weep for an innocence lost. It stirs emotions that are sleeping, but still angry—and returns my attention to an ever-throbbing pain that I have convinced myself is only the beating of my heart. The aftershocks of this tumultuous divorce will rumble throughout my lifetime, wreaking havoc if I let them and forever imprinting on my mind that instability is only a broken relationship or lost loved one away.

I have found it torturous to write this piece and to return to these difficult years. But it is a necessary story that must be told in an honest account of my childhood in my beloved Hamilton. For it is during trying times that a hometown becomes a lifelong friend. Its familiarity keeps us grounded, its institutions give us structure, and from its people come forth guardians to help us along our way. Sometimes in our moments of greatest pain, our greatest bonds are formed—and in our most dire situations—we find our purest love.

The Coterian Collection
Images of people and places from the book.
[THE **BOLD-TYPE** NUMBERS FOLLOWING NAMES AND LOCALES INDICATE

CHAPTERS IN WHICH THEY ARE MENTIONED.]

Pre-marriage photos of Tim's parents: Mona, circa 1943 and Scott, circa 1947.

Just the two of us: Tim and sister Emily, circa 1955.

The Simer family in New Philadelphia, Ohio, circa 1956. From left: Emily, Scott (father), Tim, Becky (on lap) and Mona (mother).

The Simer family in Hamilton, Ohio, circa 1963. From left: Emily, Scott, Laurie, Tim, Mona, Becky.

Emily "posing" in a photo
booth in 1958.

Tim at age six in 1960.

The siblings in 1960.
FRONT ROW, FROM LEFT: Ambrose the stuffed tiger and
Laurie.
BACK ROW FROM LEFT: Emily, Becky, Tim.

"Scottish" Becky, circa
1959.

Laurie in the Simer
backyard in 1963.

Pierce Elementary School, Hamilton, Ohio.

Elementary school classmates.
CLOCKWISE FROM TOP LEFT:
Jill Wolsefer **(2, 3, 5, 10, 14, 15)**
Ken Simmons **(3, 6, 15)**
John Timmer **(14)**
Juan "Bozo" Allen **(14, 17)**

High St. Christian Church in the '60s. **(1, 7, 10)**

Christmas, 1961.

Best friend, Mike Engel, circa 1962. **(2, 8, 10, 17, 19, 22, 23, 24, 25)**

Christmas Eve and Tim's ninth birthday in 1962.

Tim at age eight in 1962.

The "Tootsie Roll Man," Herman Dulli with wife, Lucille. **(7)**

Tim as a "Lindenwald Bill," circa 1967 (black socks not part of standard uniform). **(6)**

American Legion Post #138 Orioles in 1964. **(8)** FIRST ROW FROM LEFT: Unknown, Unknown, Mike Leck **(8, 21, 28)**, Dale Adams, Tim Roberts, Greg Bean, Jack Caudill.
SECOND ROW: Tim Simer, Ron Trester, Steve Schmitz, Rick Adams, Denny Townsend, Kevin Pendergast, Joe Vogt, Mike Banks. TOP ROW: Mr. Pendergast, Mr. Schmitz, Mr. Bean.

Lounging at the lake.
South Pond at Rees Farm.
(11)

Tim soloing in the rowboat
on the South Pond. **(11)**

The cabin and barn at the
Rees Farm. **(11)**

Tim's maternal grandparents:
Roy and Elsie Rees. **(11)**

Family photo at the South Pond, circa
1956: FIRST ROW FROM LEFT: Tim, Emily,
JoLynn Rees and Susie Rees (cousins).
SECOND ROW: Mona Simer, Becky Simer
(infant), Elsie Rees, Roy Rees, James Rees
(uncle), Lorna Rees (aunt). **(11)**

Tim's paternal grandparents, T.W. and Annabel Simer, with Tim and Emily, circa 1958. **(4)**

T.W. and Annabel photo portrait, circa 1956. **(4)**

Spreading out the blankets at the Simer grandparents' farm, circa 1960.
FROM LEFT: Tim, Emily, Becky, Laurie. **(4)**

Sherburnville Christian Church. **(4)**

Outside the lodge at
The Coterian Retreat at
Camp Luella May. **(13)**

Coterian Class members at
the retreat. **(13)**
FROM LEFT:
Sis Fath **(1)**
Jean Falk **(10)**
Evelyn Coyle
Bill Falk
Rolla Coyle **(1)**
Betty Blossom
Ellsworth Blossom **(1)**
Mona Simer
Jim Fath

Volleyball anyone?
A not-so-competitive game
at the retreat. **(13)**

The Andersons in 1972.
FRONT: Tim (son) **(16)**
May Grathwohl (Waneta's mother)
BACK: Becky Anderson (daughter) **(13, 16)**
Don **(1, 6, 13, 16)**
Waneta **(1, 13, 16)**

Seborn and Pat Wilhoit in 1972. **(1, 10, 13, 16)**

The Lemons: Red, Eva, Sandy and Mary Alicia (daughters). **(1, 10, 16)**

Red and Eva Lemon in 1972. **(1, 10, 16)**

Friends from George Washington Jr. High School (photos taken in 1971).

TOP ROW FROM LEFT:
Mike Sparks **(21)**
Jim Howell **(15, 21)**
Mike Leck **(8, 21, 28)**

BOTTOM ROW:
Bill Lasley **(21)**
Jeff Harrison **(15, 20, 21)**
Craig Gebhart **(21)**

1969 George Washington Jr. High graduation dance with date, Kim Bryant. **(20, 22)**

Ninth-grade girlfriend, Kim Bryant (1972 high school graduation photo). **(20, 22)**

1968-69 ninth-grade
English teacher, Coleen
Nelson. **(20, 21, 22, 23)**

Terrie Kinker and Alvis Cadle
(Garfield Sr. High senior prom
1971). **(22)**

A home visit from Tim's
English teacher. FROM LEFT:
Scott Simer, Mona Simer,
Coleen Nelson **(20, 21, 22,
23)**, Becky Simer, Laurie
Simer (in background).

Senior photos: FROM LEFT: Katrena Farmer **(24, 25)** (Mike's high school girlfriend and the woman he would later marry) Mike Engel **(2, 8, 10, 17, 19, 22, 23, 24, 25)** Brenda Doty **(23, 24, 25, 26, 29, 30, 31, 33)**

1970 Garfield High production of *The King and I*. **(24)** FROM LEFT: Donald Bass (the Kralahome), Dan Rommel (King) and Emily Simer (Anna). KNEELING ON FLOOR: Richard Sims and Bob Meadows (guards). Lying on floor: Stephanie May (Tuptim).

Brenda Doty, 1971 junior prom photo. **(23, 24, 25, 26, 29, 30, 31, 33)**

From *The King and I*: John Harmon (Louis), Tim Simer (Captain Orton), Emily Simer (Anna). **(24)**

Connie Combs in 1972.
(24, 27, 31, 32)

Pam Geyer in Garfield
High band in 1972.
(24, 27)

The Kaleidoscope publicity photo. PICTURED FROM LEFT: Ray Combs **(27, 31, 32)**, Pam Geyer **(24, 27)**, Nancy Wehr **(27)**, Tim Simer, Connie Combs **(24, 27, 31, 32)**, Kevin Rommel **(27, 31)**, Edwina Burton **(27)**, Laura Moore **(27, 31)**.

Cast photo, Garfield High School 1972 musical production of *You're a Good Man, Charlie Brown.*
BOTTOM:
director Joe Rosenfield.
FIRST ROW FROM LEFT:
Kevin Rommel (Schroeder) **(27, 31)**
Scott Thorpe (Linus) **(27)**
Ray Combs (Charlie Brown) **(27, 31, 32)**
Debbie Smith (Peppermint Patty) **(27)**
SECOND ROW:
Laura Moore (Lucy) **(27, 31)**
Tim Simer (Snoopy)

1972 senior prom photo with Brenda Thomas. **(31)**

1971 Garfield High School production of musical, *High Spirits* (yearbook photo). **(25)**
FROM LEFT AROUND TIM SIMER:
Barbara Larson
Pam Geyer **(24, 27)**
Connie Combs **(24, 27, 31, 32)**

Senior Photo:
Emily Simer (1970)

Senior Photo:
Tim Simer (1972)

Simer siblings in 2002.

Senior Photo:
Becky Simer (1974)

Senior Photo:
Laurie Simer (1977)

The Coterian Retreat at Camp Luella May.
Group Picture in Lodge, Fall 1963.

ROW ONE, FROM LEFT: 1-Waneta Anderson, 2-Tim Anderson, 3-Patty Burger, 4-Becky Simer, 5-Ann Falk, 6-Janet Coyle, 7-Emily Simer, 8-Karen Burger, 9-Becky Anderson.

ROW TWO: 10-Russ Burger, 11-Tim Simer, 12-Pat Burger, 13-Fred Burger, 14-Doty King, 15-Randy King, 16-Cecil King, 17-Don Anderson, 18-Eva Lemon, 19-Laurie Simer, 20-John Fath, 21-Jim Fath, 22-Jon Falk.

ROWS THREE AND FOUR: 23-Lucille Dulli, 24-Wilda Johnson, 25-Jean Falk, 26-Herman Dulli, 27-Mona Simer, 28-Bill Jenkins, 29-Diane Johnson, 30-Nellie Jenkins, 31-Mary Alicia Lemon, 32-Claude Young, 33-Mark Betscher, 34-Sandy Lemon, 35-Peg Young, 36-Pat Betscher, 37-Tim Betscher, 38-Todd Betscher, 39-Rosella Land, 40-Les Brate, 41-John Land, 42-Terry Grathwohl, 43-Vernon Grathwohl, 44-Grace Brate, 45-Scott Simer, 46-Bill Guthrie, 47-Ernestine Hickman, 48-Greg Guthrie, 49-Bill Hickman.

ROW FIVE: 50-Pete Haun, 51-Cathy Haun, 52-Gus Roth, 53-Adjorie Roth.

ROW SIX: 54-Ellsworth Blossom, 55-Betty Blossom, 56-Sis Fath, 57-Rolla Coyle, 58-Evelyn Coyle, 59-Bill Falk.

17

My Paper Route

It was a late summer afternoon in 1966, and a rare quiet had shrouded the Simer household. Becky and Laurie had escaped to some neighborhood hideaway, and Emily was upstairs in her bedroom, primping as usual. My mother and father had declared a precarious silent truce, and the temporary hush perked my ears as I listened to the uncommon serenity. When the doorbell broke the somber stillness, the interruption was not unexpected. I went to the door, peeked out and caught my first glimpse of Joe Ripberger, the district manager for my new Cincinnati *Enquirer* paper route.

I had pleaded with my parents for some time to get a paper route, and after finally receiving their permission, I had discovered there were no openings to deliver the Hamilton *Journal-News* in our neighborhood. After waiting several months for something to open up, I had decided to pursue an *Enquirer* route as an alternative. Because the Cincinnati *Enquirer* involved early-morning delivery, late risers were hesitant to apply, thus the field of candidates was shortened considerably. I had been contacted by the newspaper shortly after my call of inquiry, and this weekend meeting had been subsequently arranged.

In nearly every respect, Joe Ripberger was rock-solid. He was stocky with dark hair and fair skin and looked as if he might have been a distant cousin of Clark Kent. When he made eye contact, his purity became emphatically recognizable. But Mr. Ripberger had a nervous tic that was difficult to ignore—even upon first meeting. He continually contorted the shape of his mouth, as if he were trying to exercise his mandibles or somehow slip a dislocated jaw back into place. This habit provided some comical facial expressions as he appeared to break into obscenely overdone James Cagney impressions at frequent but unpredictable intervals. His character outshone his idiosyncrasy, though—and I was later to discover that he was highly respected by the carriers in his district.

We spent almost two hours with Mr. Ripberger that afternoon, as he explained the intricacies of managing a paper route. After carefully weighing his presentation, my parents signed the consent forms, and I was presented a new canvas shoulder bag that read "Cincinnati *Enquirer*" in bold all-capital, glossy red lettering, along with a gigantic box of rubber bands. He arranged for me to meet with the current carrier and train with him for a week before assuming my formidable responsibilities.

*   *   *

On the following morning, I sprang from my bed the instant my new GE clock radio sounded its alarm and met the carrier/trainer promptly at 5:30 A.M. on the corner of Griesmer and Clinton Avenues—only about a block and a half from my home. The route belonged to Juan Allen, an elementary-school classmate whom I knew by a more familiar name. The kids in school addressed him as Bozo, a nickname that he oddly seemed to embrace.

Bozo parted his light-brown hair so it split his eyebrows and wore a permanent dolphin-like expression on his face. He had maintained a textbook route payment book and proceeded to give me an extensive customer collection review of which even the local credit bureau would have been proud. Little did these unsuspecting adults know that the neighborhood youth network maintained a regular oral financial file on nearly every household within walking distance. Customer personalities were divided into two distinct classifications: mean or nice. And I was well-briefed on any customer special requests and eccentricities. I went home that morning convinced that I had a bright future in the newspaper delivery business.

The remainder of my week-long training went remarkably well, and at the end of the orientation period I was prepared to go it alone. For several weeks I formulated my own distinct delivery technique, as I mastered the yet-to-be-patented skip-toss, rainbow-lob and my personal favorite, the silent-slide. "The Slide" would skid across a deep porch to the base of the front door while making nary a sound. During the developmental stage of these masterworks, I additionally became a lightning-quick retriever, and when accidentally striking a door or the side of a house, a deftly skilled escape artist. My folding and banding expertise continued to improve until I became an automatically reloading, folding and banding machine—as my arms and fingers generated a whir of nimble locomotion.

On weekdays and Saturdays I would arise at around 5:00 A.M., fold my papers, hop on my trusty balloon-tired red Huffy bicycle and begin my

158

race against time. Sometimes I would commentate the dash in a hushed whisper, as if it were a sanctioned Olympic event. The course could be completed in a cool fifteen minutes.

Sundays were an entirely different story as my customer list nearly doubled that of a weekday. When the driver dropped my bundles, my porch resembled a paper-drive collection station with reams of advertising supplements, free samples—and even a token amount of editorial copy. I would either be forced to make numerous bicycle trips or load up our four-wheeled red wagon and leave bundles at strategic locations throughout my route. Because I wanted to economize my time, I would stuff my carrier bag to its expandable limits and stagger around the street like a hideously deformed hunchback, with the canvas strap pinching its imprint into my tortured shoulder.

Collections were never my forte, but initially I punished myself into regularly doing them. I purchased a metal coin-changer that could be hung on my belt, and although I doubt it induced me to approach my collections with any more diligence—it sure made them more fun. It also proved a useful gadget for stress relief as I would endlessly flip the levers and watch the change spit out at the rate of a slot-machine payout.

*   *   *

The beginning months of my paper route and the end of my parents' marriage occurred simultaneously, and my business barely survived the move of the bundle drop-off point to an address a short jaunt down the street. My emotional state made the discipline of the route more burdensome, as I had difficulty sleeping and not coincidentally awakening. My mother and I had regular early-morning barking matches, until I would finally drag myself out the door, muttering unpleasantries under my breath.

I convinced my best friend Mike Engel to accept a route near mine, and his companionship injected some new interest into my work. We often delivered together and would sometimes sneak in overnight stays at each other's house. On these exceptional evenings, we would plant ourselves in front of the television and watch our hero, Bob Shreve, and his Schoenling Beer All-Night Theatre until our newspapers arrived. Shreve was a master of sight gags and inane silliness and would appear before or after commercial breaks. He usually was dressed as a barkeep and stood behind a television studio bar, wearing a tavern bib and making a totally delightful fool of himself. Each week he would bellow his familiar commercial jingle to the tune of "Sailing, Sailing." I believe his rendition went something like this:

Schoenling, Schoenling, that is the beer for me!
It has the tastes of malts and hops of finest quality.
Schoenling, Schoenling, my choice for purity.
I've tried the rest, Schoenling's best!
It's Schoenling beer for me!

The final "me" was completed with a deafening octave slide into an off-key falsetto, which was followed immediately by a lengthy recording of thunderous applause. The movies were usually intentionally bad and the humor worse, but it was ideal late-night fare, and we held him in great reverence.

Around 4:00 A.M. we heard the loud thud of our wire-wrapped newspaper bundles hitting the front porch and knew that duty called. We quickly folded our literary missiles and were off into the still night air. The early morning hours were incredibly silent, and in the predawn darkness the sense of sound seemed to rule the streets. Breezes would rush past the ears, almost tickling them with an uncontested clarity. And an oncoming car would be heard from blocks away, as one could clearly distinguish the rhythmic purr of its tires gripping the pavement from the lonesome wail of its shifting motor.

Conversation was hushed and limited as we went about our business while surveying this neighborhood that now belonged to us. After completion, we would often make the lengthy approximately one-mile walk to Dunkin' Donuts on Dixie Highway. There we would carefully select a sackful of donuts or Danish and eat until our fingers were sticky with frosting and donut glaze. Only then would we reluctantly succumb to our exhaustion and sleep until late morning, when we would again have to share the world with the remainder of the population.

We were not always as angelic as my descriptions sound. There were rare summer mornings when we would make our rounds armed with several of Mike's limited arsenal of M-80 firecrackers. These were "special deliveries" made to select friends and enemies and were capable of temporarily arousing more than a city block of unsuspecting sleepyheads. Like our newspapers, these little treats were home-delivered, but always involved a dwelling not in our immediate stomping grounds. After igniting the fuse, we would sprint until our lungs hurt or until we spotted a car, in

160

which case we would halt on a dime and quickly assume our best looks of boyish innocence.

It must be said that this is probably the most rebellious behavior that we ever indulged in. Had there not been such sheer delight in so dramatically severing the silence, our guilt would have surely ended the tomfoolery. As it was, it ended as quickly as did Mike's short supply of artillery.

*   *   *

But I also treasured the countless mornings I went it alone. There was no hushed conversation to break the silence, and senses were heightened to almost eerie levels. Each unexpected sound precipitated an involuntary flinch, and any motion within my sight lines drew immediate focus. There was an unpredictability in the oft-interrupted stillness, but my body felt like my fortress—harboring a soul that seemed to grow stronger in solitude. I never felt more alone—or more complete. The time was often used for meditation and reflection. Problems were left at home—and although I pondered them, they added no weight to my load. My thoughts cut through the quiet, and difficult decisions were reached by listening to those who spoke with the greatest clarity.

*   *   *

As the months progressed, the *Enquirer* offered additional income and incentives for signing up new subscribers. Because of our sales prowess, we won trips to the Ohio State football game, the Reds' opening day and the Coney Island Amusement Park. Mike was a good door-to-door canvasser, and I was even better. Decades later, he would still grumble about my signing up new customers on his route who would invariably cancel immediately after the thirty-day trial period.

Mr. Ripberger, aware of our impressive skills of persuasion, would constantly seek us out on weekends to go on sales crews to various areas of the city. We did not enjoy the intrusion on our private time, nor were we fond of the prospect of tasting a steady diet of slammed doors. We began to avoid his predictable weekend phone calls, so he opted for the more direct approach of coming unannounced to our homes or cruising the neighborhood in search of his star solicitors.

Mike and I became weekend fugitives, making frequent use of our back doors and slinking about the streets, ready to duck behind a bush or shrub at a moment's notice. If we had made a clean break, we would seek the safe haven of Sip's Fountain and Donut Shop. Sip's was a wonderful little corner store with its own deep-frying donut machine located behind the fountain counter. Once there, we would stare through the machine's clear windows as the donuts danced in a sizzling pool of oil before tumbling out into a metal tray to be iced or dipped in cinnamon or powdered sugar. We would gobble down a freshly made donut or two while waiting for the coast to clear, sometimes doing dueling Mr. Ripberger impressions and always celebrating our afternoon-long freedom from buyer rejection.

* * *

Of course, the best time to have a paper route was over the Christmas holidays when I reaped added benefits for my efforts over the year. By my second December of delivering, my holiday tips had become quite substantial, and I found myself with nearly one hundred and fifty dollars in somewhat unexpected compensation. Since my father had left, our yuletide celebrations had been diminished in size, but not in spirit. I decided to spend much of my tip money to brighten the Christmas of my sisters and mother. I bought Emily an electric curler set, Becky a first-rate doll house with furniture and Laurie an Easy-Bake Oven. I also gift-wrapped a Polaroid camera for my mother, which was considered a wondrous futuristic gadget throughout the decade of the '60s. It was a heartening experience to be able to play Santa Claus—and an emotional breakthrough for me to want to.

Christmas fell on a Sunday that year, so we made the early morning delivery of the newspapers a family affair. Everyone had agreed that the entire day should be spent together—so my mother and three sisters trudged out into the icy winter with me—taking turns dragging a wagon full of *Enquirers* that would bring both good and bad tidings to holiday readers. The clock read an unthinkable 5 A.M, yet amidst the woolen caps stretched atop their heads and scarves snaked around their faces, I read a deeply gratifying contentment in their wind-watered eyes. In this see-your-breath cold, the pre-dawn present of seeing my family Christmas-wrapped in multiple layers of warm clothing was more precious than any other gift I would receive.

* * *

I would give up my paper route before another Christmas arrived. As I neared the age of sixteen, other job opportunities became available. I had

162

become consistently slow on my collections which had cut directly into my profits, and my heart was now firmly set on purchasing a car for personal and family use. Mr. Ripberger had been patient and helpful during a shaky period in our family's history, but I realized that it was time to part company with him and the Cincinnati *Enquirer*.

It had been a good run. The job had provided me with my first real taste of responsibility—and of operating a successful business and meeting deadlines. And Mike and I had shared some wonderful and unique bonding experiences that neither of us will ever forget. The route gave regimentation and continuity to my days and provided structure when I sometimes felt I was ready to crumble.

But most importantly, it provided me with quietude. In the stark soundlessness of early morning, people were meeting their needs through peaceful slumber. The footsteps I heard were mine alone, yet they sufficed as my companion. While the rest of the world remained halted and silent, I had learned to listen to my own heart.

18

Tim's Place

My father left our family in 1967 and took with him the only male influence in my troubled home life. The house was now overrun with women, and they infiltrated every nook and cranny of our new home on Pleasant Avenue. My mother and sisters and their friends and acquaintances crept through the hallways and lurked around corners like an infestation of she-devils. Their primary objective appeared to be to create such a hideously pure feminine environment that my maleness would eventually be driven from their midst. Every room was marked by their bobby-pins and emery boards, Barbie dolls, teen magazines and romance novels. A television broadcast of the World Series or the NCAA basketball tournament meant nothing to them, and they viewed Marvel comic books and baseball cards as mere household clutter. I sought refuge at friends' homes and became involved in as many extracurricular activities as possible. However, it was still sometimes necessary to roost in the family hen house. In these cases, I would seek asylum in the protected sanctuary of my upstairs bedroom.

*   *   *

The room was off-limits to snooping sisters and was regularly combed for any feminine paraphernalia. A brown wooden miniature bulldog with concentrated glass eyes and green collar served as a door stop and symbolic sentry, faithfully guarding the portal to my private domain. In the late '60s, my room was decorated in a very unladylike black and fire-engine red, the result of a furniture refinishing project my father had undertaken just before his departure. The work had been done as part of a last-ditch effort at marital reconciliation and meant much more to me because of it.

All of the furniture had been painted coal-black, except for a deafeningly loud shelving unit constructed with bricks alternately painted

164

black and red. The bricks served as support for three solid-black, eight-foot-wide plywood shelves. My bed cover was bright bordello-red, and atop my chest of drawers was a garish red-and-black striped embroidered rug. The overall decorative scheme was contemporary roulette wheel and was manly, yet properly gaudy. It was a bachelor's playland and surely would have broken a girlfriend's resistance, if my mother had allowed me to lure one into this splashy showplace.

Mood lighting set the nighttime climate. Along with a rather ordinary lamp that my mother had insisted upon, I owned a bonafide black light and several scented candles in distinctive holders that I had received as Christmas gifts. On a side wall there were two simulated-candle lighting fixtures that I had replaced with flame-shaped amber bulbs. I thus could regulate the atmosphere at the flip of a switch, spanning the spectrum from laboratory-bright to psychedelic and dreamy.

The walls were decorated with two blacklight posters purchased in the hippie-filled Old Town section of downtown Chicago. My father and I had discovered them in an incense-filled, psychedelic storefront in Piper's Alley. Directly over my bed was another poster of a bug-eyed and toothless old fart who was practically swallowing his own lips while sucking on a mouthful of cigarettes and blowing smoke from his ears. While it is true that the photo blowup was not in keeping with the sensual ambience I had so expertly crafted, I just couldn't bear to part with it. If I had, it would have been placed into my ultra-cool trash container shaped like an oversized Ballentine Ale can. I was still too young to have developed a taste for the suds and had never personally seen a can of Ballentine. But the wastebasket seemed very collegiate and conformed to my new worldly image.

At the foot of the bed was a night stand which held my Philco black-and-white television and my private stash of Blommer's chocolate. On weekends, whenever I lost the battle for the downstairs set because of some mid-afternoon tear-jerker, I would retire to my den and cheer on the latest edition of the Cincinnati Reds or Bengals. And countless late evenings were spent reclined on my red-ribbed bedspread, watching Joey Bishop or Johnny Carson while gnawing on thick chocolate bars. Eventually I would nod off and usually reawaken at the crack of dawn with an intense case of heartburn. The Philco had been purchased with paper-route money and was my pride and joy because of the freedom and autonomy that it represented.

*   *   *

165

On the night stand at the head of the bed were my beige GE clock radio and a mammoth Vlasic pickle jar that contained my live pet newt. His pickle-palace was filled with rain water, several rocks and a twig that extended far short of the gaping entrance to his glass house. The shortened twig had been a security measure because of the newt's numerous and embarrassing attempts at escape. The lizard had been purchased at a very inopportune time, just days before my parents' separation, and he somehow had managed to survive for nearly two years. Soon after bringing him home, I realized that a newt in confinement did nearly nothing except eat and stare icily. His fixed expression never altered, except that he puffed up slightly when he was submerged in water for more than a few minutes. I had tried without success to give him to someone with a suitable aquarium, but failed consistently because of his deathlike demeanor. When he sat stone-still on his twig or floated like sculpted driftwood underwater, I began imagining that he had locked in on my every move and was glaring at me no matter where I was situated in the room.

At night he would be moved to the lowest shelf on the night stand, so I could sleep without being subjected to his evil eye. And on nice days, I would put him out on the porch, using the feeble excuse that he could use some fresh air. One brisk fall evening, the temperature took an unexpected dip while I was away from home, and the newt became a failed experiment in cryogenics. The disaster was unintentional, but I underwent a bout of personal guilt—wishing that he had lived a fuller life. I must admit, however, that I also felt a great sense of relief at being freed from his neverending scrutiny. It had been a bad marriage from the start. We had never really understood each other.

*   *   *

Hanging on the wall over my brick shelving unit was a peace symbol made of hard clear red plastic that was a post-divorce gift from my father. It rested on a pair of nails and looked like an undersized steering wheel, but cast an ember's glow when it absorbed candlelight. When my room was brightened by the flicker of a candlewick's flame, and the hi-fi blared out the Byrds' "Turn, Turn, Turn," I felt very much in tune with the times.

The record player was a bulky old Zenith portable with an automatic record changer and a detachable speaker that doubled as the unit's lid. It was also equipped with an adjustable speed-selector that could play records at 16, 33 1/3, 45, and 78 RPMs or at any speed in between. A showy, but otherwise useless gauge displayed calibrations that spun by at the same rate that the record was revolving. The phonograph was a gift of a friend's parents, who had purchased a much larger stereo console and no longer had use for it. I adored the present and would stack as many LPs as the spindle would endure and escape into the music and my fantasies.

*   *   *

My shelves were lined with my most valuable personal property. On the top shelf was a large red Texaco tanker-truck that I had owned since I was seven. My parents had ordered it as part of a service station promotion and given it to me as a birthday gift. The rig was so handsome that I had refused to play with it, and instead had always displayed it as a centerpiece in my room. The truck was parked near a miniature metal replica of the United Nations building that my parents had brought back with them when they attended a church convention in New York City. It was one of the few trips that they had taken alone together, and was significant to me because I had never seen my mother happier or more excited.

Near the United Nations paperweight was a small simulated-marble bust of Abraham Lincoln that I had purchased as a souvenir of our trip to the Lincoln Memorial. I had always been fascinated with Honest Abe, and the month-long Eastern U.S. camping trip that our family had taken together when we passed through the nation's capital was one of my most pleasant family memories.

On the second shelf was a collection of hardcover and paperback books that I had gathered over the years. My most precious literary treasures included a replacement copy of my favorite novel, *The Catcher in the Rye,* a fully illustrated book of basketball fundamentals by Oscar Robertson, and a personally engraved copy of the Holy Bible that I had received for my baptism when I was eight. Next to these scholarly keepsakes was a tall stack of my most recent and favorite Marvel comics, including the Avengers, X-Men, Spiderman, and the Fantastic Four.

Alongside the comic books was a five-car windup Cocoa Puffs train that I had sent away for when we still lived in New Philadelphia. I had faithfully devoured a bowl of the sugary treat every morning for months so that I could collect enough boxtops to receive this spring-locomotion vehicle. When wound tightly, the choo-choo would circle the linoleum, while the wheelless caboose flicked back and forth like a cat's tail. The train is

167

still operable to this day, making it the best fifty-cent investment I have ever made.

Stacked on the lowest shelf was a collector's selection of *Playboy* magazines. My mother had reluctantly permitted me to subscribe to the periodical in hopes that it would satisfy my overwhelming curiosity and prevent me from obtaining less artistic pictorial compilations. Unfortunately my curiosity proved insatiable, and the *Playboys* ultimately had an effect similar to reading a quality travel magazine. It only made me yearn for the day that I could witness these wonderful sights in person. My library of lasciviousness drew frequent avid readers, and my bedchamber became the neighborhood male adolescent reading room.

An autographed Reds baseball was carefully wrapped in Saran Wrap and rested next to my *Playboys,* so that I could indulge in two divergent fantasies in one sitting. The ball was a gift from Bill Jenkins, an adult neighbor and church member, who shocked me when he handed me the ball without fanfare after one Sunday worship service. The official major league baseball included the signatures of Frank Robinson, Pete Rose, Leo Cardenas and Johnny Edwards and was handled like a museum artifact. A college photograph of my father often also lay face-down on the bottom shelf and would be displayed only when my mother was away or sleeping. I had been given the picture as a young child and simply could not ignore its existence. It remained an integral part of the room and resurfaced whenever the situation would allow it.

The bedroom floor was a tiled linoleum of blacks, browns and grays. A pair of throw rugs was strategically placed to give the room a more comfortable feel. Sounds echoed in the sparsely furnished room, and the predominantly metal furniture creaked and clanked when drawers were open or I sank into my bed. But it was my room and was filled with the things most important to me. Its safe harbor provided me shelter from my own raw emotions and sadness, and temporarily isolated me from the people whom I often loved and sometimes despised.

*   *   *

Our rooms and, in later life, our homes are essential sanctuaries. They are vehicles for our creativity, and within the restrictions of financial capabilities, demonstrate how material possessions can provide a physical extension of our moods and personalities. They hold our music and our books—and fabrics, colors, and textures that are sensory extensions of our spirit. But most importantly, they hold our memories. They are a historical exhibit of relationships that we hold dear, objects that represent significant occasions in our lives, and photographs of people and times that we have loved.

As we age, our rooms imitate alterations made in our personalities and lifestyles—or sometimes foreshadow changes we would like to make. Items and photographs that no longer tell our story are discarded and replaced by selections more pleasing to our eyes and minds. Our surroundings undergo a perpetual facelift and forever reflect what we see when we look at ourselves in the mirror.

Ballentine Ale waste cans and plastic peace symbols eventually find their way to basement boxes or garage sales and are replaced by new friends more compatible with our current lifestyle. Yet in most cases, parting with our old companions is excruciating—and tears are sometimes shed when we are forced to say our good-byes. And if they have become so weighted down with memories that they are impossible to remove from the house, they are simply added to our excess baggage—deemed worthless or useless by insensitive souls who cannot possibly understand their significance in our personal history. After all, these appointments held an esteemed position in our lives—they had resided with us and served their purpose proudly.

When in our rooms, we can either close our doors and curtains and lock the rest of the world out or open our windows and portals and invite outsiders to share an environment that is uniquely us. My room was my friend throughout my youth because it served to remind me of who I was—both in the isolation that it provided me for meditation and in the stories about my life that it retold each time I entered its refuge. It was, in fact, a mirror image of me—and when I looked into its face, I found that I generally liked the person I saw. I had discovered that even under the most trying of circumstances, I still enjoyed my own company.

19

Lainie

If someone asked me when I first kissed a girl, I would be hard-pressed to give him an answer. Initially there were experimental early childhood pecks when puckered lips collided, and I wondered why adults would engage in such a senseless and messy custom. After I had made lip contact with several neighbor girls and classmates, I decided the ritual was not for me and would have no more of it. When Donna Ernst tried to kiss me at recess in early elementary school, I ran like a jackrabbit. And when Carol Colgate decided she would plant one on me when I spent the afternoon at her house, I hid under a bed and remained there until the heat was off.

Later, when I reached adolescence, there were games of spin-the-bottle when the exploration was less clinical and my participation a bit more eager. Technique was gradually developed, and when the bottle targeted the right girl, the experience could be downright enjoyable. Still, the encounters were forced and public, and they lacked the excitement that I now believed must make the experience so special. By the time I had graduated into the eighth grade I had kissed more than a handful of bobby-soxed lassies, but none of the episodes had proven particularly inspired or memorable. It was then that I met Elaine Copelin and quickly discovered what all the clamor was about.

*　　*　　*

It was the spring of 1968 when the Copelins moved into the parsonage on Pleasant Avenue. Elaine's father had been hired as the new pastor of High Street Christian Church, and curiosity demanded that I size up my father's replacement at my first opportunity. A chance presented itself when a number of church families attended an open house at the Copelin residence.

That afternoon, the parsonage backyard patio was humming with lively conversation, as curious guests trailed the new minister and his wife like an overeager press corps searching for background information. In the interest of self-preservation, I was desperately trying to untangle my observations from my emotions. Being in my old home was difficult for me, and seeing another family perform our role as gracious politicians served to psychologically finalize the events that surrounded my parents' separation. I was feeling sorry for myself when Elaine walked out of the back door.

She was wearing tight blue shorts and a baggy short-sleeve sweatshirt and was amazingly curvy for a girl in the seventh grade. Her legs were perfection and her posterior an adolescent boy's dream. Elaine's piercing green eyes darted back and forth, scanning the crowd as if consciously assessing her next move. She was quite striking, with eyes accentuated by dark eyebrows and her cinnamon hair combed straight and curled gracefully around her ears. She glanced at me only briefly, but I felt her eyes and interest and was immediately enticed.

Initially no words were spoken, but we recorded each other's movements and interactions. I shadowed her cautiously, accidentally showing up in nearly every area of the house or yard that she drifted to. Ultimately my pursuit ended, and we found ourselves seated side-by-side on the living room sofa—staring at an episode of "Wild, Wild West." Although there were several other people in the room, they drifted one by one to mingle with the throngs. Elaine and I stayed put.

We talked sporadically and shifted our weight ever so gradually—leaning toward each other until our shoulders made contact. I nervously grabbed a couch pillow, pulled it to my lap and almost cradled it in my arms as I attempted to calm the butterflies that fluttered in the pit of my stomach. After several minutes our bare arms brushed accidentally. Our elbows dropped to the sofa seat, and opposite hands drew closer together until our fingers spontaneously intertwined. As adults would say, we hadn't planned it—it just happened. Her hand fit snugly with mine, and because the incident had not been pre-planned—my palm remained surprisingly sweat-free.

The hand-holding episode lasted only a matter of moments, because it seemed somehow inappropriate. After all, it was our initial meeting, and we had already given the gossipmongers plenty to chatter about. We had shared a romantic encounter, and my interest was definitely piqued. Elaine was our new pastor's daughter, but she was also my best friend's next-door neighbor. I would be seeing a lot of her.

It did not take long for us to become an item. We began to speak on the phone, and I spent even more of my free time at Mike Engel's house. When Mr. Copelin put a backboard and hoop on his new two-car garage, I finally had a legitimate excuse to invade Elaine's territory. She would come out to twirl her baton, while I would make a half-hearted effort at games of one-on-one basketball. Elaine had become a school majorette, and her routine commanded the majority of my attention. My eyes often strayed from the baton to appraise her form and footwork—with particular attention paid to lower-body evaluation.

On one occasion Mike wearied of my wandering eyes and left us to our flirtations. Our conversation accelerated, and she soon abandoned her wand for private basketball instruction. We exchanged shots for several minutes before the ball inadvertently rolled into the open garage, and I went in to retrieve it. As I scooped it up and pivoted to return, she blocked my path and playfully attempted to snatch the ball away from me. I resisted, and a brief tug of war ensued. Suddenly the ball fell from my grasp and took several waning bounces before rolling as far as its momentum would take it. There it rested for more than a minute, no longer a possession that either of us had use for.

I had been moved to kiss her. When our lips touched, countless hours of practice on proper technique and worrying about the most opportune moment to make my first move were rendered meaningless. My mouth had melted into hers and had temporarily shorted out all brain activity. We were leaned against a garage wall with my hands clenching her lower back, drawing her as close to me as was possible.

Her face was incredibly smooth and youthfully yielding. Her hair smelled like a woman's, and the emotions that stirred in me more closely resembled romantic passion than any I had ever experienced. The kiss felt as wonderful as I had dreamed a kiss could feel, and I reeled back when our lips parted as I tried to clear my mind and regain my equilibrium. I felt as if I had been administered a jolt of electricity—my lips felt numb, and my entire body was temporarily sapped of energy. My salivary glands were operating full-throttle, and my head did a quick shudder as my eyes struggled to regain focus. The effects were short-lived but momentous, and a part of me felt like a little boy who had just ridden a colossal roller coaster—I was dying to try it again.

The basketball found its way into the garage more times than Mr. Copelin's blue Buick that spring and summer, and I found myself madly in love with love. I gave her a Sears mail-order catalogue ring that I'd never worn, and she dressed it in angora and displayed it proudly at school. In turn, I wore her Siamese ring snaked around my left pinky, thus announcing to the world that I was desired and taken. I usually walked her home from school and would spend weekend evenings in front of the Copelins' television set, biding my time for an opportunity to steal a kiss or wrap my arms around her. We even chose a song that we called our own—"Silence is Golden" by the Tremeloes, and I played it constantly while wallowing in thoughts of our whirlwind romance. She was now Lainie to me—a pet name that made our relationship seem much more adult and intimate.

I gradually grew comfortable with being a boyfriend and learned many subtle nuances of male/female relationships. I became proficient at walking in tandem, and fine-tuned the timing and form used when slipping my arm around her while in both standing and seated positions. My manual dexterity improved, as I became adept at using both right and left arms and hands—making me an effective Romeo when seated on either side of my new steady.

Our physical contact was limited to hand-holding, prolonged kisses and my arms around her shoulder or waist. But our self-imposed restrictions only served to heighten the significance of the ardor we did allow ourselves. Our demonstrations of affection were almost always private, and the extent of our feelings for each other was known only by our closest friends. Her parents gave the relationship room to breathe, allowing us limited private access to each other while always managing to be somewhere nearby. We obliged them by policing ourselves, reasonably comfortable in our naivete, and successfully keeping the lid on adult feelings that sometimes welled up inside of us.

*   *   *

As my ninth-grade school year progressed, high school loomed in the not-too-distant future. The one-year age difference between Elaine and me became a bigger stumbling block with each new day. The newness was wearing off, and newness is what often makes young love so desirable. We had learned much from each other, but I thirsted for new romantic adventures and the freedom to pursue them. We both had other flirtations at church, she with a much-older boy named Jim Fath, I with a childhood friend and neighbor named Donna Werk. After suffering through our first lovers' quarrels and several serious spats, we broke up. There was one sudden explosion of romantic fireworks months later when we kissed in the privacy of a secluded Sunday school room, but for the most part I adjusted to life without Lainie.

She had come to me at a time in my life when I craved and wanted both to be adored by someone and to lavish my affections in return. My eagerness to know more about women was sometimes overwhelming, and my sexual desire was surfacing in physical symptoms I had never before experienced. Elaine Copelin and I were both preacher's kids, and our shared upbringings allowed us to respect each other enough to experiment in a controlled setting. In retrospect, the timing of our meeting was ideal. We each needed the other's discipline and understanding as we faced difficult transitions in our young lives.

*   *   *

I haven't had many romantic encounters of any kind that affected me as powerfully as the initial kiss we shared in that two-car garage. Its significance was certainly not known to me when we followed the bouncing ball to what I now consider to be my first real kiss. The moment had been born from my heart rather than my lips, so perhaps that is why it remains so memorable.

Having never discussed this with Elaine, I am not sure she recalls our first kiss or any of our kisses as being particularly momentous. But to me, when our lips made contact that spring day, she kissed my spirit and left her indelible imprint on my life. I hope that we meet again someday so that I may thank her—with a handshake, of course.

20

Mrs. Nelson

The troops gathered outside our fifth-period English class, and I found myself surrounded by a collection of teenage well-knowns who would certainly not tarnish my carefully crafted ninth-grade image. It was the first day of school in the fall of 1968, and I was feeling the confidence of being established in the junior-high hierarchy. During the first two years of my post-elementary-school identity search, I had associated myself with a group of friends who were not only popular in the true junior-high sense of the word, but also were fairly likeable and interesting people. Through a stroke of luck, a handful of them were scheduled to be in this class with me. We were all reveling in the good fortune that had befallen us, because the scuttlebutt that had swept the school was that a new young female teacher would instruct the course.

There were immediate inferences that could be drawn from this information. "New" meant that at least initially we had the upper hand. The teacher had to acclimate to the territory, and the longer we could keep her tentative and flustered, the longer we would remain in control. "Young" was the double whammy, because not only was the teacher in a new environment, but in a new profession as well. The fact that she was also a female eliminated the potential of a stern male disciplinarian who would not spare the rod, and thus would become a pain in the derriere in a quite literal sense.

We were discussing summer war stories and exchanging vital mental notes of the day's events when the bell rang. My friends and I inflated our chests and strutted toward the classroom door as if we were a gang of bad-men entering a saloon in a town where lawlessness ruled the streets. We were prepared to confront our new adversary and stared a hole through her back as she wrote the name "Mrs. Nelson" on the front blackboard. Suddenly she made a half-turn, and even the most hardened of us was surprised by the scenery that revolved into view. Scanning the room, her gaze was aimed directly into the eyes of each student who dared look up at her.

Her green eyes were piercingly clear, and there was something about them that almost immediately allowed me to see both her strength and her vulnerability. Her skin was pristine, yet more supple and full than a younger girl's—suggesting the contrast between the bud and the blossom. Her hair was dark brown and shoulder-length, and hinted of sweet womanly fragrances that were intimidating allures to fifteen-year-old boys. Her skirt, though properly conservative at the time, was short enough that her shapely legs kicked and then crumbled whatever was left of my tough veneer.

I struggled to regain my composure. She was, after all, a teacher and therefore sub-human. A cool, withdrawn demeanor was needed when dealing with these dangerous mutants. I decided to bide my time, to observe and test her, until I became more familiar with this enemy.

*   *   *

Over the next few weeks I pushed and prodded Mrs. Nelson's psyche. I was often taken aback by her ability to sniff out our attempts to engage her in mind games and her knack at subtly communicating that awareness to us. She treated us as individuals and gave us immediate respect that we had not yet earned. Whatever knowledge she lacked about the tricks of her trade was compensated by honesty in admitting what she did not know, and her ability to convince us that she was learning at a lightning pace. We all knew that Mrs. Nelson was vulnerable to a student revolt. Yet as she gained begrudging respect from each of us, the prospect of artfully abusing this person who became more real to us each day provided little satisfaction.

I was becoming enamored with this teacher, a realization that I would reluctantly admit only to myself. Although I observed her from the safe distance of a student-instructor relationship, I felt that I knew her on a much deeper level. Mrs. Nelson became the first adult I had encountered that, through no fault of her own, crossed the line that separates professional relationships from intimate friendships. It was not a schoolboy crush that I suffered from, but a fascination with her mind and thought process, and this fascination was amplified by the fact that she was also a stunning female in her twenties.

I appreciated her womanliness. There was a graceful completion of her physical maturation, a well-rounded and soft definition in all of her features. I studied her with a child's curiosity, yet with an eye that had begun to view women in an adult way. Her personality was my primary fascination, though—and the fact that she was strikingly attractive only offered an interesting and confusing distraction.

*　　*　　*

Mrs. Nelson was an excellent teacher—an instructor who interpreted English class as more than diagraming sentences and reading the classics. The course explored debate, poetry, music and musical lyrics—plays, speech and creative writing. The atmosphere was casual, yet controlled—with enthusiastic participation from many unlikely sources. Creative humor and wisecracks were tolerated if not sometimes encouraged, and students' thoughts and opinions were heard without a trace of condescension.

*　　*　　*

On one occasion, we were given the assignment of writing and performing a TV commercial, and my friend Jeff Harrison and I decided to compose an ad about a brand of frozen cream pies. We developed a script in which I heckled him while he was hawking the desserts until he angrily let me have it, in the proud tradition of the Three Stooges and Soupy Sales. There were two complications with our execution of this dazzling concept. We had not let the pie thaw completely, and we had neglected to tell Mrs. Nelson what we had planned to do. When the pie struck my face, it felt as if I had been clobbered with a ice-filled frying pan topped with whipped cream, as it literally shattered—leaving a trail of banana-cream slush on the walls and side bulletin board. After my cobwebs had cleared, Jeff and I offered our janitorial service and spent some private time with Mrs. Nelson after class. We explained, and she listened—with teeth clenched. I'm sure by now she actually sees the humor in it.

*　　*　　*

She was blessed with all the physical tools of an engaging speaker. Her eye contact demanded attention, and her voice was crystal clear, with a precise and resonant tone that was almost three-dimensional. It reached out to include you, and the fact that there was always so much class interchange and enthusiasm only enhanced her ability to draw you in.

177

As one of her first assignments, she initiated a semester-long project in which we were to submit a personal journal that was to contain at least six entries. There were no restrictions concerning the entries; they could be of any length and could be poetry, a short story, a diary entry or whatever our mood moved us to write about. It was only stressed that we do the work outside of the classroom and preferably at our leisure.

I found that entries often gushed out of me, and that I came to look forward to my writing as my personal therapy. The journal was a creative emotional outlet when I felt trapped by the pressures of adolescence and my current home situation. But I also used the journal as my primary method of communicating with Mrs. Nelson. The entries were not directed to her, but they offered my most private thoughts, and allowed me to bare my soul while maintaining the distance that my comfort and pride demanded. I submitted many, many more than six entries and could not wait to get my graded journal back. Mrs. Nelson would write several paragraphs explaining our marks and commenting on certain sections of our work. This red-penned evaluation felt like a reply to a heartfelt letter that I had written her.

*   *   *

It did not take long before Mrs. Nelson was the best-liked teacher in school. When the music teacher, Mr. Hill, cast a mini-production of Gilbert and Sullivan's *The Mikado,* he found he did not have the time or the training to serve as an acting instructor. Since the school was without a drama teacher, Mrs. Nelson was the logical and popular choice to assume these duties. I had been cast as the wandering minstrel, Nanki-Poo—a role and a name that no one seemed to forget over the next four years. It was recalled regularly by alleged friends and became a term of endearment that my high school sweetheart embarrassed me with—both in her letters and in carefully selected public situations.

Rehearsals began awkwardly when it was discovered that the script called for a kiss between Nanki-Poo and his lover, Yum-Yum, who was played by Pam Baumann. Pam was not an unattractive girl, but the vision of my classmates witnessing my staged attempt at romantic prowess was as frightening as the actor's nightmare of suddenly realizing that he is performing without his pants. Mrs. Nelson came up with the perfect solution to our dilemma. A red paper heart large enough to conceal both of our faces was unfolded when the kiss was to occur, drawing laughs from the audience and preserving Pam's and my dignity.

For the most part, the cast was well-behaved throughout the rehearsal schedule. But occasionally we were guilty of indulging in a game that we came to call Stalag 17. When we were left unsupervised for any period of time at after-school rehearsals, we would kill all of the lights in the theater. The cast and crew would quickly scatter and hide anywhere on stage or within the first five audience rows. Then the spotlight operator would begin his search for escaped prisoners. This bit of mischief aside, rehearsals ran smoothly and yet were often wildly creative. Some of the show's funniest moments were developed here, as Mrs. Nelson encouraged improvisation and was always open to suggestions.

The big evening performance finally arrived, and Mrs. Nelson's husband was in attendance. He was disgustingly cute and dimply—a cross between country singer Clint Black and some long-lost Osmond brother. All of the girls raved about this well-scrubbed, toothy Romeo as I buried my own incisors into my lip, concluding that he was obviously not right for her. The show went remarkably well, and I left that evening as a twenty-four hour celebrity with my girlfriend Kim Bryant on my arm. I was still slightly shaken, however, by the stark realization that Mrs. Nelson had a living, breathing husband outside the world of George Washington Junior High.

*   *   *

I vividly recall a field trip we took to see Franco Zeffirelli's *Romeo and Juliet* at the Ciné Malibu theater. I was swept up in the film and was truly appreciative that Mrs. Nelson had once again gone beyond the call of duty to expose us to the fine arts. As I climbed on the idling bus to go home, she was standing near the driver, counting students as they boarded. Our eyes met briefly, and for a fleeting moment I was overcome with a powerful urge to kiss her, as a grown man would kiss a woman. It was a thought born both out of the sexual stirrings within a fifteen-year-old boy who had just been exposed to the passion of Shakespeare, and a true love and appreciation of who she was and what she had meant to me. I immediately reeled the emotion back within me and would not let this thought cross the rigid boundaries between us again.

*   *   *

Although it sometimes feels like another lifetime, it is still quite possible to revisit the excitement I felt toward Mrs. Nelson and her classes. I recall her childlike look of delight when I gave her a ridiculous long-faced sculpted bust that I had brought in for a class assignment. The bust had remained in her room for months and came to be known simply as Fred the Head. After several months, it became obvious that Fred was much happier with Mrs. Nelson than he had ever been with me, so I allowed fate to take its course. She delighted in my present, and Fred became a classroom fixture, sporting various hats and eyeglasses befitting the particular mood of the students. It was a gift that had no intrinsic value, yet represented a wealth of shared humor—and was a symbol of the unique relationship between Mrs. Nelson and our class.

I will never forget my intense shame when she caught me altering a library pass she had written, so that it included several of my friends. No punishment could be worse than the feeling of letting her down, and no teacher's paddle hurt as much or as long as seeing the disappointment on her face.

She believed in my ability to write and encouraged me when I wrenched out an article about my parents' difficult divorce. After enthusiastically trying to help me get published, she was there to support me when I received my first rejection notice. To her, it was a battle scar that I should take pride in.

And I remember studying her femininity. It was perfectly permissible to stare at your teacher—I believe the term is attentiveness—and I took every advantage of this unintended side benefit of classroom protocol. I scrutinized her every move, intoxicated by the mysteries of the opposite sex and delighted in the care and conviction that radiated from her eyes. Mrs. Nelson was beautiful in the purest sense. Her beauty emanated from an inner source, and like waters jetting from a dancing fountain, its neverending flow far overshadowed the foundation created to contain it.

Mrs. Nelson was a teacher who wields her influence for a lifetime. She instructed with warmth and humor, she listened, and she believed in the potential of her pupils. Her intention was to explore the world with her students—to share her knowledge, and to eagerly learn from us and with us. She was an anchor at a time when I was often drifting aimlessly. Mrs. Nelson believed that there was something special about me and helped me nurture and protect my sensitivity so that the world did not destroy it.

But perhaps of equal importance, she was a woman—not a mother or sister or junior-high girlfriend—but a woman about whom I cared deeply.

180

The intermixing of raging hormones and profound respect found a comfortable home in my psyche—and taught me that it was possible to feel both simultaneously. It was inconceivable to divorce Mrs. Nelson's body from her mind—they melded naturally into an essence that was precious in my eyes. Physical intimacy was forever given a more human face.

Mrs. Nelson retired from teaching amidst numerous accolades in 1999, culminating an award-winning thirty-year career. She maintains her fiery enthusiasm for life and her former students, and has since forged a successful second career as a freelance writer and editor.

Her last name has legally changed to Armstrong, and somewhere along the line she shed her teacher's skin and became Coleen to me. She seems even more lovely now, for life has taken its best shots at her, yet she maintains a youth that looks stunning in full maturity. We remain close friends to this day, distanced by the miles between us, but eternally connected by the powerful bond we felt even as student and teacher. She is a kindred spirit who resides in my past, present and future. I will forever be indebted to her.

21

The Flight of the Eagles

As I entered the ninth grade in 1968, I was genuinely looking forward to the new school year. Junior high school had sometimes been a brutal clash of initiation among vigorous young rams, and after two years of scrapping for a comfortable identity, I could finally walk the halls without feeling that I had something to prove. Being accepted by my peers had always been my top priority, but I had consistently tested the limits of permissible noncon-formity, while maintaining the necessary masculine respect from those most likely to squelch my individualism. I was an average student at best and showed disdain for my studies, partially because indifference served to make my intelligence more permissible. I instead nurtured a reputation as a class clown and found I could use humor to both remain true to my character and keep potential adversaries off-balance.

My best friends were popular and fortunately also people I would have chosen to associate with, regardless of social ramifications. Most of them had been my chums since the seventh grade, and although our circle had expanded, our fraternity had become more closely knit. We usually traveled in a pack and drew confidence from each others' presence. Individually we were still jittery, uncertain teenagers—collectively we were kings of a very small mountain.

Basketball season was fast approaching, and many of us would be trying out for the team. Even though I had been cut the year before, I knew that I was a superior player to many who had worn the Eagles' red, white and blue. This time around, I was determined to take the tryout process more seriously.

Varsity basketball had become an obsession to me. Every season the name of each member of the George Washington Junior High varsity basketball team was listed in large block letters next to the time clock on the gymnasium scoreboard. Adding the name T. SIMER to the roster-board

182

had been my fantasy since I had first entered the gym as a bewildered seventh grader. I was confident that this year the fantasy could become reality.

*   *   *

All of my friends who had any chance of making the team showed up for the first day of tryouts. We were joined by a horde of other hopefuls as we all pulled on our white crew socks, elastic waistband gym shorts and reversible sleeveless practice jerseys, before loping countless laps around the gym's periphery. A pack of panting soon-to-be rejects inevitably trailed behind us, like a fast-fading herd of rubber-legged zebra that would soon be taken down one by one by predator/coaches' shrill whistles. The field diminished each day as realists faced the inevitable, and voluntarily removed themselves from consideration and the rigorous daily exercise. By the time the dust had settled, the majority of my pals had survived the ordeal and the roster trimmings, and Coach Hawkins was prepared to take his not-ready-for-flighttime Eagles against the remainder of the public league. Washington entered the season with the formidable handicaps of an all-white student body, the smallest enrollment of the four city junior highs and a lineup that could hardly be termed talent-laden. It would prove to be a long season.

The roster survivors were an odd assemblage of personalities that meshed far better off court than on. We were consistently undersized and overmanned, not particularly attractive to look at, and for the most part, our uniforms didn't even fit well. But we always held our heads high and by season's end, mastered the role of gracious losers. Each player was a critical cog of a spewing, sputtering machine that wheezed its way onto the court for each and every game—well-prepared to accept the inevitable thrashing that was to be administered. The outcome of the game was never in doubt—only the point differential of the shellacking provided any suspense.

*   *   *

Ladies and gentlemen, may I present to you the 1968-69 George Washington Junior High Eagles basketball team. In the interest of time, please hold your applause until all introductions have been completed.

Jimmy Howell, whom the coach affectionately called Fig Newton (although no one really knew why), ran the offense. Team members may sometimes have been at each others' throats, but everybody loved Jimmy.

183

He was sturdy and steady, seemingly unflappable—and by women's standards, teddy-bear cute. When he traded in his glasses for contact lenses in high school, he shed his shy schoolboy image and became a legitimate high-school hunk. I too stopped wearing my eyeglasses the same year, but only because electrical tape no longer held them together. My results, however, were not nearly as earth-shattering. I looked about the same, but the world sure didn't. I squinted my way through the next three years.

Mike Sparks had laser-beam eyes and dark hair that was curly when he let it grow long enough that anyone could tell. His intense, steady stare would lead you to believe he pondered great thoughts, and his dry sense of humor demonstrated that his non-blinking style had honed his world perspective. Sparky, as we often called him, didn't cave in to the social cliques so predominant in junior high. He was popular with both eggheads and pinheads, as well as the broad spectrum in between. Mike didn't worry about being seen with the right people—and for the most part was admired for it.

Jerry Johnson had blond wavy hair and was the most physically gifted athlete on the team, although not necessarily the best basketball player. Having shot out of the gate in the puberty derby, Jerry seemed at least a year older than most of us. He was sneaky-smart, and his apparent shyness drew cute girls to him like a magnet. Jerry had a way with women and often dated girls who only politely recognized my existence. Our friendship never significantly hampered his style, but unfortunately also never improved mine.

Craig Gebhart was a transfer student from the Catholic school system. He sometimes exhibited a gruff exterior, but was really just a nice guy with a loud bark. Craig was a capable athlete and had been adopted into my circle of friends without hesitation. He was quick-witted and quick-tempered, but it was easy to quell the storm by making him laugh. His laugh was hearty and distinctive—contagious when we got him going.

Bill Lasley was probably my best friend in the ninth grade. He was in all my classes, and his interests closely paralleled my own. Bill's face was boyish—with high cheekbones, exceptionally long eyelashes and a fair, freckled complexion. He overcame this gentle appearance by diligently working out with weights and boasting about his current belt status in karate. Although he found it necessary to use street savvy to mask his sensitivity, he often let his guard down with me. We were together much of the time, and although ninth grade was the only year that we were really close, the friendship was a significant one.

Harry Reasch (pronounced "rash") was the star of the team. He was a virtual colossus of a teenager—a surprisingly graceful tank in tennis shoes. Harry had an unusually soft "shooter's touch" for a player his size and was the only true scorer in our paltry arsenal. Nobody ever crossed him, and we all breathed a sigh of relief that this monster was on our side. Harry had a wrecking ball atop his short neck and a broad forehead with deep-set eyes. Opponents, when not in his formidable presence, would taunt us by feverishly scratching their private parts—muttering something about having a bad case of "hairy rash." A face-to-face encounter with him, however, brought about a miraculous dermatological healing. When you were able to cut through his stony exterior, Harry had a soft side—and was a surprisingly nice guy when you got to know him.

The bench players were cursed with the label of playing second-string on the worst junior-high team in the county. Mike Blanton was a backup at forward and was more of an enforcer than a basketball player. He was charcoal-haired and rugged, the kind of guy you'd prefer not to rankle. Steve Thomas was a red-headed backup who looked a little like a human Howdy Doody, and Randy Maltbie was a baby-faced, sweet-tempered guy who endured more guff than he deserved. Mike Hoskins was a much taller, carrot-topped version of Steve Thomas, but was a very silent character who kept to himself. We didn't know much about him, and he preferred it that way.

Tim Simer (yes, me) was a cocky, but still earnest kid whose forte was defense and rebounding. I had begun sprouting like a weed and was struggling to adjust to a body that was lengthening every day. I was all ears, arms and legs—and complained incessantly about my knobby knees. Basketball meant a pleasant refuge after school had ended. It elevated my stature with my peers, and more significantly to myself. Being a member of the Eagles was the most important thing in my life.

*   *   *

These were the names and the faces of a team that could only have been recalled in infamy. However, it is far more likely that our existence has been erased from the memory of anybody or anyone not directly associated with the team. Although the mention of our season might drum up unpleasant and even ugly images, we were far too forgettable to warrant a casual observer's recollection. After all, we hadn't committed any crime—unless there was a statute on the books against bad basketball.

Hopes had been unexplainably high at the outset of the season. There were weeks of leg lifts, rope skipping, jumping jacks, medicine balls, relay races and pushups—as we built up tremendous stamina so that we could lose without getting too winded doing it. When we finally did get our hands on a basketball, it was obvious that we should have tried playing with one much sooner.

Coach Hawkins had developed a myriad of plays, all falling under three basic offensive patterns: Abel, Baker and Charlie. None of his brain-children seemed to work, but he vehemently insisted that we run all of them. So our point guard constantly hollered out plays, and we went through a series of extravagant motions. The choreography never resulted in a basket, but it certainly was intriguing to look at. Occasionally we would lull opponents into a hypnotic state as they ogled our elaborate, yet meaningless Chinese fire drills.

*   *   *

Being on the basketball team definitely had its perks, though. There were pep rallies where we were the guests of honor, and overexuberant underclass and underdeveloped girls shrieked their orchestrated cheers. The players would sit together on the gym risers decked out in our clip-on ties, pretending to be bored by the clamor and occasionally yanking the false knot from some unsuspecting teammate's neck.

I could now stroll the hallways playing the part of basketball jock, as I had admiringly watched two years of players do before me. And I had direct access to a bevy of beautiful cheerleaders, which paid no direct benefit other than being in their proximity and receiving an occasional unsolicited smile or hearing one of them scream out my name at a game.

Vicky Helcher had always made me "ga-ga," and although she had never shown any inclination to satiate my fantasies, she still had the power to make my palms sweat. My friend, Bill Lasley, was now going steady with Georgetta Laws—the other ninth-grade cheerleader whom I secretly worshipped. Georgetta was painfully cute with mischievous eyes and an irresistibly cuddly and petite body. Both Vicky and she rarely wasted time with boys our age and usually were surrounded by hulking suitors, which only made them more temptingly inaccessible. I still occasionally sigh deeply when I recapture an image of them in those adorable royal-blue out-fits.

Considering our lack of success in game situations, I drew most of my

186

personal satisfaction from our practices. After about three weeks of sessions to improve our strength, stamina and reflexes—we spent much of our time scrimmaging in intersquad games. It was schoolyard basketball at its finest, with daily access to a large gymnasium and a head coach who could arbitrate disputes that arose using our honor system officiating.

We would run the court like gazelles, fast-breaking at every opportunity—often applying a wicked full-court press on the hapless second team. Coach Hawkins would sometimes rein us in and force us to run our designed offense, but even the straightjacket of our enemies Abel, Baker and Charlie could not prevent the starters from falsely inflating our egos against our pitiable opponents. Although we all knew that we were a bad team, we were a team nonetheless. We were united by our shared frustration from habitual defeat, and we succeeded or (much more often) failed together. Win or lose, we enjoyed the opportunity that had been afforded us.

After practice we would escape to the locker room where we would shower, dry ourselves with white towels that reeked of disinfectant and usually engage in some manner of creative horseplay or well-conceived practical joke. While dressing, we would discuss anything from the moral dilemma of the Vietnam War to our love lives or lack thereof. Tales of sexual exploits were concocted and compared—and were interspersed with several first-rate towel fights or slap-boxing matches.

Those walking home in the same general direction would grab their compulsory gym bags and exit the locker room double-doors into the frigid early evening air. If I had been negligent in towel-drying my hair, it would sometimes stiffen immediately and feel almost brittle to the touch. A corner grocery on St. Clair Avenue was our only rest stop. It was only a few blocks away, and if I had been successful in controlling my spending at lunch, I would buy a pack of Hostess Ding Dongs or Ho Hos. We would then congregate outside the store like a shift of construction workers on break—our mouths full of candy and pastries, whipped cream and fruit fillings.

On some level, even then we were aware that this was the prime of our lives. When we traveled in a group—the world took notice. Our energy level charged the atmosphere, and we were convinced of our invincibility. My teammates and I were at the door of our high school experience and entering the richest of our teenage years. When adults looked at us, we could sense their envy. We now had a firm hold on the intangible youth that had slipped their grasp, and younger children dreamed of being at our level of physical maturation and autonomy. We were the center of attention—and it was a nice place to be. Content in our innocence, time was considered a restriction rather than a blessing. It held no value and placed unnecessary limitations on our otherwise limitless lives.

After fifteen or twenty minutes of enthusiastic idle conversation, we split up and each took direct routes home. My body was still warm from our workout, and my tired muscles triggered a soothing sense of relaxation—as if an inner cleansing had just taken place. I had time to think, and the walk seemed to clear my head—providing me the calm to face whatever turmoil would be swirling when I entered my front door.

* * *

After games, we would gather at Frisch's Big Boy on Dixie Highway. The company there was selective and the conversation more diversified. Our topic might be as complex as the afterlife or world hunger, or as mindless as a debate about the best pizza in town or an open-forum discussion about Mrs. Nelson's legs. We each would make a minimal food purchase and then waste several hours licking our wounds from that night's game. Talk of females dominated the dialogue, but any issue or warped thought was fair game. Our waitresses usually exhibited incredible patience with us. Perhaps their tolerance was due to the fact that we were unusually polite, but more likely it was because when we misbehaved, we did so creatively. We were usually joined by three of my favorite sidekicks: Jeff Harrison, Bob Neiderman and Mike Leck.

I had been in awe of Jeff Harrison's ability to make me laugh since we'd met during the first week of junior high school. Jeff was not the athlete that some of my other friends were and therefore used his wit as his primary method of intimidation. He had the ability to crush the most ego-laden of adversaries by artfully pushing the buttons that hit them where it hurt. He never pretended to be macho, so threats of violence only made his angered foe appear more oafish. Jeff was lean with wavy dark hair—and sleepy eyes that smiled when his thoughts amused him.

Bob Neiderman used to carry a wad of pens in his shirt pocket and one behind his ear, but he was going through a junior-high conversion that would later find him a bronzed, buffed, football stud at Garfield High. When I first met him, he sported a razor-close crew cut with a Brylcream-drenched tuft where his bangs should be. But he was now getting with the program and had recently been initiated into our elite clique.

We now knew him more commonly as "Harvey," which we had recently discovered was his middle name. He tolerated this unconcealed baiting, but his suppressed agitation was obvious enough that the nickname stuck.

Mike Leck was blond and mischievous, with an infectious machine-gun laugh and a refreshing on-the-edge lunacy. His clean-cut appearance would deceive you, but a close look into his eyes would tell the keen observer that he was laughing at the world. Mike's high intensity humor was the perfect complement to Jeff Harrison's more subtle and sarcastic style. Put them in a room together, and you had instant entertainment.

We never ran out of things to talk about, only time to do the talking. The restaurant was packed with penny-pinching minors when we arrived, and we were usually one of the last tables to depart. The party then sometimes moved to Pizza Hut or Dunkin' Donuts, where we would continue thought-provoking discussions that I suspect I would enjoy eavesdropping on even today. The associations I shared with these people were among the richest that I have ever experienced. At no other time in my life, save the early years of college, were so many changes occurring so quickly to a core group of friends.

The temptation is to liberally expound on each important individual, but it was the flavor rather than the specific ingredients that made our conversations so delicious. Suffice it to say that we propped each other up and pooled our knowledge and humor to make a potentially difficult life transition predominantly enjoyable. These people were very close friends for a very short period of my youth. Time and varied scholastic interests eventually pried me from them, but we remained delighted whenever we could share each other's company. If George Washington was a training camp for the difficult transition to high school, then I could not have selected a better group of fellow campers with which to weather the trials and tribulations.

*　　*　　*

George Washington Junior High School did not win a single basketball game in the winter of 1968. Our best efforts were close losses against Trenton and Talawanda, and we even played mighty Roosevelt competitively in one of our league games. For the most part, we were lucky to keep things respectable and happy when the other team appeared to take us seriously. I started every game, including one that I attended in spite of the fact that I had been too ill to show up for school. I scored eight points and two

189

detentions for that effort. My last name was listed prominently on the gymnasium scoreboard for the entire school year. And my girlfriend Elaine and her father (my minister, Joe Copelin) were present when I scored fifteen points and had fifteen rebounds against Trenton.

However, my most powerful memory was our first league game at home against Harding. Coach Hawkins gave us an inspired pep talk in the industrial-arts room, and we were sky-high when we broke through the large paper-covered hoop and into the crowded gymnasium at our introduction. Parents and students cheered, and the pep band broke into the school song—although a few less accomplished bandsmen were guilty of breaking into unrehearsed split-second solos. A few overzealous members of the student body chimed in with the accompanying lyrics:

Let's cheer for Washington our school so strong.
The best that's in the land.
We raise our voices in a rousing song,
With loyal heart and hand.
Hail our team, so brave and bold,
Stalwart sons of fame.
On to victory, we shout and cry,
Now win that game!!!!!

Although I admit that the words to the fight song were laughable, I was still somehow touched. I had seen this picture countless times, but I had never been in the center of it. The crowd faces were so animated, my teammates so sincerely determined and the cheerleaders so young and vibrant. They were all hoping against hope that something good would happen.

As usual, we lost the game. But I gained something much more valuable. Through the successes and failures of our basketball season, there were lessons to be learned about the true value of friendship and teamwork. On the court or in everyday life, I realized I must rely on other people.

*　　*　　*

During the winter of 1968, I discovered that what the world perceived as failure was often laced with profound but sometimes almost indiscernible victories. Although life's indoctrinations had taught us of a world of dramatic highs and lows, reality was not nearly as heavy-handed. Story-

190

book endings were hard to come by—reality was filled with ebb and flow. Goals were rarely achieved without unforeseen obstacles. It was obvious that life wasn't going to get any easier—not even for a stalwart son of fame.

22

You Don't Tug on Superman's Cape . . .

It was late in the fall of 1968, and I sat in Mrs. Nelson's ninth-grade English class with my eyes and concentration riveted on Terrie Kinker. She sat one row over and a few seats up from me, providing me an ideal vantage point from which to leer without being caught at it. Terrie was a girl whom I had been somewhat interested in since seventh grade, having come close to having an official relationship with her on several occasions. Mother Nature had recently waved her magic wand in Terrie's direction, making her ever more appealing to the eyes and the loins of fifteen-year-old boys. Ms. Kinker was razor-sharp and widely talented with light brown shoulder-length hair and a naturally flirtatious smile. Her confident air and keen mind intimidated bumbling ninth-grade greenhorns, who generally hoped they could survive a hall dialogue without changing vocal octaves mid-sentence or drawing undue attention to angry blemishes that had erupted on their faces. There was something even more terrifying about Terrie, however. She was the steady girlfriend of Alvis Cadle.

To say that Alvis Cadle was big for his age was like saying King Kong was large for a monkey. Alvis was now in high school, a year older than I, and was a mountain in the blackboard jungle. When rising to his feet, he seemed to unfurl and inflate like a jumbo balloon character in Macy's Thanksgiving Parade—until his horizontal was as jaw-droppingly impressive as his vertical. He was not the pump-iron, fitness-fanatic brand of big. He had just grown and grown and grown up that way.

For the safety of those who might have crossed him during his childhood, he should have been tattooed "Born to Be Huge" at birth. And as if his size alone was not frightening enough, he had arms that nearly dragged the floor, bright red hair, freckles—and a huge chip on his giant shoulder. He had regularly roamed George Washington Junior High's hallways between classes with a devilish grin on his face, bruising random underclassmen's biceps with single sledgehammer punches that left the recipients' arms numb for the entire next period.

It probably has become increasingly clear to the reader why Terrie and I had only come close to an official relationship. Although the extent of our association outside of school had been attending a worship service together at my church and some first-rate junior high flirting—Alvis sensed the attraction and did not take a liking to it. Terrie had discussed breaking up with him, but each time the move was contemplated, no action was taken. All that resulted was that Alvis glared at me with just a little more venom, and I began to imagine that I heard barely audible growls when he passed me in the hall. He saw less and less of me, however, as I tried conveniently to be where he wasn't. This included some downright silly between-class detours that involved climbing and descending stairs to make connections between rooms on the same floor.

I was not as cowardly as it might appear. After all, if I were beaten senseless in a schoolyard skirmish, surely someone would eventually put a halt to the blood-letting. It was simply that I had no idea how I would go about fighting him. Would Raymond Burr take on Godzilla without a loaded weapon? Not only would I be pummeled mercilessly, but I would look ridiculous absorbing the punishment. It was a no-win situation, and I dearly hoped that the storm would blow over.

Rumblings of Alvis "looking for me" began late in my eighth-grade school year and carried over into the summer. It was much easier to avoid him, however, since we were rarely at the same place at the same time. The summer was progressing swimmingly until our Babe Ruth baseball teams were scheduled to meet for the first time. This in itself was not a dire concern, since games were well-attended and supervised. But when I found out that he was scheduled to pitch, and I was in the starting lineup, the complexion of the situation altered dramatically. I was certain that he would be throwing at me, but convinced myself that if I stayed alert and concentrated solely on preservation of my body, I might be able to survive this living nightmare.

I believe that it was in the second inning of the game that I slinked to the plate for the first time. Alvis stood on the pitching rubber and scowled menacingly at me while I went through all of the mandatory theatrics of preparing myself for my plate appearance. I rubbed a little dirt onto my palms, windmilled the bat and artfully dug a comfortable spot for myself in the batter's box. My eyes were riveted upon his hands and the ball, which not only served the purpose of making me appear as if I was a pure hitter, but also gave me an excuse to avoid any visual contact that might rankle the beast. My attention was directed solely on the unforgiving spheroid that he held like a pebble in his mammoth hand. I knew that his horsehide missile would be hurtling toward its objective in a few short seconds, and I hoped that his target was the catcher's mitt and not the bull's-eye he might envision between my ears.

Alvis threw four consecutive pitches outside the strike zone, but I survived the barrage still firmly balanced upon my hindquarters. As I trotted to first base, I believed that I had survived round one of an afternoon-long confrontation. I took a conservative lead from first base, then stood frozen with legs apart and crouched—ready to make a dash around the bases if the hitter made contact, or Alvis bounced a wild one off the backstop. He went into his stretch, glowered at me and then toward the plate, and rocked back—readying to fire yet another screaming beebee. Suddenly he shifted his weight and his delivery toward first base. I broke instinctively back to the bag—and he reared back and threw mightily. The next sound that shook the diamond was the flesh-crawling thud that is made when a Rawlings regulation baseball strikes the upper thigh of a human with such force that it leaves the imprint of laces on the epidermis.

It was the only moment of my life that I was happy that I was not more well-endowed, because if I had been I might never have heard the thud in the first place. I did not fall down. My journey to the ground more closely resembled the toppling of a bowling pin as I crashed to the dirt about ten feet from first base. The ball, having been thrown at great velocity, caromed from my leg like a tennis shot and rolled down the first base line with a trio of fielders in hot pursuit. Our first-base coach wildly gestured toward second base, urging me to advance on the errant throw. I responded with some primitive utterance meant to convey that my answer was no. Not only could I not run, I could not move.

The next few seconds were a cacophony of shouts and screams, of animated faces and players darting about in all directions. The only person who did not move was me, a situation that my competitive nature would not tolerate. Bracing myself as if I were a double amputee, I pushed my torso up with my arms and hand-walked back to the safe haven of first base. I never looked back at Alvis. Instead I accepted my new leg tattoo as his revenge and somehow felt I had gotten off easily, considering my indiscretions. After nearly five minutes of extensive writhing and rolling, I un-

194

folded myself and returned to my feet. Ever the trouper, I stayed in the game without further incident.

The new school year had given me a perceived clean slate and a school without Alvis Cadle. He had mercifully taken his strong-man show to Garfield High, and here I sat in a junior-high English class miles away, gawking at Terrie Kinker. She was now leaning on her elbows with hands on chin, her substantial chest resting comfortably on her desktop. It was a pose that drew considerable attention away from the subject of English, even when taught by the voluptuous Mrs. Nelson.

Terrie had assured me that she had broken up with Alvis and now no longer wore his bracelet-size ring on her finger. With Alvis no longer in the picture, my hormones were drowning out my common sense. I saw an opening and elected to seize the moment.

Georgetta Laws, a popular cheerleader, was having a birthday hayride. The party was actually a thinly veiled disguise for some novice high-octane osculation beneath an autumn evening sky. After Mrs. Nelson's class that day, I leapt through the window of opportunity headfirst and began plummeting toward the inevitable asphalt named Alvis that awaited me at the end of my journey. I asked Terrie to go to Georgetta's hayride with me, an invitation that she readily accepted. Although I knew I was taking a chance, I convinced myself that the risk was worth taking. I would soon wish that I hadn't been convinced so easily.

Georgetta's party was a splendid affair, as juveniles piled into a flat-bed wagon and instantaneously entwined themselves in pairs amidst a mountain of hay. Heads mated at the mouth, as everyone practiced the recently discovered art of extended passionate kissing. The boys were under intense pressure to display images of unflustered and silky-smooth Casanovas, while the girls concerned themselves with avoiding an entirely different image. It was an evening of passion, and both Terrie and I performed our roles as romantic leads with great verve and savior faire. But the evening of bliss ended too quickly, and it became apparent that it would soon be time to pay the piper.

The message was sent to me that I had once again made Mr. Cadle unhappy, and he was combing the neighborhood looking for me. After the initial panic wore off, I became increasingly annoyed by the threat. I was weary of running and felt that whatever humiliation I must endure or beating I must absorb—I was willing to do it. He had already gotten his revenge, and I was not anxious to endure additional months of fretting about

195

something I could remedy quickly—albeit quite painfully. I went about my regular schedule knowing that I would run into him and almost hoping that it would be sooner rather than later.

The showdown was not long in coming. Mike Engel and I were playing basketball in the backyard of my pastor, Mr. Copelin. The pastor's driveway and backboard were still considered our turf, since the residence had been my home less than two years earlier. Although engrossed in a game of horse, we glanced up to see the image of a red-haired Goliath filling our vision. It was Alvis, mean-stepping it up the long driveway with an entourage of five friends bringing up the rear.

I was a bit offended that he had brought so many of his buddies to witness my thumping, and also a little worried that Mike might end up in a fight that was not of his making. Suddenly a brilliant idea popped into my mind. The notion was so ingenious that a cartoon thought-cloud containing a jumbo light bulb should have instantly appeared above us—with its trailing mini-bubbles targeted directly at my noggin.

It had dawned on me that there was a rehearsal of the Garfield High production of *Guys and Dolls* taking place at my house, and it was the guys and not the dolls who were tightening up their musical numbers. My mother, who was enough of an instrumentalist to peck out vocal parts on a piano, had volunteered to assist the musical director—so an entire roomful of high school upperclassmen was only a block and a phone call away.

I dialed posthaste and asked to speak to Tom Shobe—one of the cast members who I knew would be there. He was smitten with my sister Emily, and although he was a senior in high school, he had always treated me with a surprising degree of civility. Tom was also a "Nicely-Nicely" beefy fellow in his own right. I explained my dilemma and asked him if a few of the "guys" could come over to back me up. He took down the address, and within five minutes we could hear the faint but crescendoing echo of a male chorus singing "Luck Be a Lady Tonight." Mike and I shot out the door to witness the fireworks.

Approximately ten brawny juniors and seniors, including a regional karate champion and a Golden Gloves boxer made their entrance, and the scene took on the qualities of a demented dream gang battle between the boys of Damon Runyon and the Jets in *West Side Story*.

The appearance of this collection of good-natured and oversized hooligans and the immediacy with which they had arrived obviously came as a shock to Alvis. I am certain that considering he was not a connoisseur of the arts, he never made any logical connection to the musical. In fact, only one sentence was spoken among the mass of humanity that nearly collided there. One of his friends stared at the oncoming pack of "Sarah's sinners" and exclaimed, "Jesus! He brought a whole army!" Shortly thereafter, Alvis and his entourage silently vacated the premises. My army escorted me home to a rousing rendition of "Good Old Reliable Nathan."

I never had another negative encounter with Alvis Cadle. I spoke with Terrie and broke off our short-lived romance until she and Alvis both agreed that their relationship had been terminated. It was simply not worth the headaches to tease the situation. Terrie attended Fairfield High School the following year, and I became intrigued with a transfer student named Kim Bryant and went steady with her until our relationship failed the test of a summer separation.

To this day, I am certain that the incident that took place in Mr. Copelin's backyard did not frighten Alvis in any way. He was too massive to experience fear when faced with physical confrontations with mere mortals. The element of surprise may have caught him off-guard, and in reviewing the situation perhaps he was intrigued by my ingenuity. Although we never became friends and almost never spoke, he later backed me up in a tense situation in high school, and there was never any evidence that he held that earlier encounter against me.

I can only hope that if he is alive and well today and places his enormous hands on these pages, he is smiling. I'm too old and tired to run, and I now reserve my fighting for battles that I have a reasonable chance of winning.

23

Have Mop—Will Travel

I sat in the privacy of my bedroom with door closed, feverishly scribbling numbers onto a sheet of notebook paper. I knew I had a tough decision to make, and it had to be made that night. It was the fall of 1969, and I had been attending tryouts for the high school basketball team—attempting to fulfill an aspiration I had held since I first stepped onto the hardwood in elementary school. Unfortunately, another priority had crept into the picture, and it now held equal importance to me.

Ever since my mother and father had separated when I was thirteen, our family had survived without an automobile. This situation had been barely tolerable while I was without a driver's license. But my sixteenth birthday was fast approaching, and my hard-fought reputation as a free-wheeling teenager was now at stake. The only way a car would find a permanent home in our driveway was if I earned the money to make it happen.

My ninth-grade English teacher, Mrs. Nelson, had arranged for me to be interviewed for a janitor's position at the Ciné Malibu Theater—the recently remodeled Linden Theater on Pleasant Avenue near my home. I now had to choose between dreams, and the mathematics I had just completed provided me a target date for holding title to a fully operational automobile. The correct decision was obvious, but painful. Basketball was more of a pipe dream with fewer concrete returns. I would pursue the janitor's job.

*   *   *

When I walked into the theater for my scheduled interview, the process was only a formality. The manager contacted me the following day, and training began almost immediately. I felt a tinge of excitement about being handed the keys to a movie theater. The lobby and auditorium were a wonderland of state-of-the-art audio and lighting—decorated with the rich fabrics and handsome appointments that make a theater a magical place.

198

There was a clear-glass candy counter carefully stacked with movie munchies. And at show time, an aluminum and plexiglass popcorn machine was usually piled high with newborn puffs. Their playpen was kept warm by an amber heat lamp that cast a buttery glow onto a mound of cottony faces. A crowd-bingeing backup of at least one monstrous storage bag full of pre-popped kernels was carefully tucked away behind the snack bar, to be craftily added to the mix when volume exceeded production.

On either side of the counter, entrance doors led into the auditorium, and near the more frequently used entrance was an old pop machine that dispensed soft drinks in cups. Customers could peer through the small, clear retrieval door and watch their selections being poured. A paper cup would drop into the clutches of a metal mechanism that held it stationary. Then it was pelted with ice and filled exactly to the brim with a steady flow of syrup and carbonated water. I would polish the retrieval door each day, leaving it spotless so that those who delighted in this mini-show could receive a crystal-clear view of the high action.

The lobby and theater rugs, as well as the acoustical drapes on the side walls of the auditorium, were regal-red—and a double curtain concealed the movie screen. A sheer white curtain was overlaid by a heavier gold one, made of a fine and textured fabric. These could be opened simultaneously or separately, and the screen's nightly unveiling was a pre-feature event not to be missed. The curtains were electronically controlled, and whirred impressively when drawn and closed from the projection booth upstairs.

The theater could be lit with floodlights when cleaning, or illuminated romantically by using dimmer control panels that brought the room to a subdued glow. When the theater was cast in this manmade twilight, the subtle glimmer of aisle lights bordered the two carpeted runways and lent an air of sophistication to audience seating.

When the auditorium was clean, and this dreamy ambience had been created, the room had the feel of history—a location where decades of theatergoers had laughed, cried, applauded and cheered. But the next day, the floodlights cast their harsh radiance on the less artistic aspect of movie-going. Their white glare exposed a sporting event's rowdiness with popcorn strewn everywhere. Empty and half-full beverage cups blanketed the now-sticky cement flooring. Other cups had been stomped flat and could be likened to empty shotgun shells that had sounded ear-popping explosions during the evening's presentation.

The task ahead of me was a simple one. I was to make it look like the movie party that had created this disaster of debris had never occurred—no

199

matter how long it took. This substantial chore could be done any-time—from the moment the last audience member left in the evening, until the first ticket buyer arrived on the following day. The position offered flexibility of scheduling and freedom from direct supervision. I rarely saw the manager, whom I knew simply as Pete, and we usually communicated only by leaving notes for each other. His notes to me were scotch-taped to a shelf in the cleaning supply closet, and my replies and inquiries were written on refreshment-stand napkins and left attached to his office door.

After a brief adjustment period, I found a comfort zone in which I could schedule the cleaning around my extracurricular activities and important social events. I enjoyed going to the theater and locking myself in. My seclusion offered uninterrupted silence and a respite from annoying people. I would sometimes take extended breaks and climb up to the projection booth, where I would thumb through whatever adults-only tabloid the projectionist had left behind. And occasionally I would flip the switches that opened and closed the theater curtains, while introducing the current feature in my best radio voice.

If my budget allowed it, I stepped out to the Mt. Pleasant Bakery. The bakery was only a few doors down the street and usually had a tray full of peanut butter cookies to titillate my taste buds. Once inside, I would fill my head with the glorious scents of powdered sugar and icing, and their wide variety of breads and rolls—all wafting tempting odors that smelled as if they had been simultaneously squeezed from a long row of atomizers.

*   *   *

The job at Ciné Malibu was proving to be a perfect fit. Not only was I padding my bankbook, but I received the added benefit of attending films free-of-charge. These no-cost nights on the town transformed me into an eligible connoisseur of the arts. A simple nod to the ticket taker put a female companion and me into the cushioned comfort of my not-so-private screening room. And because the theater was part of a local chain, I could pull a few strings if there was a feature playing elsewhere that might enhance my dateability. But soon my weekly trips to the West Side Federal Savings and Loan with my paycheck and blue savings passbook convinced me that my earning efforts must be accelerated.

My sister Emily had been working at Frisch's Big Boy Restaurant on Dixie Highway as a car hop, and she told me of a dishwasher's position that had become available. I could work at the Big Boy on weekends and would still be able to maintain my position at the theater. I mounted a persuasive case to present to my mother, convincing her that I could absorb the added burden. She relented, and a subsequent interview bolstered by my sister's recommendation landed me in the steamy confines of the dish room at Frisch's restaurant. I was issued a uniform that consisted of a pair of baggy black-and-white checked pants, a highly unflattering starched white work-shirt, and one of those ridiculous paper and mesh hats that instantaneously reduces the wearer to a Neanderthal ninny. As I made my way up the stairs from the employee lockers into the kitchen, I gazed upon a gleaming room of stainless steel and intimidating kitchen apparatus. Waitresses flitted by with bottoms swaying, while service personnel pushed mops and scoured countertops. Everyone seemed to have a regimented agenda, and a new face in the kitchen seemed an obstacle rather than a curiosity.

The first morning was spent being trained by another dishwasher, a sad-faced man in his fifties named Joe. He was bald beneath his ill-fitting cap, and his prominent nose had obviously seen and smelled better days—as it appeared to have been broken more than once. Throughout the day, he poured out his tale of woe, seemingly trying to explain how his life's journey had brought him to this semi-permanent rest-stop. As we worked, his hat continuously slid slowly down his perspiring forehead—until it settled at nearly a 45-degree angle and rested on his left ear. Joe's spiritless eyes and aura of hopelessness pierced my heart, which had not yet been numbed to such resigned sorrow. My soul branded the image into my memory—never to be forgotten. Joe would work with me only during that first week. Unfortunately, as the speed of my work increased—he was phased out of a job.

*   *   *

The dish room was in a secluded area of the kitchen near the restaurant service doors. It was sweltering hot, and a cloud of eyeglass-fogging air billowed from the industrial dishwasher each time a rack of recently dirtied dishes was inserted, and a scalding-hot collection of spotless dinnerware was removed. Dirty dishes were brought into the room in large gray tubs that had been placed on service carts in strategic locations throughout the restaurant. The table scraps were then emptied into a small round opening in the stainless steel counter that fed waste into a large receptacle on wheels. Plates were scrubbed when necessary, then hosed down with a high-power shower nozzle connected to a long flexible metal hose suspended from somewhere near the ceiling.

There was no time for conversation. The only sounds that could be heard were the liquid drumming of the dishes within the dishwasher, and the ceramic clatter of plates being shuffled and then dealt onto plastic racks for cleaning. Occasionally, the dishwasher would change cycles, and the rhythmic tempo would be altered. And sometimes a flat rack filled with silverware would be prepared for cleaning, and the emphasis would be shifted to metal percussion.

For the most part, I was left alone to my work. The managers, both predictably named Chuck, steered clear of the area. And the waitresses only came in when they needed something. For the first three weeks of my employment a twentyish carhop, whose name I've forgotten, would wander in pretending to search for dishware—and then would brighten my day by firmly goosing me. However, as soon as I came to anticipate the routine, I discovered that she had been terminated—as was an unwritten benefit of my employment.

As I became more proficient in my job, I was continually given additional duties. When I worked days, I would prepare the vegetable soup and chili. This entailed a trip to the walk-in refrigerator where I would remove several wax cartons filled with the prepackaged potage. The contents were often frozen solid and needed to be broken up with an ice-pick before being placed in the steamer. Cleaning the drive-in lot was also often on the morning agenda. I would wander the grounds picking up the discarded wrappers of thoughtless litterbugs and grumbling about their lack of consideration, while frequently retrieving my paper hat after it had either slipped off or been blown from my head.

The rest rooms were my other major area of responsibility. After everyday latrine duty at Ciné Malibu, I had received more than my toilet bowl's fill of scrubbing commodes. I would, however, reluctantly drop to my knees and complete the dreaded chore. Immediate upliftment was available in the ladies' room, though—for the words "Brenda loves Tim" were scratched into one of the stalls, placed there by the newly discovered woman of my dreams.

Employee meals were my favorite part of the work day. We could order anything we wanted on the extensive menu, and I had dearly loved Frisch's fare since I had first moved to Hamilton. I would place my sandwich order with Vi, the head grill cook, who was a jewel of a woman in her late forties. She was everybody's mother and had a comforting Southern lilt to her voice. Vi appeared to have survived a few storms in her lifetime, but emerged with a nobility and grace which made her irresistible. On most days, she artfully prepared two Big Boy double-deck cheeseburgers for me. I then piled the plate with french fries just emptied from the deep fry and made my way to the employee lounge.

My fellow workers were friendly, but my solitary confinement in the dishroom kept me from developing any real relationships. The waitresses were either of the high-turnover variety or were seasoned veterans who had loyally worked at the Big Boy for years. Each day I would see some combination of Ina, Wilma and Judy work the dining room and caught glimpses of master waitresses at work. They had reduced the job to an exact science. These old hands glided about the room, juggling any number of items on their serving trays and subtly shifting their weight or making ballet-quality foot maneuvers to avoid passersby.

Frisch's was taxing work, and it soon took its toll on other aspects of my life. I was almost always exhausted and would occasionally nod off in my high school classes or even while cleaning the theater. But my bank book always offered me some revitalization, as I was fast approaching the financial goal I had set for myself. Because my leisure hours were so limited, my girlfriend Brenda would sometimes help me out at the theater. It gave us some much needed privacy and cut my completion time almost in half—unless, of course, we had the desire and energy to inject some romance into these quite unromantic surroundings. I was flattered that she offered me her assistance in this unglamourous endeavor, and it only bolstered my confidence that she really cared for me.

I scrimped and saved throughout my sophomore year—then purchased a 1967 sky-blue Rambler American from a friend of my mother's during the subsequent summer. The car was in mint condition, and I was impressed with its clean lines and classic grill. A Rambler would not turn anyone's head, but it was free of body damage and was modestly impressive. I adored the car and considered it my second home. I would escape to its front seat when family emotions reached a boiling point, or I temporarily needed to shut out my personal problems. The driver's door would slam, and I would be sealed in—enclosed in my self-contained world. I had instant mobility, the entertainment of a solid-state AM radio, a functional heater, and the room to invite visitors into my bachelor's pad on wheels. There was a fulfillment in rewarding myself for my hard work. The automobile had once been only a faint vision in my imagination, but I had plugged away until it became reality. Although it had been officially designated a family car, I knew in my heart that it was mine. I had earned it.

*   *   *

I survived that exhausting summer working both jobs, as I put in a full schedule at the Big Boy along with my part-time janitorial duties. But soon I grew tired of the smell of mop water and the eyelash singeing trips to the restaurant incinerator. No matter how many times I washed the dishes, it seemed there were never enough of them clean—and I yearned to involve myself in more after-school activities. I decided to give up the position during my junior year. Although I was told by management that I was sacrificing a real career opportunity, I honored my two-week notice and left the dishes for someone else to do.

The theater continued to be an ideal job for me, as I cagily drafted helpers who would accompany me following my extracurricular activities so that the theater would be spotless prior to the first scheduled feature. I held the janitor's position until the end of my senior year, when I took a government-subsidized position at National Lead Company—a U.S. nuclear contractor. My friend Mike Engel took over at Ciné Malibu while he was attending Miami University in Oxford and living in Hamilton with his new wife Katrena.

I would always have fond recollections of my days at the theater. I had taken many females there to see free movies during operating hours, and did my own operating while indulging in after-hours, low-key hanky-panky when the theater was empty. It had provided me regular income while still allowing me to enjoy my days in high school. With the turn of a dead bolt, I could work or play at my leisure. I took pride in my job performance and enjoyed the independence and trust that my employer honored me with.

The cost of liability insurance for my car became more than I could afford during my senior year. I had been involved in two accidents and received a citation in the final one. My rates skyrocketed, and the car subsequently sat in our driveway until I sold it during my early college years. I would never, however, lose the sense of gratification I had received by earning it.

*   *   *

I regret the fact that I didn't have the opportunity to win a spot on the high school basketball team. But if I had not developed the discipline of aspiring to a long-range goal and worked diligently to obtain it—college may have never been a possibility. Most of us would rather swish basketballs than toilet bowls, but I was learning to make choices based on a future that existed beyond the upcoming weekend. For one of the first times in my life I was charting my own course, recognizing roadblocks and investing time and effort without expecting immediate gratification. Basketball would have provided a collection of press clippings, but the rigors of manual labor slapped me in the face with the less glamorous aspects of life that most of us are forced to endure. It was not life in a storybook; it was a huge slice of humdrum reality. And the experience provided precious fuel needed to propel my transportation—to my desired destiny.

24

The King & Me

It was midwinter in early 1970, and I was staying after school by my own volition. A substantial group of classmates had joined me in Mrs. Ireland's room, having asked for a meeting with her because of her much-deserved reputation as a caring teacher. The topic for discussion was a student request that we be allowed to present a spring musical. Even before the confab began, we knew that there were two strikes against us. Unlike the more affluent Taft High School on the west side of town, there was no drama teacher on Garfield's staff. And probably more importantly, the voice teacher had decided that he was unwilling to help with the music. This left us without an advisor and lacking the additional instruction and assistance necessary to mount any type of theatrical production—let alone a musical.

The students who met with Mrs. Ireland that day did not, however, accept that these two strikes meant that it was time to toss our bats and walk quietly away. If the answer was not within Garfield High, we believed it might lie somewhere within the Hamilton public school system. Whatever the results, it seemed necessary to put up a respectable fight. This was the last chance for many seniors to smell the greasepaint, and the sophomores and juniors did not want to set a precedent that might carry over for several years. There was a broad spectrum of students present at that meeting, from the perennial stars of the music department to potential backstage volunteers—who only hoped to have some of the magic of musical theater spill in their direction.

The meeting that day was in no way confrontational. Mrs. Ireland was a diminutive and extremely proud woman with wavy dark hair, and eyes that had sustained years of genuine concern—yet still held their sparkle. After listening intently to the gathering's convictions, she seemed deeply moved by our desire to take action. She promised to do all that she could—and because of her track record, that answer was satisfactory to all of those attending.

Mrs. Ireland did more than keep her promise. Obviously, strings were pulled that we did not even know existed. John Stalls, the superintendent of music for the Hamilton public school system, met with our coalition before a week had elapsed. The get-together was brief, as he attempted to gauge the sincerity and raw numbers of those interested. He left the building convinced that our conviction was quite real and vowing that he would seek someone to pull together this unbridled enthusiasm. It was only a matter of days before Mr. Stalls returned with a decision regarding who would coordinate our spring musical, and the official announcement only heightened the furor that had been building since the superintendent's involvement in the matter had begun. To our surprise, Mr. Stalls named himself as the director and then further declared that we would be presenting *The King and I.*

Those readers unfamiliar with *The King and I* should realize what an ambitious undertaking the musical is. The script calls for not only an extended cast of lead characters and various other inhabitants and visitors to the royal palace, but also requires a large collection of King's children—ranging in age from approximately five to teenhood.

Mr. Stalls' talents were widely known in the local community, his having served as director of the Hamilton Choral Society. His name regularly appeared in the *Journal-News,* and he was forever involved in music-related area activities. The fact that he had accepted this awesome responsibility—and had selected a production that seemed to be a nearly impossible undertaking—placed a public eye on all the preparations that followed.

*   *   *

Perhaps it is time to interject some background information that will help the reader understand the magnitude of the decision made on that day. For years and years the city had but one high school. Hamilton High had enjoyed a rich history and tradition that prompted alumni to regularly spew endless tales about the glory days of "The Big Blue"—the team moniker. In 1959, the city felt it necessary to divide the students into two new high schools—Garfield and Taft. Garfield was constructed for the students on the east side of the river, Taft for those on the west.

A wide socioeconomic discrepancy existed between these two sections of Hamilton. The mean family income was much higher on the west side, primarily because nearly all of the impoverished neighborhoods were located across the river. Not coincidentally, Hamilton's Afro-American population was almost exclusively made up of east-siders—meaning that Garfield was much more racially diversified than Taft. This situation resulted in the unspoken but recognized labeling of the two schools as the haves versus the have-nots. Students at Garfield often felt they were viewed as the teenage social outcasts of the Hamilton/Fairfield community. The decision by Mr. Stalls to direct our show helped to somehow legitimize Garfield High, and gave us unusual positive citywide publicity that seemed to energize the school in general and would-be cast members in particular.

*   *   *

As the auditions neared, I became captivated with the idea of winning the part of the King of Siam—a lofty goal for a mere sophomore. My sister Emily, who had starred in musicals in both her sophomore and junior years, seemed a shoo-in for the role of Anna, and I envisioned a brother and sister teaming that would take the town by storm. I wore out my mother's copy of the movie soundtrack, committing each song to memory and regally strutting about the house, while developing a convincing Yul Brynner accent. At any semi-appropriate moment, I would exhibit my exaggerated and majestic stage persona—occasionally thrusting my index finger skyward and proclaiming mock-confusion by uttering the words, "Is a puzzlement!" I became so swept up in the moment that I purchased a latex bald wig at Spencer's Gifts, convinced that this would put the finishing touches on my chameleon-like transformation into His Royal Highness.

Tryouts finally arrived, and the auditorium was jammed with sweaty-palmed auditionees. Mr. Stalls and Mrs. Ireland patiently listened to reading after reading, panning for gold in a stream heavy with human gravel. John Stalls would prove to be a wizard, though—exhibiting a natural charisma and confident authority that made prospective talent as malleable as clay. He was a tall man with coal-black hair and a maestro's eyes. His proud posture and commanding carriage made him an imposing character, and although he did not strike fear in everyone he met—he certainly had their ear.

Emily was the clear choice for Anna, and I honestly believed that I had read the part of the King better than anyone else. I left that evening with stars in my eyes, convinced that I would follow in the footsteps of my sister and establish myself as the leading man of the Garfield stage. When the casting sheet was finally posted, I was crushed to find that although Emily had been cast as predicted, the part of the King had gone to Dan Rommel—a very popular senior who had simply not done very well in auditions. I had also been nixed as Lun Tha, the secondary romantic lead. Instead, I would play Captain Orton, a lowly seafarer who never sets foot in Siam, and only has—as I repeated endlessly—"eleven stinking lines." I was devastated and went home crying foul, feeling that I had not been given objective consideration.

The facts bore me out. The next day, Mrs. Ireland took me aside and told me that although I had read extremely well, the roles had quite intentionally been given to seniors. She smiled, firmly grabbed my arm, and spoke from her heart. "Your time will come," she said encouragingly. She was right. I would have other moments on the high school stage.

*   *   *

My emotional wounds healed quickly, particularly after it was announced that I would understudy both the roles of the King and Lun Tha. The appointment was more honorary than functional, but it meant that I would be involved in nearly all of the rehearsals—which offered significant social benefits. Rehearsals proved to be a delight, as the cast and crew gradually came to know each other. With an ensemble that large, many of the students had never met. Therefore, not only was there coordination necessary in the staging of the show, but the cast members and scores of volunteers had to mesh into a cohesive unit.

Loyalties and friendships were generated that carried over into the classrooms and hallways. The cast became a working family, and their warm feelings for one another became apparent to the entire student body. A community feeling swept the school, as cast and crew began to associate outside the auditorium—and their friends and acquaintances were put in a convenient position to do likewise. Racial tensions were diminished as students recognized faces rather than skin color—and new dialogue brought personalities to perceived enemies.

Rehearsals were always particularly riveting when the King's harem was present—and flirtation possibilities skyrocketed. I exchanged frequent furtive glances with Connie Combs, who played Lady Thiang. Connie was a friend of my sister, and Emily enthusiastically played our go-between so that I could avoid actual extended interaction. And I had re-

209

cently dated Pam Geyer—one of the King's many wives—whom I also regularly made eyes at in biology class. Both would become close friends and eventual love interests of mine. The sheer number of women in the cast and crew created endless possibilities, and the after-school sessions offered all the high romance and sizzling gossip of a high school summer camp.

Dan Rommel improved daily in the role of the King, and he brought a maturity to the part that I could not have duplicated. Dan was good-looking, tall and athletically built—with red-brown hair and a well-scrubbed countenance that was a bit deceptive. He was both quick-witted and adept at physical humor—and surprisingly approachable, considering he was a popular senior. I grew to accept that he deserved the role and appreciated his many talents. Dan and I later became friends, attended DePauw University together and even roomed with each other during one college summer.

Donald Bass played the stern Kralahome and was the chief "character" among the cast members. He was a large, giggly, acid-tongued black senior who seemed to effortlessly draw attention to himself. Donald was a close friend of Emily and a frequent visitor to our home. He rarely displayed his serious side, which made him pleasant company, but meant that most people only knew him on a superficial level. There was a sweetness about Donald that few had the pleasure to know.

Garey Carson played Sir Edward Ramsey, Anna's acquaintance from England. He was my sister's first love and longtime boyfriend, and we first grew to really know each other during the span of these rehearsals and performances. Garey was wiry, with dark blond hair and deep-set and serious blue eyes. Always a philosopher, he possessed a very dry and not instantly perceptible sense of humor. He would be my roommate at DePauw University and during our college summers, and we shared rent on an apartment for more than a year after I graduated into the real world. Garey would become one of my closest friends.

Tom Lorance and Stephanie May played Lun Tha and Tuptim. Tom was a very pleasant gangling senior who, unfortunately, was not blessed with overwhelming theatrical talent. He had the fluidity of movement of a Disney World animatron, and was so stiff during romantic exchanges that pained spectators hoped the couple would seek intimacy counseling before Tuptim made any serious commitments. Stephanie May was an attractive, well-endowed brunette with a lovely soprano voice heard frequently in public performances throughout the area. She was reasonably patient with

Tom, and after hours of instruction and encouragement from Stephanie and Mr. Stalls, Tom made great strides and seemed only slightly uncomfortable during actual performances.

*　　*　　*

The story behind the mounting of this production did not go unnoticed by the local newspaper. As rehearsals proceeded, it became necessary to cast the roles of the children. Brothers and sisters of cast members, as well as other adorable children related to Garfield students, came to the rescue. This recruitment effort only served to amplify the feeling that the entire cast was extended family. Connie Combs had two sisters and two brothers in the production—while Wanda Cooley, one of the King's wives, added her irresistible set of twin brothers to the King's onstage lineage. My own little sister, Laurie, was cast as the Princess Ying Yaowlack, who reads a touching letter aloud to the King just prior to his tear-rendering death. This casting and the ongoing rehearsals became semi-regular feature stories in the *Journal-News*. Stage parents brought in their small children and developed good-natured relationships with the older cast members, and student body interest in the show swelled as more and more people became directly or indirectly tied to the musical.

I was pleased with my limited role in the show and relished my opportunity to be an on-the-scene observer of so many aspects of bringing the production together. I took great pride in watching my sister play the role of Anna and occasionally tried to view her as if I were an unbiased observer. Emily was both beautiful and incredibly talented, and often dominated the stage in her elegant hoop skirts. Her performance gave me a total appreciation of her that I often could not let myself feel. If possible, the musical brought us even closer together. And Laurie was perfect as the little princess. Her natural purity made her ideal for the role, and I could not help but marvel that she maintained a child's innocence, even though circumstances had in so many ways soured her youth. She was a great kid.

As the opening grew near, things came together for me as they never had before. I had my eyes on a damsel whom I had spotted several times standing in the lunch line with Katrena Farmer (the steady girlfriend of my buddy Mike Engel). This newfound Juliet was lithely slender with auburn hair, and brown eyes that burned with a fire that left me a little dumbstruck. Her name was Brenda Doty, and that spring marked the beginning of a lengthy romance that will always be a crucial part of who I am.

At the same time, I was being wooed by several other girls—a situation that was quite unfamiliar to me. I confide this to the reader not to brag of my good fortune, but to emphasize the peculiarity of it. Suddenly I found myself blessed with a charisma that even my Hai Karate cologne could not explain. The spell was short-lived, but thoroughly intoxicating, and hardly a moment passed when I was not retesting my mystifying allure or overindulging in it. Miracles like these often occur only once in a lifetime—and I managed to make the most of it. It was the height of spring, I owned a newfound self-assuredness, and the musical was only days from opening. My life was being driven by an inexplicable positive force, and I decided I would ride this wave to wherever it took me.

*   *   *

On opening night, the backstage area and the nearby dressing and music rooms were swarming with hyperactive Siamese squirts and cast members admiring each other in full regalia. Mrs. Stalls—who had been drafted to handle the colossal task of costuming—straightened hats, tucked in loose shirt tails and patiently helped the younger set put on their finery. Amazingly, she kept a smile on her face as she issued instructions and bolstered confidences, while almost always keeping at least one straight pin in her mouth. Orchestra members picked up their instruments from the band room, and they, too, seemed consumed by the moment, as they voiced words of encouragement to their participating friends and other cast members.

In the makeup room, there was the strong scent of still-wet pancake, along with the sounds and smells of a youthful styling crew shaking and then spraying black Nestle's hair color from aerosol cans. I had meandered into the middle of the hubbub while the King's wives were receiving their body makeup for bare areas not covered by their harem costumes. This stroke of luck was almost too good to be true.

My own hair had already been sprayed a silvery grey, and I was continually being told how distinguished I looked. With each compliment, I felt my confidence swell. We had received strict orders from Mr. Stalls to keep the coloring in our hair for several days as a cost-cutting measure. It was a brilliant but unintentional public-relations ploy, as these eyecatching makeovers served to remind the cast and the entire student body of our magical week of performances.

That evening, the show went superbly. Dan Rommel had developed into a convincing and powerful King of Siam, and Emily was mesmerizing as Anna Leonowens. The children were properly irresistible on the stage and reasonably well-behaved off it. Laurie's speech had brought tears to my eyes. Each cast member was as good or better than they had ever been, as they seemed energized by the audience and the moment. Afterwards, Mr. Stalls skillfully worked the theater lobby, obviously puffed-chest-proud of the students and their accomplishments. The show was a big hit and was the talk of Hamilton, Ohio.

The production improved with each performance as the cast and crew became ever closer. Nearly everyone who saw the production was moved by it, not only because it was so well-produced—but because it was obviously such a labor of love. Each night, the solidarity and sincerity of the company seemed to wash over the auditorium and create one of those rare communions of spirit—as audience members, stage hands, orchestra members and even concessionaires unwittingly shared in the moment. Everyone sensed we were a part of something much, much larger than a stage presentation—the production represented a historic triumph for Garfield Senior High School. For one brief, fleeting moment the city's spotlight had shifted—and we had responded by stealing the show.

On closing night, I felt a deep sadness that this overpowering wave I had ridden was dissipating. But I also experienced an ecstatic joy at our accomplishments and fraternity, and a comfortable satisfaction at where this wave had ultimately taken me.

That night played out like a real-life fairy tale that everyone knew would end happily. We allowed ourselves to let the moment take us where it might, and it whisked us through the performance with a natural fluidity the likes of which I have never again experienced. Eventually, the final curtain fell on our sweet dream, but rose once again for extended curtain calls. The applause surged as a parade of cast members appeared, seemingly igniting the raw energy in the air. Dan and Emily took their final bows, he offered his arm, and the orchestra rang out with its final reprise of "Shall We Dance?" They began to waltz gracefully, and circled the stage as the entire ensemble beamed uncontrollably at the couple and at each other.

A group of male cast members hoisted Mr. Stalls on their shoulders and brought him downcenter, as those on stage and in the wings drifted to him without prompting. The standing audience broke into a chorus of vocal cheers. A shaky and exhilarated Mrs. Ireland was escorted onto the stage and presented a dozen long-stemmed roses.

213

At that moment, I thought about what Mrs. Ireland had said to me after the auditions and have thought about it quite often since then. I was one of the stars of each school production for the next two years and would appear in numerous plays and musicals in my lifetime—having a lead role in many of them. When Mrs. Ireland offered me her support after casting had been completed, she spoke of what my theatrical future might bring to me. Little did she know that the future would arrive so quickly. As I stood on stage that night, my time had come as it never had before or has since. Theater and life would never be better than this.

25

Brenda

I stood leaning against a wall in the school cafeteria, wearing my best expression of nonchalance as I waited in the food line next to Katrena Farmer—lady love of my friend Mike Engel. My contrived boredom was not for Katrena's benefit. My sights were aimed on the luscious target standing next to her, and experience had taught me that the worst way to exhibit interest in a girl was to appear too eager.

The object of my attention wore a wide, easy smile while we exchanged banter and tentatively waded in romantic waters. She had feisty brown eyes and a near-perfect complexion, high cheekbones and dimples that became obvious when she was delighted. Her name was Brenda Doty. I had met her only recently, and our interaction had been brief, but the fact that she was Katrena's best friend made it quite tempting to exploit the connection to find out whether she was unattached and potentially interested.

*   *   *

It was mid-spring in 1970, and I was in the midst of a string of good fortune. The opening of our production of *The King and I* was just around the corner, and my confidence had been bolstered by an inexplicable pre-production success with the opposite sex. My ego had become artificially inflated and could now absorb the blow of a thumbs-down response if I made an official inquiry into Brenda's availability. I decided to swallow my pride and ask Mike to be my emissary. His instructions were to convey my interest and await the lady's response. This contact was either never made or happened simultaneously with a similar effort on Brenda's behalf. The word got back to me that she thought I was cute—a description that boys my age generally had disdain for, unless the observation came from an attractive girl. I had hit pay dirt. We arranged to go on a double date with Mike and Katrena—the safest way that we could imagine for us to test the spark.

Brenda and Katrena's world was completely foreign to me. Both of them had attended Roosevelt Junior High, so their social circle differed greatly from mine. They lived in an area of town that I was only slightly familiar with, and neither was in any of my classes. Brenda and I had little common ground when we went out that first evening, but it made little difference. It was the most refreshingly easeful date that I had ever been on. When we hugged at the end of the night, it was as if she belonged in my arms, and when we kissed, there was a tender respect that we gave each other's lips. When I dropped her off that evening, I felt no hesitancy. I was prepared to venture into uncharted territories. I was ready for my first high school romance.

*   *   *

Our relationship developed about as quickly as was humanly possible, as every revelation that she made about herself made her more precious in my eyes. There was an inherent goodness about her that I desperately needed and a sensitivity that made her both eminently reachable and adept at gentle reaching. Of course, there were the typical high school flirtations of passing notes in the hall and plastering each other's names all over notebooks and in the margins of every sheet of paper that was not submitted for grading. But there was also a maturity with which we approached our relationship. We were committed to each other and talked openly of our thoughts and feelings. We assigned our relationship immediate importance, because we knew that there was so much right about what we had. It was only a matter of weeks before we began going steady and exchanged rings. I loved the look of my class ring rubber-banded to fit her finger. She was beautiful and caring—and she was *my* girlfriend.

Transportation became our first obstacle, as I had no access to a car, and she was rarely able to borrow her parents'. Double dating offered little privacy and sometimes felt like sitting inside a rest room stall that had no door. We became overly familiar with back seats and blaring speakers, while wishing that someday we would be the couple with the keys. The coup de grace occurred one evening while we cruised several remote country roads with Mike and Katrena. They decided that we would seek our seclusion on Maud-Hughes Road—parked atop a bridge where a host of similarly amorous couples claimed to have been approached by unearthly orbs of light. When Mike finally killed the engine, and Brenda and I locked in passionate embrace, we felt as if we must be in a bad Japanese movie. The sounds of lip-smackings and labored breathing echoed throughout the car, but were often out-of-sync with what was occurring between us in the back seat. Vinyl squeaked and seat belts made their marks, while we contorted our bodies to alleviate muscle cramps and tried to dodge each other's flailing elbows. The only orb of light that we saw that evening was the spotlight of a sheriff's patrol car that pulled up alongside us. Our interrogation was brief, but mood-destroying. Group amour was highly unfulfilling—it was definitely time to get an automobile of my own.

*　　*　　*

During the summer of 1970, I was finally able to purchase a car with the money I had saved working part-time jobs at Frisch's Big Boy and the Ciné Malibu movie theater. I purchased a '67 sky-blue Rambler American from a friend of my mother's. The car was well-maintained, and though officially a family car and not a make or model that held any standing in the high school community—it symbolized my personal liberation and gave our romance some room to breathe.

The first evening that I owned the car, Brenda and I were parked in front of the garage of our home on Pleasant Avenue. There was a light drizzle, and we listened to the pleasant patter of raindrops on the car roof. The AM radio blared, and the coolness of the night air made our bodies feel nearly fused when pressed together. Our kisses were sometimes passionate and always adoring, as we celebrated the unbridled freedom of our new-found independence.

In that moment, I knew that I was in love with her. True, the emotional tumult of infatuation had welled up within me, but I also felt an inner peace and assuredness in the depths of my heart. In truth, it was this comfort that frightened me. Its safety felt almost confining. If I fell into its trap, I would not have the strength or desire to explore my destiny. I was all too aware of my young age and held high aspirations for my future. This persistent anxiety would continually gnaw at me throughout our times together. But all my fretting did not prevent our romance from unfolding in a progression of wonderful discoveries—as we reveled in the newness of each other and this feeling of love. The non-threatening nature of our rela-

217

tionship wore at my defensive barriers and allowed for moments of free-flowing devotion.

Each day of that emotion-packed summer seemed devoted to bolstering our interconnection. We saw each other as often as possible and talked daily on the phone. I grew to know her family but often felt alienated from them. They were a blue-collar Catholic family with southern roots, and I found their lifestyle and background strangely intimidating. The Dotys' ways were unpretentious, and their approach sometimes dauntingly straightforward. They wore their hearts on their sleeves and spoke their minds freely and often. Their hard-nosed, brass tacks way of life was foreign to me, and I had difficulty adjusting to it.

Brenda's mother, Barbara, was a forceful yet deceptively warm woman whose matronly manner could not disguise her natural beauty. Her father, Spencer, was a gruff, intimidating character with rugged good looks and an authoritarian command. Brenda also had three siblings—two brothers and a sister. Ricky was two years our junior and had his father's good looks and athleticism. He was ornery, but good-hearted—and our relationship was polite, but superficial. Larry was a sensitive kid who was about four years Brenda's junior. I liked his vulnerability and moxie and could empathize with the ongoing battle he waged with his own earnestness. Sue Ann was the youngest sibling and a bit younger than Larry. She was a pretty girl who received more than her share of attention but seemed to take her pampering in stride. My primary tactic in dealing with my difficulties with her family was to avoid them whenever possible. Brenda served as a buffer, and they tried to meet me halfway—but she needed more effort from me. I was too immature to oblige her.

Nonetheless, the bright skies and warm breezes of summer's days always seemed to wipe our slate clean, and our daily access to each other increased with the passage of time. It was a season filled with double dates, swimming, softball and picnics—an open-air arena of sweet kisses and lazy evenings on her porch swing. Our summer romance felt almost hypnotizing. It cast a spell that made so many moments together seem magical. I found myself gazing into Brenda's eyes and being engulfed by her love. My resistance to letting myself care too much was melting. It was succumbing to the warmth of the summer sun.

*   *   *

The beginning of my junior year provided a snoutful of smelling salts

218

that sent me tumbling back to reality and prompted an inordinate amount of soul-searching. I began testing and retesting our union and was unable to simply appreciate its rich bounties. The relationship suddenly became a timed event with a constant eye on the clock that counted down the days to my high school graduation. Brenda had no aspirations to attend college—I very much wanted to. Brenda seemed content with staying in the immediate area. I believed I could conquer the world. These philosophical differences began as thoughts pondered in my mind, but mushroomed into subconscious anger that surfaced at regular intervals.

But even while we struggled with our long-term future, Brenda and I had become an accepted item at school—and were usually mentioned in the same breath. We rendezvoused in the hall whenever possible, saw each other daily in choir and received reports from loose-lipped associates about our activities in between. After school, I would have rehearsals for our fall musical, *High Spirits*—a musical adaptation of Noel Coward's *Blithe Spirit*. Brenda would attend marching-band practice where she and Katrena performed as majorettes. Her gold-and-red sequined twirler's outfit showed off her seemingly endless legs and perfect posterior and often prompted an involuntary gulp—as I fought off my impure thoughts. On nights there were home football games, I would throw my coat or jacket over her shoulders, and we would huddle together to stay warm. There was a mutual protection in the act, and the love I felt from her made me feel cloaked from significant harm—even amid the melodrama that often surrounded our relationship. Everything, I kept telling myself, would be all right.

*   *   *

Away from the school front, it became more and more difficult to find private time. Both of us had large families, so someone always cramped our style at both of our homes. She would occasionally come to the Ciné Malibu to help me clean the theater, and although we were alone there—it was not the most romantic of spots. There was something about the odor of bathroom cleaner and the feel of a sticky theater floor that could instantaneously squelch an amorous moment. So we sought occasional privacy by inconspicuously parking a few doors down from her home—until her brother Larry walked by one evening while we were in a reclined position. Not recognizing my car, he rushed back to their house bearing the tale of an ill man who was writhing in the front seat of a mysterious auto. Brenda's parents called the police. I was thoroughly embarrassed, and Brenda was thoroughly grounded.

Against my mother's strict orders, I decided that it was imperative that we begin going to the drive-in. It would provide a chance to finally be left alone and sometimes even watch an entertaining movie. These moments that we spent together provide some of my most significant memories. Ardor and passion superseded sexual desire, as it was a chance to really lock ourselves away from the rest of the world and relate to each other as partners. If it was puppy love, I didn't realize it—and to this day, I still don't. My feelings toward her were as real as any I have ever experienced. I have gone to great effort and expense to try to recreate the kind of romance that occurred inside that four-door Rambler with fogged-up windows, but our innocence and trusting vulnerability can, unfortunately, not be duplicated.

But as the school year progressed, I spent less time enjoying our moments together and more time worrying about what my future would be. My fears and uncertainty about the next two years made me feel trapped by our romance and became barriers that blocked our intimacy. I resented her lack of interest in her future education and began to interpret her precious simplicity as intellectual inferiority. My failure to understand her parents and family corkscrewed into an antagonism of their lifestyle. And I became obsessed with seeing other girls, not because I really wanted to, but because I felt the walls of our partnership closing in on me.

Having neither the strength nor real desire to end our relationship, I felt myself withdraw and tried to drive her away. I became distant and angry, cold and unfeeling. This iceman tactic had provided me relief when dealing with my parents' divorce, but now it was only wounding someone whom I loved. I have vivid and haunting memories of Brenda weeping on my shoulder that still cut me like a knife. She would feel the wrath of my rejection until her wounds came to surface, and I would then try to somehow make it all right. When I returned to her, she accepted me with open arms, but I was not aware of the permanent damage my behavior had wrought.

Still, it seemed that my fears could never smother my love for her. And when I allowed myself, I could still get lost in the glow of her eyes or delight in the way she would playfully snap, "Tim, quit!" when I would tease her, or we became involved in a torrid tickling battle. For our junior prom, she had her hair done and wore a gorgeous taffeta lavender dress. I still have a framed photographer's pose taken on that day. In my mind, she was unquestionably the prettiest girl there. Unfortunately, Vernon Shobe felt similarly and continually asked her to dance—because I wouldn't. I don't think I've ever been more jealous, and dramatically and quite impressively burned rubber when I dropped her at her home.

I finally tried to break up with her prior to the tryouts for *Arsenic and Old Lace*. We had returned each other's rings, and I was feeling hollow—as if my soul had been ripped out of me. When I went to the auditions, I was shocked to see her there. She gave an impressive reading, and although she did not receive a part, she snapped whatever will I had left to remain unattached. When I took her home that evening, I had a sense of how gut-wrenching it would be to lose her. It was early-winter cold, and when I reached inside her white fur coat to hold her, the contours of her body seemed a part of my own personage nearly forfeited. I could feel her cautious trust in me returning.

The summer provided some short-term relief from our now-chronic pain. She spent time camping with her parents, and I visited my father in Illinois. The lazy season of sun provided a psychological respite from my incessant brooding. I temporarily lived only in the present and savored the times that we did have together. When I returned from my trip to my father's home, she surprised me by greeting me at our house. She had on my favorite of her casual outfits—a pair of tight blue jeans and a black-and-white checkered shirt. We hugged, I put my hands around her petite waist, and she leaned back and looked up at me. That face is the one that I will always see when I now think of her. Nothing could be more beautiful.

*   *   *

The approach of fall brought back all of my fears and anxieties—amplified by the awareness that it was my senior year. I was now obsessed with ending our relationship and symbolically entering a new stage of my life, free of the emotional burdens that I had silently carried on my back for several years. I viewed Brenda as one of those burdens, and all of the anger that I felt for not being strong enough to leave her was used as a weapon to punish her.

We broke up again, but I just couldn't let her go completely. She stood by me through a traumatic injury I sustained in the early fall and offered her sincere friendship until the tempest surrounding the incident subsided. Brenda had entered a distributive-education program and was working half-days at Lane Public Library. It was there that she met the person whom she eventually married. There were a few more fireworks between us, but ultimately the damage had been done, and I lost her. I phoned shortly after Christmas, and I assume her new boyfriend was at her home. She asked me not to call anymore, and we did not speak again until Mike and Katrena's wedding more than a year later.

*   *   *

I have spent a lifetime of speculation regarding Brenda Doty. But all the what-ifs and might-have-beens do not change the fact that we are not together. I met a wonderful woman in college whom I married in 1977, and I sometimes feel that she is an angel that God sent to me. I have apologized to Brenda, both in a letter I wrote her early in college when I asked her to come back to me, and later in person at our ten-year high-school reunion. She said that she had forgiven me, and, as far as I know, she is still happily married to the same person she met while working at the library during her senior year.

I still love Brenda—I will always love her. Although I have grown to accept that this was not our time, it in no way lessens the intensity of my feelings toward her. Relationships sometimes blossom to fill immediate needs—and if this is true, Brenda filled my cup to overflowing. Lamentably, true loves do not always make life partners. I take solace, though, that I can occasionally close my eyes, feel my hands around Brenda's waist and see her beaming face gazing up at me. It is an indulgence that even my wife has grown to understand.

26

High School Summers

High school summers were a cause for great celebration and ceaseless exploration. When the bitter Midwestern winter melted into spring, Hamiltonians once again ventured into the great outdoors unwrapped and unencumbered. Each year, winter proved a formidable adversary, punishing us with its harsh extremities and forcing us to reluctantly respect its unbounded power. We flirted with winter's dangers as one gambles with fire—pitting ourselves against its dominance and assuming the inherent risks. But as temperatures elevated, nature reached out a conciliatory hand and welcomed us to return to its embrace.

Soon we grew restless in the confinement of our classrooms and yearned to break the school-year restraints that kept us bound to our desks. Young love and infatuation simmered in spring's sunshine, as seasonal feminine fashions uncovered shapely and previously veiled works of art. We became antsy to run and roam, and summer vacation seemed the only solution to our cabin fever. In June, when we finally packed up our hall lockers and escaped into the blinding light of day, a chief regimentation had been removed from our lives. Structure loosened and friendships tightened. Days would slow to a near standstill, as the populace bathed in the fresh air and sunshine. It was summertime in southwestern Ohio—and the living was easy.

The time was June of 1970. My sophomore year had concluded, and although I relished the freedom from my search for knowledge, I fretted about a schoolbreak separation from my new girlfriend, Brenda Doty. Her home was located near the high school, and I resided an approximately fifteen-minute drive away in Lindenwald—with no immediate access to an automobile. Our relationship was only two months old, and my trust in our bond was tenuous. After all, it was June, and an operable car elevated a male's summer stock considerably. I envisioned Brenda cruising Erie Boulevard in a jacked-up Chevy Supersport with a savvy senior, while I labored at my dishwasher's job at the Big Boy Restaurant—clad in my over-starched jumbo service outfit and an apron stained with a sampling of every food item available on the dining-room menu.

It took me less than two days to recognize that absence does, indeed, make the heart grow fonder. I craved the scent of her hair and yearned to wrap my arms around her and draw her to me. The memory of her eyes burned a hole in my brain and uncoupled my train of thought. From the moment summer had officially commenced, missing her was my driving force and negated all interest in other females. I became increasingly aware of my addiction, and—much to my relief—our phone conversations confirmed that the feeling was mutual. Our isolation had only enhanced the high drama of our romance. She confessed suffering similar withdrawal symptoms, and when I finally reunited with her twenty-four hours later, we again felt complete.

That evening I saw her in shorts for the first time. Her legs were shiny smooth and somewhat rosy from their early season unveiling to direct sunlight. She wore her hair off her face, and her cheeks were slightly flushed from the heat of the evening. The red sleeveless-pullover knit blouse she wore exposed her bare shoulders and my vulnerabilities. Brenda's eyes smiled and glistened with adoration, and I felt her delight pervade my heart and soothe my soul. Triggering sights and smells of future summers would again bring this picture into focus, and with such regularity that it has become a permanent fixture of my seasonal experience.

I worked persistently to arrange transportation to see her regularly until I could finance my own set of wheels. Double dates abounded, and occasionally we were blessed with private access to her parents' Toyota or Chevy. Friends would drop me off at her house and retrieve me at specified times while I saved conscientiously to purchase a piece of gas-powered freedom. Our careful and patient planning provided us the access to each other that we needed and assured that our romance would survive the summer. I was buried in a passionate relationship—and was loving every minute of it.

Summer was the ideal opportunity to gallivant about town with a carload of friends, touring public parks and swimming pools where females might congregate. On weekends the four public pools were jammed with youth of all ages, and beach towels carpeted the cement periphery of the pungent chlorinated waters. Transistor radios blared, while just about as many people walked laps around the pool's edge as entered its basin. Eyes darted nervously, as nearly everyone sneaked peeks at members of the opposite sex. Some girls achieved instantaneous and previously unobtainable popularity, as formerly unnoticed attributes became readily apparent. Curvaceous lovelies a few years our senior were worshiped as goddesses, while younger girls were largely ignored and artfully avoided.

Some people submerged themselves in the cool water, bouncing up and down in water-induced slow motion as they motored about by pushing off the pool floor. Others treaded vigorously in deeper waters, struggling to keep their coconuts above the surface while swallowing splashes from fellow flailing bathers. Actual swim-strokes were impossible without inflicting accidental blows to several of the congregated collection of bobbing heads. Occasionally, a smiling face would unexplainably be sucked under, which would usually be followed by two heads resurfacing only moments later—the second being the cackling culprit who had performed the unrequested baptism.

Adolescent male-female grappling ran rampant, as couples indulged in hands-on voluntary human anatomy classes with everything not securely bound within a bathing suit considered fair game. Lifeguards' whistles trilled like mating calls, as the white-nosed dictators sat perched atop tower chairs, pointing at the accused and shaking their heads vigorously—or worse yet—dramatically giving them "the thumb," meaning their swimming day had just concluded.

Those who were not tanning, scouting or bobbing could be found in the designated refreshment area, where flirtations could continue in quieter surroundings. It was here that summer romances were kindled while seemingly ravenous, snot-nosed children chomped on ice-cream sandwiches and frozen Snickers bars or slurped ice-filled sodas or rainbow snow-cones.

The entire pool area and accompanying bathhouse were enclosed by a chain-link fence that separated the paying customers from those there simply to watch the show. Carloads of testosterone-charged Romeos would drop by just to hop out and strut their stuff as they circled the outside of the security fence and their female prey. Girls would occasionally wander over to the protective wall to make conversation with the gapers—and the scene strongly resembled an enclosed backyard that housed prized female poodles, and drew would-be suitors from every corner of the neighborhood. On a productive Saturday afternoon, my fellow cruisers and I would hit several of these human zoos, with particular attention paid to Washing-

225

ton Pool in Lindenwald and Ford's Pool on the north end of town—where there were also several softball diamonds.

If our mood was less amorous, we would buzz all of our favorite recreational areas in search of some softball or hardball action—or even an out-of-season basketball or football game. Seeing recognizable faces at a local park was enjoyable, but sometimes challenging a group of unknowns was even better entertainment. Playing against foes whose abilities were uncertain brought out our fierce competitive nature. However, if no enemies could be found, we reveled in the wonder of the game alone. All of God's children should be blessed with the experience of standing on a dusty dirt infield on a sunny summer afternoon, pounding on a prize ball glove and adjusting the brim of a comfortable old cap. The quiet serenity and peacefulness of the moment defies description. The competition of our games was usually secondary to the camaraderie we shared and the thoughtful moments that we didn't. We each drew our personal joys from the afternoon's action and kept those joys to ourselves as males are often wont to do.

An afternoon of cruising was never considered complete without a trip to the A&W Root Beer Stand or Hyde's Drive-In, where we downed icy mugs of dark draft that were brought to us on a metal serving tray that affixed to our partially rolled-down car window. A car hop would bustle out to serve us, roll her eyes when realizing our order included no food and curtly deliver the heady brew to our auto posthaste. We would savor the drinks like conquering Vikings, enjoying the feel of the thick wet mugs in our hands and scoping the lot for bawdy wenches that we might have our way with. When our tankards and/or our pockets were empty, we revved the engine and rolled down the highway, our radio blaring loudly—proclaiming to the outside world that we were on the cutting edge of cool.

I had earned my driver's license by my sophomore year and befriended a junior who was both generous and naive enough to let me drive his car. His name was Doug Rogers, and we had met in concert choir and initiated a friendship that extended well into my college years. Doug was plain-faced and beefy—a good-hearted and generous fellow who became a regular "running buddy" and generally provided our transportation to run. His car was a sky-blue Impala, a rumbling V-8 that was generally jammed with a varying passenger list of eager cruisers on Friday and Saturday evenings. The car represented our hope for chance encounters—a fantasy that was rarely fulfilled, but doggedly pursued. We intentionally happened by our favorite females' houses, feigning surprise if we were lucky enough to catch them outdoors. And occasionally we took the twenty-minute drive to Oxford, the home of Miami University, where we pretended to be college students and probably provided a few good laughs to any coed we encountered.

We buzzed every restaurant drive-in and fast-food place with a youthful clientele and, like unsuccessful fishermen, generally rolled home empty-handed—except for a full string of well-reasoned excuses. But even when we struck out, the night seemed endless and electric. Air-conditioning was a luxury reserved for the wealthy, so many people hit the streets to beat the heat. The days were sweltering, and the evenings the time to prowl. Night after night, I remained convinced that something magical would happen.

My magic could be found at the Doty residence on Kahn Avenue, and although I enjoyed trolling with a carload of friends, I remained true to my new girlfriend and spent as much time with her as parental restrictions allowed. For Brenda and me, it was a summer relegated to back seats, where warm breezes whistled past our ears from open car windows and swelled to hair-fanning gusts with quick acceleration. Intimacy could be found in the interlocking of hands or the exploration of the contours of her shoulders or waist. The feel of her lips and the art of kissing was new, and the passion was enhanced by the vibrant summer nights. Our summer was balmy evenings gently rocking on a porch swing while children still engaged in yard play even after the sun had set. It was the tempting chimes of a passing ice cream truck and the shadowy outlines of her smooth soft cheekbones at dusk—when she looked at me as I hoped a woman someday would. It was a summer that fills me with a lifetime of curious anticipation which swells from within each time the thermometer once again exceeds eighty degrees.

Almost surprisingly, fall eventually arrives, slapping its chilling rains onto our faces and splashing flashy autumn colors to ease our dread of the upcoming winter. Summer is a time of hope—a season to daydream of youth and romance—and an instant when the brilliant sunshine convinces us that wondrous things are about to happen.

In the Midwest the seasons are in sharp contrast, and summer owns a powerful mystique that evokes our most nostalgic of memories. The summer of 1970 was a real-life dream that I often re-experience whenever I smell freshly mowed grass or see a young amorous couple walk in tandem down a sidewalk on a brilliant July afternoon. It is an enriching dream that does not make me mourn the loss of my youth, but instead reinforces how wonderful my life can be. Every summer carries its own special and unique memories, and each year when the mercury begins to rise, we allow ourselves to believe that summer's enchantment will touch us again.

27

The Kaleidoscope

Eight friends and acquaintances sat in a small living room in Lindenwald on a chilly autumn evening in late 1970. I sat on a sofa next to Kevin Rommel, a newfound friend, as we all made small talk and half-listened to Pam Geyer poke out a melody on a small upright piano. What was to occur was a meeting and rehearsal of a collection of choir members interested in forming a singing ensemble. These auditions had not been sponsored by the school music department. Instead, those attending had been hand-picked by a core group of three founding members (myself included) based on each person's vocal ability, stage presence and personality. Our little get-together was simply a gathering of talented individuals who loved to sing and wished to perform in a more intimate group than those offered at Garfield High School.

The idea was not an original one. The previous year, my sister Emily had been in a similar group called The Bel-Airs. Numerous graduations had disbanded the ensemble, although they had blazed a path that we hoped to both follow and expand on. We were meeting at Laura Moore's house that evening to lay the groundwork and to rehearse a few numbers that we were all familiar with from choir—so that we could determine how well this combination of voices would blend.

*　　*　　*

The individuals in that room would all eventually become integral people in my high school experience. Two of the attendees had been members of the Bel-Airs, and I had become acquainted with them through Emily. Our friendships had been bolstered in the school choir and during Garfield's production of *The King and I.* Connie Combs had an exquisitely rich soprano voice—probably the finest in the school. She had light brown hair and well-formed womanly features with almost Oriental eyes. Connie was a striking girl, with a buxom hourglass figure and a consistently sweet nature. Joe Scherzinger was a first-class tenor with a baby face and a stock-pile of unabashed earnestness. He was diminutive and surprisingly soft-spoken—a welcome counterbalance to this assemblage of dominant personalities.

Pam Geyer was still shamelessly pounding on Laura's piano one key at a time. She was a dark blonde with knowing blue eyes and a pristine complexion. Pam was slightly built with almost feline facial features. She was both dainty and wise—a female to be both respected and revered. I had known her since junior high and was attracted to her both physically and mentally. We would date both in high school and college, and our relation-ship with each other and how it eventually ended (or more appropriately dissolved) has always been perplexing to me. Laura Moore, whose house we had intruded, was the most classically beautiful of the girls present. She was a petite brunette with ashen skin and fascinating green eyes. We had been school mates since I had moved to Hamilton, and our paths had crossed quite frequently. Laura was strong-willed—a personality trait that I, too, had been accused of. We sometimes clashed, but always maintained a tenuous friendship. Perhaps we knew each other too well.

Kevin Rommel, the sophomore planted next to me on the sofa, was multi-talented and brimming with good humor. He was a vital athletic type like his brother Dan—who had played the male lead in *The King and I*. Kevin had large animated eyes that he used effectively for comedic em-phasis. He and I would be the basses in the group, but with his additional instrumental background, he was a far superior musician. Edwina Burton was the only person present with whom I had not socialized. She had a cheery round face and kind eyes, and epitomized the phrase, "pleasingly plump." Edwina was quite attractive just as she was, and the weight that she carried seemed to belong on her. Because I initially had difficulty re-membering her name, I began calling her Edgar Bergen, and since it tick-led her, she suffered this indignation for months afterwards. I loved to make her laugh.

Also in attendance was Doug Rogers, a stocky senior who had a re-ceding head of dark-brown hair with unstylishly long sideburns. He was making an honest attempt to sing tenor, although he was really a baritone. The experiment did not work. Several weeks later, I was given the unpleas-ant chore of representing the group in asking him to step down. One of the most gut-wrenching tasks in life is to tell someone that he is not good enough. Doug was miffed, but resilient. Within days, wounds healed, and as is usual with male friendships, the incident was never discussed again.

The conversation picked up gradually, as a natural chemistry developed, and people subconsciously determined if and how they would fit in. By the time our pianist, Mariann Julliard, arrived—mouths were in overdrive and laughter flowed freely and effortlessly. Mariann had been the accompanist for the Bel-Airs and was a pretty dark-blonde with a rosy complexion and eyes that were always filled with wonder. She offered a rare combination of being both highly intelligent and painfully naive. Mariann had a captivatingly precise and enthusiastic voice, and I often found myself completely enthralled with her. Being a senior, she provided a challenge to me, and I eventually coerced her to date me several times before I left for college. I received a lengthy "Dear John" letter from her my freshman year, and it remains forever in my memory because it is the only one that I ever received. I was baffled by her detailed rejection of me, but appreciated her thoughtfulness.

Mariann had started to pound out some of our more popular choir selections, so we got down to the business at hand. The rich tones that filled the room nearly shocked us, as this crackerjack choir made instantaneous adjustments in modulation to intermix with their partners, and in turn with the six people singing the other three vocal parts. We toyed with the blend and occasionally revved the singing machine up full-throttle, so that when we performed "The Girl From Ipanema"—a song we were already quite familiar with—everything came together. There was an interconnection and instantaneous communication in our performance that was exhilarating. We parted company committed to practicing one night a week and trying to obtain a few of the bookings that the Bel-Airs had done the year before. That evening it seemed that our possibilities were endless.

The group practiced diligently for several weeks. Rehearsals were held at various members' houses, and although we were perfecting our available repertoire, we were limited by the pieces of sheet music that we could pilfer from the school choral department. We knew that it was time to cut the umbilical chord and begin to truly operate independently. The ensemble made its first public appearance when we sang the national anthem at a Garfield football game. Although the on-field miking was practically nonexistent, and the response was less than overwhelming, our appearance proclaimed to the world that we were now officially a group. As happens with nearly any significant human relationship, we had needed to make a symbolic commitment to each other. Now it was time to tighten our alliance.

Each of us began putting out feelers, searching for any excuse to perform and any group who would listen to us. Our concerts took place at PTA meetings, churches, clubs and fraternal organizations. And we sang at elementary school assemblies, in parking lots and at rest homes. If the audience was healthy enough to breathe and well-mannered enough to refrain from hurling objects at us, we would walk bravely into the spotlight (or any light for that matter). We began accepting donations for performances and used the funds to purchase new sheet music that included recent pop hits and selections from Broadway musicals.

*　　*　　*

Our group was eventually named The Kaleidoscope. In our interpretation, the name properly expressed that fact that we were divergent personalities and voices integrated to create beauty. The organizations that booked us seemed delighted by our performances. We were clean-cut, attractive kids who were painfully polite to adults. The group had banded together without benefit of adult supervision because we loved to sing, and we sang songs that were instantly recognizable.

The Kaleidoscope was now considered the elite singing group in school by our peers in choir—although we were not school-affiliated. In fact, the choir teacher was becoming increasingly annoyed because bookings were offered to us rather than the school choir. The group was providing us more pure enjoyment than even we had anticipated.

We spent the first year of our existence building our reputation, performing whenever asked and developing a close fellowship that we shared at least one night a week. The members also enjoyed each other's company away from the piano. Although a romance developed between Joe Scherzinger and Edwina Burton, for the most part, the relationships between the young men and women in the group remained primarily platonic. It took months before our professional veneer wore thin, and callow carnality cracked through the surface. Before we were finished, nearly no one had escaped Cupid's arrow.

The group was compensated for shows more than a dozen times during the school year, as we continued to polish our performance skills and expand our musical variety. We also made many gratis appearances and did some old-fashioned Christmas caroling during the holiday season.

Gradually we were making a name for ourselves in the Hamilton/Fairfield community.

*　　*　　*

The conclusion of my junior school year brought my most memorable high school summer and two vacancies in The Kaleidoscope, as Joe Scherzinger graduated, and we searched for a full-time replacement for Doug Rogers. Connie Combs had a younger brother named Raymond who was an incoming sophomore, so he was an automatic choice. Raymond was a fireplug with a crew cut—a magnetic character with an impish grin and solid tenor range. He immediately found a niche as the clown of the group, and audiences seemed to love him. The other tenor slot was filled by Tim Sparks, who was also turning into quite a crowd-pleaser. He was a trim junior with dark eyes, curly black hair and an almost passable moustache—an impressive achievement for a high-school student. Tim was boyishly mischievous, and the competitive banter he maintained with Ray was usually worth eavesdropping on. Our pianist, Mariann Julliard, had also graduated and was replaced by Nancy Wehr—a tall, thin brunette with a striking long face that exposed her kind-hearted nature. She owned an easy manner that served as the same calming influence that Joe Scherzinger had provided the year before. This combination of personalities clicked immediately, and our on-stage persona seemed energized by our new additions. With a host of repeat bookings and a small operations budget, the ensemble often dominated much of our leisure time.

Rehearsals continued throughout the summer, and we were invited to sing at the Italian-American Picnic gala fireworks display on the Fourth of July. The event was held at the Butler County Fairgrounds and was the place to be seen on Independence Day. The grounds were illuminated by a tantalizingly brilliant white light that spotlighted the festival to anyone who passed by on foot or in autos. Youth were drawn to this intoxicating glow like moths to a flame—and they pleaded with and pulled their parents through the gates as if their summer's significance hinged on it. The air was filled with the scent of Italian spices and the hubbub of bingo games in motion. Recognizable faces manned booths and concession stands, while tattooed ride operators frightened small children by barking instructions like drill sergeants.

We were scheduled to perform in the infield of the grandstand area—the distinguished showplace where plug-horses often loped the track for charity or decaled junk-heaps battered each other to a not-so-merciful demolition-death. The stands were jammed with action-hungry spectators, and a temporary stage had been constructed specifically for the festivities. A grand finale fireworks extravaganza was to take place directly behind us immediately after our performance had concluded.

The Kaleidoscope was formally introduced, as we kicked off what we believed would be an approximately forty-five minute set. The unruly crowd had other ideas. About halfway through our first number, we realized that no one was listening. Either they couldn't hear us, or they just didn't give a hoot—but they definitely weren't listening. Having never been ignored by so many people simultaneously, we weren't prepared to cope with this collective cold shoulder. Our requests for increased amplification went unheeded, so we bullheadedly continued our act—hoping that eventually someone would acknowledge our presence and pluck us from this twilight zone.

Mike Woodward, a folk singer with red shoulder-length hair, accompanied us on acoustic guitar throughout the fiasco and eventually attempted to scream out a few numbers himself. A last-place plug-horse would have received a warmer reception. Mike broke into an uncensored tirade, hurling expletives at the audience and anyone else who would listen. No one did. He ended his act mid-song, stomping off the stage with face flushed and clutching the neck of his guitar like a caveman's club. James Taylor and John Denver would have been mortified.

About five minutes later during a solo by Pam Geyer, someone pulled the switch on the lights in the grandstand area and the fireworks commenced. As we huddled together in almost total darkness, we assumed—quite properly—that our contribution to the evening's entertainment had been unceremoniously concluded. It did not, however, conclude the incident. An angry swarm of parents and family members confronted the entertainment coordinator after the show. When all the head wagging and finger pointing had ended, it was difficult to decide which fireworks display had been more impressive. Somehow we survived this Independence Day debacle and were subsequently informed by indignant family/groupies that our set had played out like a presentation of mime theater—no one had heard a word. I suppose our most appropriate musical selection of the evening had been "The Sounds of Silence." We would laugh about it later.

We returned to the scene of this accident later in the summer to enter the talent contest at the Butler County Fair. The fete dominated a week in August, and nearly everyone in town made at least one appearance there. It was a classic Midwestern fair with a full slate of agricultural activities, local craftsmen peddling handmade goods, and rows of booths sponsored by clubs and fraternal organizations. There were cooking and dance demonstrations, all of the essential carnival rides and games of chance, and a multitude of junk food vendors—all thriving amid the powerful aromas created by confined farm animals. The day that we were scheduled to compete, there was the threat of rain—but we frittered away the overcast afternoon and met at the sheltered contest site just before show time. It was a night for our scrapbooks, as we won first prize in the group-senior division and also took top honors as the best overall act. We had been redeemed. They scheduled a separate night during the week for us to return to sing an entire concert, and the Hamilton *Journal-News* gave us a major write-up with an accompanying photo. The phone rang for days with calls from friends and church members.

*   *   *

My senior year was the heyday for The Kaleidoscope. We performed quite regularly and earned enough money to purchase matching outfits. My girlfriend Brenda Doty and I had broken up, so I could officially express interest in both Connie and Pam. Connie's brother Ray and I became close friends—and Ray and Laura Moore enjoyed a brief flirtation. We were all experiencing the joys and the pains of familiarity, and it made the group's interrelationships both more interesting and volatile.

A television show called *Jim Scott's New Faces* had debuted on the Cincinnati CBS affiliate. Jim Scott was a local morning radio personality, and *New Faces* was a series showcasing area talent. We received an audition, took the intimidating journey to downtown Cincinnati and were chosen to appear on the show. When we arrived at the television station the day of the taping, we discovered our segment would be shot in the same studio where the local kiddies' show *Uncle Al* was produced. It was a bit disconcerting to see numerous shelves of lifeless puppet carcasses and set-props gathering dust. Years of suspended disbelief were immediately negated. Television could be an ugly business.

Other than experiencing an unexpected acute awareness of all of our bodily limbs the moment the dreaded red light clicked on—our two segments went remarkably well. We bounced about enthusiastically and had

235

the look of starstruck children who were acting out their fantasy. A few days later, we had the thrill of seeing our listing in *TV Guide,* and the show was taped on video cassette and shown regularly at Garfield High. We had made all of this happen without adult assistance and rightfully took great individual and group pride in our accomplishment.

*   *   *

The Kaleidoscope faded away after my senior year. We had not intended for it to happen that way. We auditioned unsuccessfully for summer work at Kings Island—a major amusement park in nearby Mason. Unfortunately we had only brought the sheet music necessary to perform our prepared selection, and they asked us to do a few additional numbers. Our pianist could not accompany us without her music, and it probably cost us the audition. After racking our brains for other alternatives to keep the group alive, we reluctantly gave up, split the money remaining in our music and wardrobe fund and ultimately went our own ways.

I have not sung in an ensemble since then, and I often long to relive the experience. There is pure joy in singing four-part harmony. It is a skill that involves listening carefully to the other singers and then adding your own voice to make the mix somehow cleaner and more precise. Collectively, our ensemble always worked toward an unattainable perfection. We could never be perfect—but we could always be better. The exhilaration is similar to emotional highs experienced in athletic team competition. And just as often happens in sports—our divergent personalities were not only acceptable, but necessary. Differing dispositions and approaches made the vocals more interesting and gave the music its life.

The Kaleidoscope had fought ferociously to keep the group a cohesive unit, yet I have now lost track of nearly all the members. Ray Combs went on to become a highly successful comedian and television personality until he met his tragic death in 1996. And I have talked with his sister Connie several times on the phone since our formal schooling and have occasionally run into their parents during my visits to Hamilton. Pam Geyer is now married and is a physician in Cleveland. But the remainder of the ensemble has disappeared from my life—relegated to second and third-hand accounts of their suspected whereabouts and occupations. In high school, they were some of the most important people in my life—in adulthood they are only thriving memories. Year after year I fail to pick up a phone to reach out to them. I've convinced myself that our stories have become too lengthy to tell easily, and I wonder if my overtures would be welcomed or considered an awkward inconvenience.

I miss the people who were in The Kaleidoscope. I miss some of them immensely. And I miss the life that the music breathed back into me. The Kaleidoscope banded together because we shared a passion—and our achievements were rewards resulting from that passion. Too often, it now seems that people only have the passion to achieve. When it seems that the drive for success supersedes the joy of traveling the road to it—my inner voice is sometimes drowned out by life's dissonance. It is then that I hope that my memories of The Kaleidoscope will sing to me, so that I can hear my part in the music once again.

28

Class Clown

Hamilton, Ohio, is a tough town. Its people are unabashedly blue-collar, with a sizable contingent of residents who have relocated from the hills of Kentucky and Tennessee. It is a town of corner taverns and gloomy factories, of sometimes uncomfortable racial disharmony and close-knit neighborhoods. Hamilton wears its emotions on its sleeve and a chip on its shoulder. It has little use for pretense or rhetoric and holds disdain for those who choose to look down on its deliberate simplicity.

My years in elementary and junior high school were spent isolated in a predominantly white middle-class neighborhood known as Lindenwald. There was no racial tension because there were no black people, and the poorest and roughest of Hamilton's juveniles attended other schools in other areas of town. Thus my early youth was spent in relative security, insulated by my middle-class surroundings and Hamilton's carefully etched lines of segregation. I'd been exposed to my share of schoolyard skirmishes and prearranged fistfights in neighborhood parks and vacant lots. And I sometimes marched home an exuberant victor and other times slinked through the back door with my bloodied nose pushed to one side of my face.

But my altercations were few and far between and were of the sort that many boys must endure as one of the less-desirable rites of growing up. The skirmishes posed no lasting threat except to my fragile male ego. I selected my battles carefully and bluffed much more often than I came to blows. By the time I was in junior high school, I was big enough and growled enough that I was not frequently challenged. And I learned to placate those who relished brawling, allowing them to throw their weight as long as it wasn't flung combatively in my direction. In general, I used my wits rather than my fists and managed to thrive in my sanitized surroundings.

By the time I entered Garfield Senior High School, I had survived more than two tumultuous years of life without my father and had become adept at swallowing my emotions and enduring my days with nagging inner pain. Garfield High offered a climate that suited me. Exposure to a broad cross-section of inner-city youths and the introduction of people into my life who might be considered a "less-desirable element" felt both intriguing and somehow necessary. While several of my fellow junior-high classmates' families had moved to the west side of Hamilton so that they might attend Taft High, I welcomed the opening of the invisible gate that separated me from people that I had long been allowed to observe, but not interact with.

From my first days as a flustered sophomore, I sought my higher education in interaction with the students I was surrounded by rather than the books and instructors that the school system had provided me. The mixed bag of personalities that I encountered astounded me. There were leather-jacketed rednecks with whom you avoided eye contact, black activists and white separatists who avoided eye contact with anyone of another race—and underprivileged social misfits who avoided eye contact with nearly everyone. The halls were filled with cheerleaders and athletes, illiterates and geniuses, untainted innocents and tired-eyed delinquents—who had seen and done far too much too soon.

I wanted to be accepted, but my conservative upbringing and straight-laced appearance limited my ability to reach those from other backgrounds and lifestyles. Although my grades were unexceptional, I had been placed in classes filled with honor students and was cursed with a reputation for intelligence. My interest in choir and theater further estranged me from a large segment of the male student population. I was both artsy and brainy—two traits that would have spelled certain harassment if I had lacked a calculated plan of action.

My solution was simple. I proved my lack of intelligence by essentially switching off my mind during classes and avoiding the completion of homework whenever possible. After all, only a pinhead would jeopardize his future merely to gain social approval. Although I was unwilling to sacrifice my love for the arts, I used my sense of humor to display what a regular guy I was. My wit kept potential enemies off-stride and sometimes won over people who otherwise would have written me off. Making people laugh came easily to me, and it seemed to offer me some positive recogni-

239

tion. My humor afforded me the luxury to pursue artistic endeavors that were not considered traditionally masculine. Unfortunately I was not yet mature enough to know when and where to get serious.

Initially my clowning was limited to wisecracks in classes and showcasing my humor in social situations where I could impact people whom I wanted to impress. Eventually my reputation preceded me, and I felt I was expected to be amusing most of the time. It became more difficult to find convenient opportunities to turn it off. Many of my friends were nearly as silly as I was, and we continually egged each other on and tried to schedule as many of our classes together as possible. We creatively wreaked havoc in most of our courses, exhibiting disdain for those who weren't in on the joke. If you weren't the brunt of our humor, we were funny—if you were our target, we could be downright vicious.

By the time I was a junior, I had become a smart-ass extraordinaire. I was receiving outstanding grades in subjects for which I had a passion and terrible marks in courses that I barely tolerated. I failed chemistry and physics, often not even bothering to complete the required exams. And I skipped classes frequently, submitting counterfeit excuse slips to allegedly rehearse a play or upcoming choral concert. If a teacher consistently failed to take attendance, I consistently failed to attend—opting instead to hang out in the auditorium with other adolescent outlaws or to leave the building entirely, in search of a way to kill an hour or two. I was far too responsible and principled to engage in any truly destructive acts. Instead I delighted in beating a flawed system and defiantly proving to the world that I was no goody-two-shoes.

Most of my teachers either liked me or shook their heads and washed their hands of me. A few eventually erupted, weary of my incessant testing of their boiling points. Others gave me credit for being much more diabolical than I actually was—and appeared intimidated by my never-ending shenanigans. Among students I was broadly known and, for the most part, well thought of. I was only cruel to those who could not hurt me and made a conscious effort to develop a broad base of friends and acquaintances. My humor had provided me unexpected power, and I found that the more people gave to me—the more I took. Make them laugh, I discovered, and even the most vicious hall hooligans would not want to harm me.

As I started my senior year, I felt that I had the run of the school. My primary cohort in crime was Mark Troxel—a tall, wiry, bass-voiced minister's son who shared many of my classes with me. His comedy was cerebral, and although he was less a troublemaker than I, his humor inspired

240

me to no end. Being a preacher's kid, Mark had garnered his own labels and had augmented his parental handicap by joining both the choir and the band. Our partnership was deadly. In choir rehearsals, we intentionally sang hideously off key, causing the choir teacher, Miss Johnson, to scurry about the room listening for the culprits and wincing as if someone had just passed gas. In history class, we butchered the name of our student teacher, Miss Hoffmaster, as we addressed her as Miss Halfmelon, Miss Hallmaster, or Miss Hangnailer. And in English, when an irritated Mrs. Williamson put us on the spot to "entertain the whole class," we broke into a rendition of "The Sounds of Silence"—billing ourselves as Simer and Gartroxel.

In a course called Problems of Democracy, we were joined by Mike Leck, a longtime friend and fellow crazy. The period, which was regularly interrupted mid-class by our lunch break, was filled with an all-star collection of some of the cutest girls and most popular guys in the senior class. The course was also attended by a poor chap who had the misfortune of being named Gregory Peck, a curse over which he held little control. He endured a barrage of verbal name torture along with a daily ceremonial ritual in which Mike Leck chicken-strutted around his desk, quickly bobbing his neck and head, flapping his arms and squawking, "Peck . . . peck . . . peck . . . peck" as if on a search for strewn corn kernels.

At lunch break, Troxel, Leck, a fellow named Mike Blizzard and I dined out each afternoon—even though it was forbidden by school regulations. After several weeks of defying the status-quo, the thrill began to ebb, and we decided to raise the ante. For the next few days we placed our empty McDonald's wrappers on Mr. Florio's desk after our meal—challenging him to dispose of the litter and the mystery. An elaborate trap was set that included the vice-principal. We unsuspectingly wandered into it, and each of us received three nights' detention.

Substitute teachers were sacrificial lambs offered up to the gods of tomfoolery. A seating chart was a ticket to play the role of an absentee or exchange identities with a classmate—if only to inject some levity into the proceedings. Our unspoken rule was that under no circumstances was a substitute to be burdened with the truth. There was, after all, great entertainment value in a state of confusion. On one occasion, I had failed to attend my scheduled class and instead took a seat in a science course that was being taught by a first-day substitute. I disrupted the proceedings to the extent that the flustered teacher demanded that I report to the principal's office. I left the scene, and I understand that she followed shortly

241

thereafter—arriving in the administrative office with a tall-tale of a phantom rabble-rouser whom they were never able to identify.

*   *   *

My record, however, was certainly not squeaky clean. Mr. Lucia booted me from the marching band, although I was an irreplaceable virtuoso cymbal player—and I was tossed from English class, despite the fact I had been receiving A's for my academic efforts. That permanent ejection was for disputing the meaning of a poem by Robert Frost, a hot-button topic that I have since consistently sidestepped. Discussions about politics, religion and Robert Frost poetry should be avoided at all costs.

I was a master at getting under teachers' skins and was generally admired for my expertise. I never got into any hard-core trouble and had friends and acquaintances who traversed the spectrum of personalities that coexisted within the walls of Garfield High. My education was flawed yet full, and although I was aware of my controlled anger, I saw it as an inevitable process of toughening up. Throw a few jabs and keep my guard up—I believed—and no one could harm me.

When I look back on my high-school shenanigans, I occasionally chuckle at some of my pranks and delight in the good humor that I shared with a number of close friends. But these feelings are always tempered by the faces of people I managed to hurt. There was a host of people like Greg Peck who were the brunt of my jokes and suffered great emotional pain simply because I wanted to be amusing and well-liked. They did nothing to incur my wrath, and I picked on them primarily because they were not in a position to retaliate. So often we inflict pain on others for no other reason than because we too are suffering. I hurt when I think of those I needlessly abused and hope that they have healed and can forgive my selfishness and brutish behavior. I'm not sure that I have.

And I recall a handful of quality teachers who left during my years at the school and hope that I was not partially responsible for their departure. Our choir teacher, Miss Johnson, was hardworking and dedicated—and was a truly fine individual. I expressed my gratitude for her efforts by exploiting her weaknesses and toying with her sincerity. She was largely responsible for our senior musical, *You're a Good Man, Charlie Brown*, and orchestrated a choir trip to New York City that I still hold as one of my most precious memories. For this, I send her my unspoken thankfulness and hope that I can someday express my gratitude and apologies in person.

242

These high school memories carry with them a sting that I have always allowed myself to feel. They serve to remind me that life does not exist in a vacuum. People's feelings are at stake nearly every time a decision is made, and a person's contributions can be measured largely by the dignity they have afforded the people they've come in contact with. Hamilton, Ohio, was sometimes intimidating in the 1970s, and the passing years have done nothing but hone life's sometimes razor edge. Sooner or later, all of us find ourselves on the receiving end. If we choose to lash out to survive—it seems that everyone bleeds. But afford life and people the respect that they deserve, and you may go to the grave with your precious nose intact and still squarely centered upon your face.

29

Saturday at Bill's

On just about any Saturday night in 1971, Hamilton was a virtual hotbed of activity. The parking lots of bars and taverns were crammed with automobiles and pickup trucks, and the handful of hot nightclubs resonated with the blaring sounds of local country and rock bands. All of the Frisch's Big Boys and McDonalds in town were teeming with newly licensed teen drivers and their thrill-seeking passengers. They circled the eating establishments, peering into each car they passed, hoping to see the friendly face of someone they either knew or would very much like to. Drivers revved engines and occasionally heartbeats, as would-be couples exchanged longing looks and conversed in sometimes graphic body language spoken from the hips.

In the Simer household, my sisters and mother were changing into their most stylish new outfits while I disgruntledly sat in my basement bedroom—agitated because my girlfriend, Brenda Doty, was spending the evening at a family get-together and would be unable to go out with me. Instead I would be driving to Greenhills, a Cincinnati suburb, to spend the evening at a gathering held twice a week that was known simply as "Bill's."

* * *

Bill's is a particularly difficult phenomenon to describe, since to this day I am not exactly sure what I witnessed when I went there. It should be explained at the outset that "Bill's" refers to an individual rather than an actual location. Bill, whom you will meet later in this piece, shepherded a flock of followers who met routinely for spiritual enlightenment. I suppose one might have called these assemblages religious services, but the converts who attended did not describe them in those terms. In reality, the meetings were probably an outgrowth of the self-awareness and meditation movement of the late '60s with the added enticement of an alleged psychic/faith-healer. At Bill's, peace of mind and divine health care were offered up in a single attractive package—all neatly wrapped in Far Eastern spiritualism. However, to a more detached and less receptive critic, Bill's would have appeared to be only a Midwestern gathering of San Francisco-style eccentrics involved in some downright peculiar behavior.

Unfortunately, the women in my family were fascinated with the possibilities of expanding both their minds and their datebooks. The meetings had an enthusiastic underground following and had evolved into a super-hip curiosity for Cincinnati-area cloud-climbers. There were four eligible females in our house, and the get-togethers offered a more cerebral version of skirt-chasing than encountered at most of Hamilton's lowbrow social gatherings. The ideology was intriguing, the psychic feats mystifying, and the men always at least superficially sensitive. It was a chance for my mother and sisters to schmooze, and although I was often resistant to joining in—an evening at Bill's was not without its charm. It was on the lower echelons of my Saturday night options, but I enjoyed the experience a bit more than I was willing to admit. I considered it a guilty pleasure—but vehemently denied my interest to anyone who was not receptive to these cursory spot-searches I conducted into my own soul.

That evening the meeting took place in a school gymnasium where tumbling mats had been unfurled parallel to the base of the side walls. As we entered the room, many attendees greeted my family with extended embraces and effusive social kisses. I stiffened and jammed my hands into my pockets, trying to ward off any attempt to extend this love-fest in my direction. Because we had arrived late, we sat on the edge of the gymnasium stage—surprisingly the location furthest from the action—in this painfully deliberate attempt at informality.

More than a hundred people sat on the linoleum floor, many with legs crossed in yoga fashion, and stared up at a slender, nearly bald, red-haired man who spoke eloquently—painstakingly crafting each sentence that he uttered. His eyes overflowed with compassion but also divulged a no-nonsense stability that set him apart from many of those attending. The speaker's name was Bob Rothen, and during business hours he practiced dentistry in the Greenhills community. Bob was my favorite of the people I had met at these gatherings. His approach to the meetings was scholarly and grounded—in sharp contrast to the highflying fireworks show that would follow.

He was acquainted with me, but more through my family's descriptions than through personal contacts. When he saw me, he usually addressed me as "The Rock," a name Christ had given to Simon Peter, and a characterization Bob used to describe the strength he felt I exhibited throughout my parents' messy divorce. Outwardly, I had sloughed off the designation as an example of the foolishness I felt occurred in these celestial sensitivity sessions. But in my heart I had respect for the man and appreciated his perception of me.

Bob spoke for nearly twenty minutes, and although I have no specific recollections of the speech, I always found his thought-process provocative. His demeanor was intense yet deliberate—his delivery low-key and respectful. It was obvious, however, that he was considered simply the warmup act for the megastar who waited in the wings. Following Bob's talk, there were several minutes of pensive silence before two denim-clad and rather wilted flower children fluttered forward to warble their way through a selection from *Godspell*. Immediately after their number had concluded, they placed their guitars out of harm's way and plopped down upon their iron-on pocket patches—patiently waiting with the throng for the much-anticipated main event. Suddenly, a man who appeared to be in his mid-thirties bolted into the room to take command of center stage. All eyes followed his every movement, as if each step and facial expression held deep underlying meaning. Bill had made his grand entrance.

From what I understood, Bill's full name was Bill Boshears. He was an ex-truck driver, and although not an ordained minister, he certainly had an evangelist's flair. Bill was a balding, plain-faced man who attracted electric glances from female audience members as if he were a lightning rod. His eyes were wide and other-spirited, and his controlled mania made him resemble a middle-aged Alistair Sim in *A Christmas Carol*. As he spoke, he darted back and forth, making quick exaggerated gestures and dramatic pivots, creating an almost rhythmic choreography to his spoken words. Bill did not possess an impressive physical countenance. He was a man of quite average looks and size, with a slight paunch and an unexceptional wardrobe. But he had undeniable charisma and a wild, unbridled energy.

Bill talked for nearly forty minutes, and the actual text of his speech paled in comparison to Bob Rothen's articulate presentation. But his remarks were delivered with great fervor and zeal, and were filled with pet catch-phrases that I carefully collected for later personal amusement. Lampooning Bill was always one of my most effective weapons against my sisters. I would masterfully mimic his routine by nervously pacing the living room floor, ministering to my greatly annoyed siblings. Expressions that he repeated week after week, like the profound "Live it and give it!" or his more mysterious "I'm not where you think I am," became verbal darts that I would throw at precisely timed moments to elicit laughter or wound an indignant family adversary during a war of words.

After Bill's speech had ended, he asked all interested parties to come forward so that he might perform a feat that our family came to know simply as "the zap." To perform this miraculous act, he would make use of the tumbling mats carefully situated on the gym floor, as well as several volunteers designated as "catchers." People who wished to be zapped would line up on one side of each mat with their backs facing the thickly padded floor coverings. Bill attended to the human guinea pigs one by one, rubbing his hands together rapidly, then tapping each person's forehead or dramatically grasping both sides of his or her face before spasmodically withdrawing—as if he had just placed his hand upon a hot stove. His body contortions and pained facial expression made it seem that he was possessed by some higher power. As he made physical contact with each participant's face or neck, he/she would fall straight back—with body held rigid as if under deep hypnotic trance. On good nights when Bill worked the line, bodies faith-flopped at split second intervals and could nearly have been set to music—as if the group were water dancers entering a swimming pool in an Esther Williams movie.

If things went according to plan, catchers would break the fall of the zap victims and place them gingerly onto the mat. If things did not, their unpliant bodies would strike a quite unyielding mat full-force—resulting in a resounding thud that made even the strong-stomached a bit queasy. Subjects dropped like human dominos, as the catchers worked furiously to keep up. Very occasionally, overeager subjects would flump down out of sequence and before Bill had ever reached them. In these cases, there was nothing that could be done except to rush to their sides, wait for the cosmic cobwebs to clear, and welcome them back to the very real world of back pain and head contusions.

A few forlorn souls whispered to Bill about physical or emotional problems they were experiencing, which usually resulted in a zap with just a little extra mustard. After people had toppled to the mats, their reactions varied greatly. Some bounced up as if they had just experienced a teeth-jarring tackle in a football game, while others remained in a meditative state for minutes—with arms crossed and bodies as straight as ironing boards.

After everyone had returned to earth and an upright position, Bill

247

used his psychic powers to describe the thoughts of troubled audience members, sometimes protecting anonymity by addressing his remarks to the entire crowd, and other times attempting to pinpoint the person whose mind he had invaded. The clear majority of the audience appeared in awe of his remarkable sixth sense, and each person whom he attempted to heal or help seemed convinced of the authenticity of his gift. I will not attempt to pass any personal judgment on this impressive display, since I rarely attended these assemblages. It should be stated, however, that for pure entertainment value, it was not the worst way to spend a Saturday evening. I had usually taken advantage of these girls' nights out to spend private time with Brenda in our empty house—a confession that is surfacing for the first time with this writing. But considering the circumstances of this particular evening, it beat the heck out of NBC's *Saturday Night at the Movies.*

*   *   *

After the session, the regular attendees held an informal social club, mingling enthusiastically and raising each other's consciousness. I constantly shifted my positioning, using my family as a human wall to form a buffer between myself and the flock of strange birds that approached us. We encountered an alleged expert at identifying past lives who insisted that the Simer clan had formerly walked the earth as the Swiss Family Robinson. I didn't have the heart to inform her that we would therefore have been fictional characters. Several men who wore crosses around their necks that were large enough to crucify smallish midgets floated over to impart their infinite wisdom upon us. And a young man in his twenties who apparently believed he was some sort of self-ordained priest sullenly worked the room, graciously blessing those who dared make eye-contact with him. He conscientiously made his pastoral rounds with arms locked behind his back, looking like a young Alfred Hitchcock with hair.

Mike Tewell, a good friend of my sister Emily, approached us with his girlfriend Diane. Mike was a good-hearted man of about twenty who was drowning in self-realization. He was a relic from the '60s, and although he didn't always have both feet on the ground, he was usually able to land on them. I had seen him only at Bill's or at our home—except for an isolated incident when I encountered him on Pleasant Avenue, as he stood unfazed, but with mouth agape, watching flames shooting wildly from his car engine. No additional explanation for this peculiar image can be offered—for I was never provided with one. His girlfriend Diane was liber-

248

ated, dark and sexy—with a calculated look of seductive comfort. Seeing her was the most powerful zap that I would be administered, but I disliked the fact that I was just young enough that she did not recognize me as the grown man I envisioned myself to be. I also spotted the only girl there who seemed attracted to me—a redheaded buxom girl named Kathy. Her smiling eyes provided a much needed boost to my earthly ego and connected me as much to this fellowship as I felt comfortable with.

After rubbing the elbows and the backs of just about everyone present, my mother and sisters finally ascended into the parking lot and anchored themselves to the ground long enough for the drive home. My Rambler American was rife with discussion of the afterlife and the most recent "Bill's" gossip. We stopped off at Dixie Hamburgers to pick up a dozen or so of their scrumptious and greasy burgers—which were sold carryout at six for a dollar. Although the night had bordered on the bizarre, it had been strangely satisfying.

*   *   *

Whenever I recall this brush with characters and philosophies that were foreign to me and their biweekly flirtations with the supernatural—it is dangerously easy to paint the picture with broad two-dimensional strokes and write the experience off as pure poppycock. It can make for a more humorous account when a person ignores one or more angles of a picture that he describes. However, I will not treat the experience that lightly. It cannot be denied that many people found these Saturday night encounters deeply enriching. True, the meetings attracted a contingent of oddballs who have probably since astral-traveled their way to the Psychic Friends Network. But they also drew people like Bob Rothen, whom I have described in this account, and others like Bob Dister and Paul Brock, whom I haven't. These were real people who offered real friendship to our family. Their faces do not appear in this picture I have taken, but they appear vividly when I view these same circumstances from a different point of view.

Sometimes we drift to the most curious places in our quest for truth—and we often flock together with other lost lambs in search of an earthly answerman. Convinced that someone out there must be privy to a quick fix, we will blindly follow people who appear to know something that we don't. And as long as we believe that they are feeding us solutions, we devour their words. I have always taken a neutral position on others' divine inspiration. As long as a person in convinced that his life has been positively changed, and he is not ramming his beliefs down my throat—more power to him. A placebo is an effective cure for the common cold, as long as the patient believes in its effectiveness and keeps his handkerchief in his pocket. In short, I am certain that Bill's was working for somebody—and equally certain that it did not work for me.

But life's lessons have taught me that no single perspective can accurately tell a complete story. Every moment in time can be viewed from a myriad of angles. And differing perspectives can be in conflict, yet still be honest and factual. The key to true understanding is the ability to see the world through others' eyes—or sometimes just with all the senses with which we alone have been blessed. So be careful not to read too much into my occasionally snide commentary and sarcasm. I have lived this evening at Bill's in several substantial ways that are not described here. In other words, to paraphrase a cryptic quote oft-repeated by the man himself—I may not always be where you think I am.

30

The Incident

It had been a rocky beginning to my final year at Garfield Senior High. The Simer family had recently moved to the west side of Hamilton and away from our precious Lindenwald—our neighborhood for nearly all of my childhood. Although school administrators permitted me to finish my senior year at Garfield, the move placed distance between myself and many of the people I had grown up with. My girlfriend Brenda and I had survived the summer, but the approach of September classes ignited my desire to prepare for post-graduation life away from Hamilton. I did not know where I was headed—I only knew that I wanted to get my affairs in order before I left. Brenda represented a powerful deterrent to making a clean break, so I was driven to sever the bond before I lost my nerve. But up to this point, neither Brenda nor I could muster the strength to leave the scene of this accident.

It was a November morning in 1971, and we had met in the hall between classes as we had so many times since the spring of my sophomore year. There was little conversation between us, and we seemed to be walking together only because the routine soothed the sense of loss we now endured whenever we were together. The traffic in the corridor was thick as we neared the main bank of stairs. Many students were in no hurry to reach their destinations, while others searched for avenues to accelerate through the rapidly developing bottleneck.

We had broken through the primary congestion and had reestablished a little breathing room, when an unfamiliar and very tall male student walked toward us—fast approaching the backup of students we had just wormed our way past. He held his hands just below his chest, as if prepared to create his own opening in the snarl-up, and had his palms faced outward and held unusually close to his body. He appeared to be on a collision course with Brenda, as he forcefully passed those moving more slowly in front of him. Brenda's attention was focused elsewhere as he neared her, and his upraised hands seemed zeroed in for contact with her chest area. She never saw him until their paths intersected, and his hands briefly touched her breasts. It did not seem unintentional, and his icy stare at no one in particular made me realize that an apology was not forthcoming.

Brenda angrily pushed his hands away from her, and my muscles drew taut as I became aware that an intervention might be necessary. I was quite cognizant of my left arm that was in a cast from elbow to hand—the result of tendon surgery on my ring finger performed only two weeks earlier. The finger had been injured in a pickup football game, which was probably how I had also broken my eyeglasses—which were now beyond fixing and tucked in a drawer at home.

I aggressively stepped between them and made a brief attempt at verbal communication—for no other reason than to satisfy my curiosity regarding his bizarre behavior. "You shouldn't have done that," I stated matter-of-factly. I wanted a response—an explanation—that would make his actions forgivable. His answer came in the form of a right hand being launched at me with considerable force. Our altercation encompassed only a matter of seconds but seemed to transpire in underwater slow-motion. I raised my injured left arm to block the blow, but still felt its impact on the left side of the middle of my back. He suddenly retreated a few steps, his eyes fixed in a trance-like glare. I experienced a sudden rush of heat, felt warm liquid spill from my back, and heard someone tell me that I was bleeding. The crimson drops that had already collected on the corridor floor offered instantaneous affirmation of the fact. Without my eyeglasses, I had failed to see that my attacker had wielded a knife. I had been stabbed.

I will not speculate on why this assault occurred. To this day, I have no firm answers—only endless hours of reflection and conjecture that have provided me little satisfaction. I do not now provide the assailant's name or description, because if my wishes have been realized, he regrets his actions and has put the incident behind him. His name is insignificant to this story—the fact that he used his knife is not.

*   *   *

Even after I became fully aware of what had taken place, I remained amazingly unemotional. The moment seemed surreal, and the incident had happened so quickly and had become so suddenly violent that I had not had the time to form my emotions. It was as if a brilliant burst of light had exploded in my brain and had temporarily stunned my mind's eye. Someone mentioned taking me to the school office, and I began to head in that direction—leaving a trail of blood in my wake. I did not make a decision to go—I just went—as rote reaction seemed to supplant all reasoning.

I walked through the front office doors where Mrs. Schweinfest, a receptionist/secretary was stationed at her desk. My only words to her were, "I've been stabbed." My reputation was one of an incessant kidder, and I teased her whenever an opportunity arose. Mrs. Schweinfest simply smiled and shook her head—until I pivoted and exposed my left back to her view. "Oh, my God!" she shouted, and her exclamation triggered an avalanche of activity as a number of well-intentioned faculty members appeared before me, offering their assistance and attempting to piece together what had just occurred.

I was now seated in a wheeled office chair, as several strong-stomached souls unsuccessfully attempted to control the flow of blood and bandage the wound before the ambulance arrived. Finally, Mr. Florio, the head football coach and an instructor of mine, came to the rescue. He drew a tourniquet securely around my torso, and the paramedics rushed in shortly thereafter. They whisked me off, rolling me, chair and all, down the hallway to an awaiting emergency vehicle. I was on my way to Fort Hamilton Hospital.

*   *   *

After they scooted me through the emergency room doors, admittance papers were hastily processed while we waited for my mother—who had been notified by school officials at her place of employment. Once she arrived a surgeon was selected, and they carted me into a painfully bright operating room, where they attempted to halt the bleeding so that the wound could be closed. I remained quite calm. In my ignorance, I believed that because I was feeling no excruciating pain and experiencing no faintness, I would only need to be stitched up and then sent on my way.

The surgeon requested that I lie on my stomach, and after undressing the gash, he began applying pressure to the surrounding area to determine the specific source of the bleeding. The damage was more serious than originally anticipated, and a decision was made to place me under total anesthesia. By then everyone was scurrying, and I was surrounded by concerned faces. But with the sudden prick of a needle, their conversation melted into indistinguishable garble that seemed to steadily increase in

253

volume. I was asked to begin counting backward from one-hundred—and would not wake until several hours later.

I regained consciousness in the recovery room to the unfamiliar voices of staff nurses as they administered to the patient in the bed next to mine. My brain felt as if it were stuffed with cotton, and I struggled to overcome the effects of the anesthesia. I was too groggy and physically depleted to worry, but when my mother popped her head in the door, I felt a force field of protection that allowed my vulnerabilities to once again surface. The surgeon, Dr. Smith, made a bedside visit, and he told the tale of the surgery. The attacker's knife had severed an artery and nearly punctured my lung. A perpendicular incision had been made for surgical accessibility, and the operation was then successfully completed. After an overnight stay in the hospital to receive blood and for observation, I would be free to go home.

The subsequent early-afternoon hours afforded me time to ponder my situation, and I began to recognize the impact of what had just happened. An incident such as this would be major news in our community. And the fact that it took place in the confines of the school building would concern parents for the safety of their own children. But that was not the primary reason that this altercation would be the talk of Hamilton. It had been an episode between a white student and a black student.

Initially, my assailant's race had seemed insignificant to me. I did not know him personally, and no racial epithets had been uttered prior to his surprise attack. Although I now felt a simmering fury within me, it was because I believed he had improperly touched my girlfriend and then nearly killed me for no apparent reason. The anger had nothing to do with the color of his skin. But race relations at Garfield were always strained, and this would only aggravate the situation. Additional tension could be expected, and an eruption of violence was a distinct possibility. Some people looked for reasons to fuel the fire, and if this was twisted into a race issue—troops would gather on both sides. It was the early '70s, and integration was being met with stubborn resistance. I did not wish to become a cause to rally around.

My thoughts diverted to Brenda. My masculinity would probably be questioned, because I had not—nor did I intend to—avenge her violation. It was not fear that prevented my retaliation. My overpowering emotion was one of resigned confusion. The motivation for this unprovoked attack would probably never become clear to me, and my anger was directed at a face in the crowd rather than a known personality. Revenge was, therefore, not my natural impulse. I hoped that she could understand.

*　　*　　*

These thoughts continued to torment me until visitors began to trickle in after school ended. They came bearing the news that the perpetrator had been apprehended. I was told that after the incident, he had simply gone on to his next class as if nothing had happened. Brenda was one of the first people to arrive at the hospital and sat loyally with me for quite some time. Members of the Kaleidoscope, the singing group of which I was a member, visited and gave me a favorable report about the concert that we had been scheduled to perform that afternoon. The show had gone off as planned, and the group had done quite well without me. Several members had then traveled to the Ciné Malibu and had cleaned the theater to fulfill my janitorial obligations.

Other friends, parents, teachers, church members, and even the principal stopped by to check on me. My coterie could not have prevented the accident from happening, but they were now present to apply emotional salve to initiate the healing. I offered to make a tape for our principal, Mr. Kinch, telling the student body that I was recuperating quickly and not bitter about the events of that day. We had high hopes that the tape would douse developing flames of hostility.

In stark contrast to the violence and insanity that had erupted into a personal tempest that morning, the nurturing love I now experienced seemed to calm my emotional waters and create an internal climate of unusual serenity. My dear friends' thoughts and efforts had not gone unnoticed—in fact, they had served as a counterweight that now uplifted the incident. The stabbing no longer represented only a meaningless catastrophe—an event that I would forever seek to suppress. It instead would eventually feel like a trying, but poignant moment in my life, from which I could draw additional strength.

After the last visitors left that evening, I listened eagerly to TV and radio accounts of my adventure. Of course everyone mispronounced my name as "Simmer," and that helped water down whatever melodrama I could have reveled in. After tossing and turning in my unfamiliar surroundings, I eventually slept restlessly with the aid of pain killers. I would have a few rough weeks ahead of me.

Cards, letters and phone calls streamed in for the next few days. Many well-wishers expressed concerns regarding my health, some praised my Christian attitude in not seeking retribution, and a few openly questioned why I had not plotted revenge. Racial tensions at the high school had increased, but I had successfully diffused a major explosion. I did so, however, somewhat at my own expense.

Our local newspaper ran a story that was of no benefit whatsoever to my cause. The headline read, "Youth Held in Stabbing—Victim Says No Hard Feelings." The banner sounded as if I had passively accepted my assault, shrugged my shoulders and consoled the assailant by telling him that these things happen. I began to feel pressure to defend myself for doing the right thing and allowing the legal system to handle the matter. Clearly no action that I could have taken that day would have provided me satisfaction. Retaliation and forgiveness both appeared to be weaknesses in character—depending on who was evaluating the situation.

The majority of the communications that I received were filled with love and compassion, however—and I tried to draw from the outpouring of warmth to cope with my unwanted short-term notoriety. My eventual return to school was trying. Everyone seemed to be staring, and I spent an inordinate amount of time telling and retelling my account—until I became somewhat desensitized to the actual occurrence. I had several sessions with an area detective investigating the case, and he informed me that I would be testifying in the upcoming trial. The court date had been arbitrarily set to coincide with a trip our choir was taking to New York City, but was rescheduled to allow me to go on the preplanned journey.

*   *   *

New York City was thrilling, and the escape from Hamilton briefly took my mind off the ordeal. When I returned, Brenda and I had a brief reconciliation—but before the trial commenced, we had again drifted apart. Our court appearance was nerve-racking, but never in doubt. The defendant received two weeks in jail and five years' probation. His father went out of his way to apologize to me at the trial. It made me sad when I viewed my attacker as a human being, with a family who was undergoing their own version of pain. When I could bear the frustration and hurt of trying to understand, I could see that almost nothing in life was simple.

My healing had begun. The scar on my back would eventually no longer appear inflamed, and it began to fade—but it never went away completely. Neither have the emotional scars that are not readily visible to the indiscriminate eye. I can throw on a shirt, and only those who are most intimate with me know that the scar is even there. Similarly, I can throw a mental drape over the episode and not allow myself to feel the sting of its recall. If I conceal the emotional scars the incident has left me with, no one will know the lifelong impact that the episode holds. But I find that my recollection of this event is sometimes necessary, because if I do not recognize the hurt—neither can I understand the healing.

An insanity named violence had invaded my comfort zone, and there was no asylum from its angry clutches. It could reach into my school or my home. And it arrived without announcement and struck with the fury of a natural catastrophe. Neither locked doors nor supervised hallways could halt its entrance, and the safety of numbers had not prevented its access to me. Hatred and anger seemed a disease that sapped the mind of reason and pointed out the tenuous peace that ruled my daily routine. For a time, I was always prepared to dodge a falling sky—and saw the human condition as an explosion in search of a catalyst.

I had been initiated into the world from which parents try to protect their children. After several weeks, circumstances resembled what they had been before—but life would never be the same. It had become a measurable commodity, because death had become real, and I realized my own destructibility. I would learn to calmly look over my shoulder and developed a healthy respect for life's madness as well as a practical fear of it. I could not prevent catastrophe, but I could try to stay out of its way.

We walk through our lives every day, never knowing when or if a disaster will strike. Impending danger always looms over us, and no one knows when the hammer may drop. But if disaster does strike, we struggle with whatever strength we possess to recover. And if we are lucky, our friends and families bolster our strength and our resistance. I choose to remember and tell this story because I was a survivor. Because of the assistance and support of a community of friends and perhaps a little dumb luck—the hammer's blow was not a devastating one. For this, I will always be grateful.

31

Senior Year

I was in the homestretch of my high school experience, and although it had been a bumpy ride, my final year of public schooling had offered a smooth but bittersweet conclusion to a gratifying three years. The Simer family had settled into our house on the west side of Hamilton, and although we now resided in the Taft High School district, I commuted across town each day to complete my final year at Garfield. Brenda Doty and I were no longer speaking, and I was regularly dating a girl named Brenda Thomas—who lived only three doors from the Doty residence. Intimidated by my impending graduation, I buried myself in activity to avoid confronting the prospect of life without the structure of high school. Time spent at home had become increasingly difficult since Emily had transferred from a local women's college to DePauw University in Indiana. My mother's mood had worsened, and I structured a regular weekly schedule filled with time-consuming distractions and many late night and overnight options—all designed to keep me away from our new house on Herman Avenue during waking hours.

*   *   *

As my home life turned more volatile, and my fears regarding life after graduation heightened—I became a far less pleasant person to be around. I had begun to use my sense of humor to keep those around me at a safe distance—afraid that if someone touched me too deeply, I would surely bruise. My wit became angrier and was often brandished as a weapon. I elevated my own stature at the expense of others, and although many people found my abuse of innocent and nearly defenseless victims as clever and entertaining—more sensitive souls saw the hurt that my humor of degradation caused. There were those who could still access my softer side, but anyone who had not already earned my trust usually met stiff resistance when approaching me.

Brenda Thomas and I began dating in the early winter of 1972, almost immediately after Brenda Doty had permanently terminated our relationship. Armed with the knowledge that Brenda Doty did not care for her, I pursued a love interest to punish my ex-girlfriend for having the strength to walk away from me. But even after my first date with Brenda Thomas, I found that comfortable conversation came easily for us. And after we had gone out for several weeks, I was surprised that she placed no demands on our relationship. I enjoyed both her companionship and her family—and spent a great deal of time at their home. She was a sophomore with pale blue eyes and an aching shyness that prevented casual observers from recognizing her intelligence and sense of humor. Brenda was wholesomely pretty with thick, light-brown hair—and her face glowed when a smile broke the lines of her frequently somber expression. But she often seemed burdened and sad, and was struggling through a difficult period in her own life. Ours was not an association of passion and adoration, but instead we had a respectful friendship sprinkled with a dash of romance. We began seeing each other regularly, and she continued to allow me the unreined freedom that my pre-graduation mentality demanded.

Her family was warm and accepting of me, and I often spent one or two nights a week watching television with them in their living room. Brenda had two sisters—one slightly older named Bambi and a younger sibling named Tammi. Both were cute and vivacious and sometimes overshadowed their more sedate sister. In fact, Brenda considered herself the black sheep of the family and waged a constant battle to gain more trust and confidence from her parents. It seemed to be a fairly typical parent/teenager confrontation to me, but I had become all too aware of the difference between surface appearances and underlying truths. I therefore recognized her feelings as valid ones and afforded her the same respect with which she had so consistently honored me.

I enjoyed a cordial relationship with each member of her family, though, and anticipated our Friday evenings watching "Room 222" and "Love American Style" while eating Chester's Pizza—a wondrous delicacy available only in the Cincinnati vicinity. It was (and still is) a culinary delight with a thick, chewy crust that tasted similar to a warm pretzel. The dough was brushed with an ultra-thick layer of pizza sauce, which melted in the mouth when accessed through the combination of cheeses and liberal toppings. It was a treat that my family could not afford and one that I never grew tired of. Later in the evening everyone would graciously slip from the room—giving us a little private TV time. A touch of amour was then injected into this all-American evening—all the while keeping one eye open as we watched for surprise walk-throughs. We were capable of separating and striking innocent poses on a moment's notice, and the potential of interruptions actually injected some additional excitement into our encounters.

Although we were free to date other people if we so desired, I rarely exercised the option. However, I insisted on the concession to establish my independence. I felt that I had to send a clear message to Brenda Thomas and to myself that I was unwilling to be tied down. After all, I was convinced that a college opportunity would provide the impetus for me to leave Hamilton in a few short months.

My thoughts often returned to Brenda Doty. Our relationship had ended so abruptly that I had never really let her go. As the season of our estrangement ended and spring arrived, it finally penetrated my thick skull that there would be no reconciliation and that my regular rendezvous just down the street had only provided her additional strength to make a clean break. It was ironic that I had tried so consistently through my actions to force her to leave, yet was now convinced that I was the aggrieved party. I still loved her, but she wanted nothing to do with me. The realization was a tough pill to swallow.

*　　*　　*

The advent of the spring season brought the fresh air of new beginnings. Auditions were announced for the spring musical, but it appeared that I would be unable to participate. My job at Ciné Malibu required that I clean the facility either shortly after school was dismissed or during the wee morning hours. When I had lived near the theater, late-night cleaning was a viable alternative—but our move to the west side added a half-hour or longer commute to an already late evening. Several of my friends graciously offered to help me clean following after-school rehearsals, so that the task would be completed before the evening's first film presentation. I was touched by their offer and took advantage of this opportunity to participate in my final high-school production. I auditioned and was cast in the role of Snoopy in *You're a Good Man, Charlie Brown.*

The cast was heavily laden with members of the Kaleidoscope—the singing group that we had formed the year before. Ray Combs, a sophomore and close buddy, played the role of Charlie Brown. Laura Moore, a classmate since grade school, was Lucy, and Kevin Rommel, my bass counterpart in the Kaleidoscope ensemble, was co-cast as Schroeder.

Other players included Jonathan Settles, a portly sophomore who shared the part of Schroeder with Kevin, and Debbie Smith and LuAnn Riddle who alternated in the role of Peppermint Patty. Jonathan was one of those guys who often wore a pencil behind his ear and tried much too hard to be liked. We usually remained first-name friendly and arm's-length distant. Debbie was a dark blonde whom I found almost intimidatingly intelligent. She was a confirmed free spirit, and I enjoyed the mental calisthenics we underwent when conversing. LuAnn Riddle was on the Homecoming Court and had been the girlfriend of Dan Rommel—Kevin's older brother who had played the King in *The King and I.* LuAnn was an exquisite sight to behold, with beautifully straight light-brown hair that extended to her lower back—and a smile that turned my brains into butter. I would go out with her once after we had both graduated, but could not muster the nerve to kiss her goodnight—a faux pas about which I still beat myself up. Scott Thorpe was Linus. He was a smallish junior with long brown hair that nearly surrounded his thin face and a very animated but bewildered look. Scott was perfect for the role. He was almost elflike and had a natural sense of comic timing. And he was also one of those effervescent males who was a confidante to loads of cute girls.

*　　*　　*

The show was directed by Joe Rosenfield and our choir teacher, Miss Johnson. Mr. Rosenfield was a former student teacher at Garfield who attended Miami University in Oxford, Ohio. Our school had commissioned him to return after his teaching stint to assist Miss Johnson with the theatrical aspects of the production. He was very Jewish with a wicked sense of humor and a natural gift with teenagers.

Miss Johnson handled the music—and she had been a godsend since her arrival at Garfield. She was vastly underappreciated, and although she only taught at our school one year, her impact was nonetheless significant. Miss Johnson had followed a lackluster one-year stint by a teacher named Mr. Black and had inherited a voice program that was in considerable disarray. She was a likeable soul, but did not possess an electric personality that would immediately win over the multitudes—particularly at a tough-as-nails school like Garfield. The year had proved a struggle for her, as student vultures had consistently circled—waiting for the first indica-

261

tion of her surrender. She had proved resilient and combative, but the battles had taken their toll, and she resigned that June. Her departure was a loss to future students who would not reap the benefits of her enthusiasm and hard work.

The cast clicked from the onset, and rehearsals were professionally conducted but loaded with laughter and creative flow. Everyone in the ensemble was blessed with substantial natural talent, so individual instruction was limited. Instead, much time was devoted to creating amusing stage business, fine-tuning comic timing and tightening musical numbers. The accompanying instrumental sextet was well-prepared and effectively created the proper mood for the little musical. Our set was sparse and simple—consisting primarily of multifunctional giant building blocks, an oversized doghouse and a small wooden construction that resembled a piano.

Emphasis was placed entirely on the music and book, and the actors' ability to interpret it. The show was comprised of vignettes, many taken directly from the comic strip—interspersed with musical numbers. Every cast member had opportunities to shine, but the role of Snoopy—although not the largest part—was an absolute showstopper. I wore a white turtleneck sweater and black trousers, and it was my responsibility through my stage persona to convince the audience that I was the world-renowned beagle. The script gave me numerous opportunities to sell the part, as I barked, crawled, soft-shoed and even tinkled my way into the hearts of ticket buyers. In my biggest number, simply titled "Suppertime," I crooned and pranced about the stage as if I were Joel Grey in *Cabaret,* before erupting into a series of Russian leaps and handsprings exalting the praise of "Super-duper-dupper-time." My routine was very loosely choreographed because I couldn't dance a lick—but I sure knew how to make a comic ass of myself.

All these opportunities at physical humor did, however, present potential risks. One night, while in search of an imaginary stage rabbit, I hiked my leg to relieve myself, as male dogs have a propensity to do. It was a piece of stage business I had done countless times, but on this occasion when I popped up my leg—my pants zipper popped simultaneously. The gaping opening in my crotch area exposed my whiter-than-white jockey briefs, creating an almost spotlight effect on my now-public privates. Of course, as the old stage adage states, "The show must go on!"—and it did. My search for the rabbit was to continue into the audience, so I reluctantly made my way off stage and down the aisle. It was then that a kindly mother in the third row leaned forward to inform me that my fly was open. Oh, how I knew that my fly was open! If the words "My fly is open" had been written on my underwear, the entire audience could have read it—that is how open it was. I was probably beet-red, but no one would have noticed. All eyes were riveted directly on my BVD's. Afterwards, I was convinced that I had gotten an extended taste of what hell is like. Fortunately, this hell was not permanent, and I was finally able to slink offstage, where an emergency crew stitched the area so tightly that I would later need scissors to remove my pants.

The role of Snoopy was a gratifying challenge. It gave me an opportunity to play pure comedy, and nearly all of my scenes had the potential of eliciting a roar of laughter. The show was critically acclaimed, and the entire cast was stellar as we put on a college-caliber performance. Elementary schools throughout the Hamilton/Fairfield area were given the opportunity to see the show because several weekday afternoon performances were added. The children were mesmerized by the production and lined up to get autographs from their cartoon heroes following the final curtain. For weeks afterward I was flagged down by exuberant youngsters overcome by the fact that they had spotted Snoopy roaming the streets of Hamilton.

*   *   *

It was my final hurrah at Garfield and was taking place in a world that I now kept carefully separated from my rocky home life. The move to the west side had been extremely hard on my mother. Emily was now away at college, and I would be joining her in a matter of months—and Mom's future looked lonelier than ever. I was trying to cut loose from Hamilton and strong family ties at the very time that she needed to draw me in. Whenever possible, I hung my hat in other homes. When not parked on Brenda Thomas' sofa or toiling at the theater, I could often be found at the Combs' abode—my newly discovered weekend retreat. Ray was portraying Charlie Brown, and our working together on this musical had only solidified our friendship. His sister Connie remained one of my favorite people throughout our years in high school, and their parents were generous and fun-loving and always treated me with respect and kindness. As the need arose for me to avoid the added pressure of my family's turmoil, they opened their home to me and offered me an acceptance that buoyed my fragile spirit.

They had a large family, with Connie and Ray being the oldest of six children. Their comfortable home on Alsace Avenue was sometimes a madhouse, but was always over-full with casual comfort and good humor. Many weekend overnights were spent sleeping on the living room floor near their baby grand piano. It was there that Connie and I, who had consistently flirted with a more intimate relationship, had allowed our emotions to expand the boundaries of our past association. We had several brief, but passionate outbursts of romance—and my memories of kissing her during night-owl broadcasts of roller derby have always provided me a joyous mental escape. Saturday mornings brought the cozy smells of bacon and eggs frying in the skillet. The breakfast was monstrous, and the aromas and clatter surrounded us with the precious feeling of family. I will never be able to thank the Combs family enough for their gracious temporary adoption of me, as I reached a significant crossroad between my adolescence and adulthood.

The closing night party for *Charlie Brown* was held in a banquet room at the new Holiday Inn in Fairfield, and several cast members booked a hotel room to which we escaped after the official celebration had ended. Everyone was basking in post-production euphoria, as the run had been impressive by any standard. There was even a pie-in-the-sky suggestion of the show being moved to a local dinner theater for the summer. The evening's festivities were topped off when the band director's daughter, Linda Lucia, appeared to flirt with me. She was a stunning and quite shapely girl whom I had always tried my hardest to impress—but all my efforts had failed miserably. My brief notoriety had perhaps prompted her approach of me—but the occurrence, aided by my vivid imagination, supplied several months of pleasant ponderings.

I was bouncing on my toes by the end of the party, and when I went to the registration desk to obtain the key for our overnight room, perhaps my demeanor was a bit overexuberant. I was still in my white turtleneck and wore full stage makeup with my hair heavily sprayed into place. A police officer on duty in the lobby decided to question and frisk me, perhaps fearing that I might be contemplating converting our hotel room into a miniature bathhouse. The incident shook me slightly, but my recovery was complete by the time I turned the lock on our suite and scrubbed my face back to masculinity in a bathroom that had been "sanitized for your protection." We whiled away the early morning hours, extensively discussing every nuance of that very special evening. Our dream night concluded at the Perkins Pancake House (open twenty-four hours a day), where I dug into the lightest stack of pancakes that I had ever tasted—drenched in a puddle of blueberry syrup. The following day I received a Snoopy dog dish and a brand new Dave Cash model, Wilson baseball glove from Brenda Thomas. I was humbled by the fact that she was so proud of me.

*   *   *

My senior year in high school was not one of my happiest school years. It was a time of bold transitions—of terminating a potential life relationship, and preparing for new adventures with unknown faces in unfamiliar places. I had grown restless to leave my family nest, and those remaining in the nest were sometimes anxious to see me go. It was one of those rare times of significant transition—when you step away or are pushed from safety—and you suddenly realize that you are falling. Circumstances and personal development demanded that I become more independent, but everything was happening too rapidly. My past was quick-fading from the picture, and the future had not yet come into view. Again, good friends propped me up and kept me standing until the structure of university life could put me on a straight course again.

It would require courage to leave Hamilton. Life had afforded a litany of reasons why I could not escape my situation. I was too poor, I was too wounded, and I had become too used to making excuses. But I sensed that if I did not transplant myself, I might become permanently rooted. If I didn't at least temporarily sever ties to my hometown—I would be smothered by it. It's funny how life often provides us just enough to force agonizing decisions. It creates a crack in a door that is almost too heavy to move or an escape hatch that does not guarantee freedom. The option is nearly always ours. Inaction and fear dangle as an enticing alternative. Or we can snatch up the chance and take the hike—knowing full well the risk that we might pop our zippers—and praying that we are blessed with a few friends who own sewing kits.

265

32
Ray

The first time I met Raymond Combs, I was entering my junior year in high school. His sister Connie had become a class chum and occasional flirtation of mine, and while making routine rounds one summer afternoon, my mobile wolf pack and I had targeted Connie's home as a designated checkpoint to search for outdoor activity. If she was sighted on her porch or in her yard, we would appear surprised by the chance meeting, strike up a conversation, and feed the flames of adolescent desire.

On that day, things had fallen into place beautifully. The female Combs that we sought had emerged from the safe haven of her parents' dwelling and was now displaying a bit more flesh than we had seen during the school year. The difference in wardrobe was purely seasonal—and though not drastic, our powers of visualization were mighty. The verbal mating that we were engaged in was not particularly memorable, but Raymond's grand entrance was. He emerged from the house to survey the situation, and scanned the terrain as if the world belonged to him. He walked like a miniature bulldog on a mission, chock full of determination and unbounded energy. He was short and rock-solid, and his blonde/brown hair was cropped as to be nonexistent except for a prominent tuft that rose straight up from his forehead as if God had chiseled him from a block of granite and had not rounded the edges.

His face was an entirely different matter. It appeared to be almost cartoon-animated, rubbery, and erupted into a variety of exaggerated expressions—most of which were generated to instigate laughter. His eyes gleamed with impishness, but they were wise and did not threaten or confront. Raymond had shot from his house like a gunslinger emerging from the double-hinged doors of a corner saloon. The moment was his. He commanded everyone's attention—though he was at least two years younger than any of us.

I quickly recuperated from admiring his countenance and properly took charge of the situation. After all, he was a mere junior-high fledgling. But Raymond seemed more than willing to test the limits of both my mind and my tolerance. He never appeared even slightly intimidated and taunted me playfully, knowing full well that any real confrontation was laughable. After trading barbs for several minutes, I threw him over my shoulder like a sack of potatoes and conveniently deposited him in the flatbed of a nearby truck. Undaunted, he sprang from his corral like an unbusted bronco, all the while restraining a wide grin. There was no keeping Raymond Combs down. From that moment forth, he had received my seal of approval. I liked him.

*　　*　　*

Our relationship over the next two years is well-documented throughout this book. He sang with the Kaleidoscope singing group, a project that we both poured our hearts and souls into, and he appeared as Charlie Brown to my Snoopy in the musical, *You're a Good Man, Charlie Brown.* We spent countless hours together involved in extracurricular activities. And evenings were devoted to buzzing the town, playing off each other like a comedy duo, or perhaps just lounging lazily—stretched out in front of the television set at his home. He was not my best friend, but he was a close buddy—and his home provided safe harbor to me.

His sister Connie was one of my dearest friends—even though romance often confused our semi-honest intentions. Their father, Raymond Sr., was a gem of a man, with the same wickedly comical eyes as his eldest son. He was always eager for a battle of wits and usually emerged the victor. Unlike so many parents, he energized a room when he entered it and seemed to delight in the many youthful visitors who frequented his house. Mrs. Combs was an attractive and kind woman who rolled with the punches and loyally played the straight man to her family's comedians. Mr. and Mrs. Combs actually enjoyed spending time together, and the fire thrived in their marriage—the subtleties of which did not escape my keen eye. It restored my faith that it was possible for passion to survive a life-long relationship. They had four other children, all much younger than I, who each maintained their own collection of friends. They entered and exited the scene at the pace of a frenetic stage comedy—keeping the house forever electric and maintaining a constant barrage of fascinating sibling spats. Raymond was always the star, working the room and orchestrating the action. Because I was older, I maintained an elevated stature—but he was always the center of attention. From the moment I met him, I recognized that there was something special about him. He had been doused with a charisma that made him nearly irresistible.

My departure for college, and increasing miles and passing years, eventually created a distance between us. We contacted each other semi-regularly and managed to get together several times, but our relationship became an occasional long-distance phone call or a chance meeting in Hamilton. I heard rumors that he was trying his hand at stand-up comedy and remember thinking that if anyone could do it—Ray could. Then several years ago while I was mindlessly flipping TV channels, there he was, staring at me—his face filling my television screen. That impish smile and his raw energy were alive in my electric fantasy box. I shrieked for my slumbering wife to come see this miracle—my friend Raymond Combs was on Johnny Carson. I called his family immediately and eventually spoke to Ray personally. I was so proud and happy for him. In some strange way, it was my success—it was Hamilton, Ohio's success.

*   *   *

So Ray went on to make a substantial name for himself. He hosted the *Family Feud* game show on CBS and in syndication, opened comedy clubs in Cincinnati, found a niche in Hollywood and became a local hero. He had remained married to his high school sweetheart throughout his ascent to the top and generously gave back to his community. The last time I spoke with him I was in Hamilton, and he was scheduled to appear at a city festival. He was all that I heard about.

We spoke for about a half-hour on the phone, newsy things mostly, and then I excused myself because I didn't want to hold him up. After all, he was so important. More than a year passed, and then the shocking story came over the wire in June of 1996 that he had committed suicide by hanging himself in the mental ward of a hospital. I have never recovered from the news and probably never will.

*   *   *

This story is not about Ray Combs. He has filled its pages, but the text is a thumbnail sketch of a boy and a man who deserves so much more. It will not delve into the controversies surrounding his death or whether the act was suicide or merely a cry for help. Those stories are left to tabloid newspapers and gossip-mongers, who relish broad simplistic strokes and

268

thrive on the dramatic. My intent in this book is to make Ray Combs one of many people who became a part of my coterian retreat, and that is who he remains to me. He cannot be neglected in my own story, because he was too important. He cannot dominate my story, because he was not that important. Yet his death has gnawed at me and demanded that it too must be a part of this book. And so I try, as I often do, to make things fit.

The Ray Combs I knew was alive and vital—solid and grounded. I remember his physical being so vividly—his eyes and his hands, and how he felt when we playfully grappled, or on very rare and exuberant occasions, embraced. His essence is as real to me as anybody's whom I have known—including members of my own family. The Ray Combs I knew would never have contemplated suicide—never would have given it the slightest consideration. And so, I must conclude that somewhere along the line, Ray lost a part of himself—perhaps even a substantial part. It is easy to forget who we are and what we want to be when we spend so much time trying to live up to other people's expectations. We often get caught up in a mob-race to a finish line, before discovering that we are headed in exactly the wrong direction.

*   *   *

I see life as a series of photographs. Some are happy, some are sad—some evoke sheer ecstasy, and others are deeply tragic. Over the course of our lives, we develop a substantial album of these snapshots, and each picture represents a very real part of our time on this planet. Occasionally, I need to look back at each and every picture that has been imprinted upon my mind—for that is the only way I can really remember where I've been and how I got there. But there are those special snapshots of moments when I felt complete and whole—when life and I each offered something to each other—that I want to keep looking at again and again and again.

These are often photos that would bore guests at a cocktail party and draw yawns from those who yearn to be impressed. They are pictures of people whom nearly no one would recognize and places that would take no one else's breath away. But they are the unique memories that seem to cleanse my soul. They resuscitate me and allow me to breathe life on my own again. I cherish and celebrate these captured moments in time, for they are the refuge I now know as my coterian retreat. It is where I always find myself again—and where my protection lies.

269

33

The Final Days

The summer of l972 is one of the few blurs in my memory of my upbringing. It was as if my life's observations were made from a speeding vehicle careening down a highway that led away from Hamilton, Ohio. I caught brief glimpses of the passing days, but my primary concern was to keep the wheels turning on an out-of-state college opportunity that would take me away from the only world that I had ever really known. I could not possibly leave fast enough, acutely aware that the more totally I immersed myself in my plans for my escape, the less I would dwell on what I was leaving—and the less fearful I would be of my ultimate destination.

High school graduation had been joyless, considered not so much an accomplishment as a foregone conclusion. The congratulations I exchanged with fellow graduates were really melancholy good-byes, as I underwent an excruciating and arduous passing from my symbolic womb—an inevitable process that would never allow me to complacently coexist with Hamilton's present again. I had been selected to participate in a summer jobs program for financially disadvantaged high school students at the massive National Lead nuclear plant in Fernald—a twenty-minute drive from our current house on Eaton Avenue. The factory and the commute forced a revision in my lifestyle and were representative of the kinds of drastic adjustments in structure that I would soon need to become accustomed to.

Our stay at Herman Avenue had been short-lived. The landlord decided to reinhabit the home, and we were sent packing after less than a year. The Eaton Avenue residence represented only a structure that provided me shelter and a place to sleep. My bed and furniture could be found in the unfinished basement, as I could feel myself being nudged from a family which was now weaning itself of me. During evening hours I took a curious solace from the sounds the washer and dryer made while in operation. They offered me a feeling of normalcy and order. Things rarely looked, sounded or smelled like they used to. The position at National Lead kept me away from my subterranian room during the week, while evenings and weekends were spent with friends and with my current female companion, Brenda Thomas.

My acceptance into DePauw University in Greencastle, Indiana, had come about almost too easily. Barely average high school grades had properly reflected my indifference to study. Luckily, my college entrance exams had been considerably more impressive, and since Emily had transferred to DePauw the prior year—it had been the only school to which I had applied. Their mailed response was more than I could have expected. Scholarships, grants and financial aid would nearly cover my tuition, room and board. I needed only to obtain a small loan that my mother would co-sign for, and I could pack my bags and begin life as a full-time student.

DePauw's generous financial assistance had taken me aback and had forced my hand regarding my seriousness about attending college. I had expected a struggle to cover expenses or perhaps even a rejection of my application. Instead, a broad path had been cleared for me, and logic dictated that I take advantage of it. Bragging about leaving Hamilton to attend school in Indiana was pleasurable, but confronting the reality of an alien environment isolated from all that I knew was quite intimidating. My preparations for leaving were machinelike, as I detached myself from my emotions while filling out all the proper paperwork. And I bid farewell to many of those who had become part of my daily routine. Although I would be plucked from their lives, they would undergo a mild regeneration and would continue to thrive and flourish. On the other hand, I would sacrifice an identity that I had spent years etching out for myself. It would become necessary to develop new bonds with people who did not understand my history and had not shared my battles. I was starting over. My slate had been wiped clean—and that both invigorated me and filled me with terror.

*   *   *

The summer seemed stuck in a hazy dream. My days existed in limbo as I went through the necessary motions and simply waited. Although I socialized and partied at a breakneck pace—it proved ungratifying. I had emotionally divorced myself from the people and places I was surrounded by, and it tortured my heart whenever they penetrated my defenses and connected with me. My thoughts often returned to my best days with Brenda Doty, when she and Hamilton seemed to provide all the answers.

271

Ultimately, fate and restlessness had dictated that my search continue—though the thought of what I might or might not find unnerved me. I restrained this thought process whenever possible and generally chose spontaneous reaction over preparation.

The final days before my departure I was morose and anxious, feeling like a ghost who was forced to remain in a realm where I was no longer recognized. I made my final rounds, talking of the school breaks and summer when I would return, but knowing that I would then be a visitor rather than an inhabitant. I did not know if I might return to live in Hamilton someday, or if I would even graduate, for that matter. But I was mindful of the fact that I had opted to open my eyes to a world that would change me forever.

My final days in Hamilton were spent visiting the town that I had grown up in. It is the same tour that I often take whenever I return for a visit. My first stop was Lindenwald and the streets and alleys that I had roamed with Mike Engel throughout my youth and adolescence. We had considered them a fascinating maze of sidewalks that each led to and were extensions of our own homes. I continued on to Joyce Park—where I had played organized baseball and softball, cavorted with my friends, went to church picnics and awkwardly visited with my father after my parents' divorce. I drove to Pierce Elementary, George Washington Junior High, Garfield High School and past friends' and girlfriends' houses. I rolled down River Road and through the heart of downtown, sucking in the memories and winding down the clock so that I could turn off the lights on my Brigadoon. The Hamilton that I saw on those final days would now awaken only in my memories. Time would take its inevitable toll on many of the buildings, streets and people who remained after my departure. But the Hamilton that lived with me was forever vibrant and thriving—and could be shared with all who heard me speak or write of it.

The day of my departure, I battled tears from the moment I arose. Emily's boyfriend Garey Carson, who also attended DePauw, came to our house midmorning to take me to Greencastle. A friend would transport my mother several hours later so that she might attend the first-day festivities. Before leaving, I embraced my family members quickly, recoiling each time for fear that I would squeeze too urgently and not let go. My first step out the front door felt as if I were toppling over the edge of the earth. The somber walk to the car and subsequent short trip out of the state seemed a free-fall that became less dangerous the farther we tumbled from my beloved Hamilton. My consciousness finally descended into reality when we passed an interstate bank advertisement on the other side of Indianapolis.

The advertisement consistently flashed the current time and temperature—the clock reading one hour earlier than it would have in Hamilton. It was a powerful roadside reminder that I had entered another time zone, another dimension—and a new life experience.

*   *   *

There is no tidy conclusion to my story. I survived my first day and my next. I graduated from DePauw University in 1976 with a B.A. in Speech and Secondary Education, met my wife and was married in Chicago, Illinois, in 1977. Garey Carson became my college roommate and later one of my closest friends. I returned to town for one year after graduation and entered a circulation management development program through the Hamilton *Journal-News,* where I had been employed as a distribution district manager. My training began in Anderson, South Carolina—and I have never lived in my hometown again.

I still love to visit Hamilton. Crossing its city limits is like entering a thick cloud of memories, joys and sorrows. Every identifiable building and established street is frozen in my mind as it was in my youth—vivid sensory images that I carry with me like snapshots in a wallet. Each building that has been raised or altered dramatically takes me aback, as if someone has defaced my precious past. But when I view my town as a living entity—our meetings resemble a reunion with an old and dear friend. Although the city ages and changes, its spirit remains true. Its essence remains intact.

But the Hamilton of today is not the place that burns within my soul. Time and trends have weathered the face of the town, and I now look through eyes that are older, wiser, and may sometimes see less hope than there really is. Instead, I see the Hamilton that remains a part of me—with all the people I cherish at their most vibrant and each building at its peak of condition. This is the way I choose to remember the people and places I love—as the best of what they have been and as the best of what I believe they can be. It is the positive force that continues to drive me and the reason I continue to believe.

Epilogue

I have felt driven for some time to preserve my childhood memories on paper—so that they may breathe on their own long after I am able to resuscitate them. Nothing in my life has been so impactive as the days of my youth. But why should these tales be important to anyone else? The stories are not particularly extraordinary. They are nearly void of high action and not heavily sprinkled with notable names nor connected to significant historical happenings. Why should anyone give a whit about an elementary-school field trip to a local amusement park, a high-school musical production or a weekend retreat at a church camp? And even if they did—why not opt for fictional accounts that are unbridled by mundane facts that place a straitjacket on my creativity, or inconsequential characters that add nothing to the ebb and flow of the stories? When I first picked up my pen—I was uncertain of the answer. But the stories, like unborn children, made it painfully evident that it was their time to come out. I was certain that I could rationalize their existence when they saw the light of day. Everything would come together when the stories emerged and took shape.

*   *   *

Few conclusions can be drawn from charting the paths of the key characters of my childhood. The update is a mixed bag at best. Most of my immediate family has drifted westward, the majority settling in the Chicago vicinity. There is a genuine respect among us, and although we might not be able to swallow large doses of each other—time spent together in no way feels like taking medicine.

My sisters are all still thriving and energetically tussling with life's formidable challenges. Among their pooled experiences, they have survived the hardship of divorce, financial strain, alcohol addiction and numerous counseling sessions. They have made tough-minded career and domestic decisions and blossomed into beautiful and freethinking women—maintaining their sense of humor in a world that sometimes tries

275

very hard to keep us from smiling. Each has severed ties with Hamilton with varying degrees of reluctance—broadening their horizons and perspectives far beyond the reach of their initial expectations. And Becky has brought my two nieces into the world—marvelous creations who are knowingly and unknowingly imprinted with all of our strengths and frailties. Sara and Lisa reap the benefits of their mother's experiences and the fact that she has been able to learn from them.

My mother still lives in Hamilton and has been remarried since 1973. Tragically, arthritis has gnarled her body and left her in considerable pain and confined to her bed. The disease has contorted her skeletal system in much the same way that life has twisted and wrung her soul. Her mind is quite well—thank you—but never seems to be at rest or at peace. She owns a life force that is electric, and it will be sapped from her feeble frame only when it is called to duty elsewhere. Her body breaks while her nobility grows; she is living proof that you are never too old to grow up. Her questions and curiosity are inexhaustible, and the answers have always come too slowly or not at all. Happiness never seemed in the cards for her. But if she deems her life a failure, others see it as a portrait in courage—having withstood the most taxing of emotional circumstances. When I look in the mirror, it is her face I most often see.

My father divorced again and has since remarried. Fate has placed us in close physical proximity to each other for a number of years. He, too, has continued to grow and evolve—and has recently been walloped with the realization of the havoc that was created when he left his children. His apologies have been frequent and heartfelt. Our childhood now haunts him as a grand opportunity missed. He has become a man whom I am proud to call Dad, although he is a much better friend and confidante than he ever was a father. When he leaves this earth, I will miss him terribly.

My own life has seen its ups and downs. I have been married to the same wonderful woman since 1977 and have done stints as a newspaper-circulation manager, stockbroker, options-exchange floor broker, financial planner and theater manager. I've waged battles with my own demons, including ill-health and a never-ending fear that catastrophe is just around the corner. I will not elaborate on my current status, though some readers might hope that I would. It is a project in work—a tale that would hopefully become outdated as soon as it is told. I am not done living, and facts and feelings that I now hold within are not pressing for their release so that they might take on a life of their own.

The people who were my Hamilton primarily reside in a place that others would recognize as the past. I keep in contact with a sparing few, occasionally hear from many more, and cross paths with familiar faces almost every time I visit my hometown. I realize now that, in most cases, significant moments that we shared were at a fateful intersection in our respective journeys. We were never intended to travel together. Our vision has become acclimated to the shades and shadows of differing realities. When we look upon each other, our eyes cannot adjust to the stark contrasts between our worlds quickly enough. But we can see that the years have creased our faces, reshaped our bodies and stored baggage beneath our eyes. When we part company, I am acutely aware that I may hear gossip about them that provides fodder for mealtime conversations or grim news that might profoundly shake my world. Their lives go on, as the late Beatle George Harrison aptly put it, within me and without me.

*   *   *

Hamilton has suffered through some difficult growing pains. The economy has crippled its industries and sometimes given it sea legs amid numerous tempests. It is not fashionable to say you were raised in Hamilton. Cincinnati is big-city and all-inclusive, Fairfield is vital and expanding. Hamilton is—well, Hamilton *remains* its lovable self. It is kind, yet scrappy—comfortable, yet binding . . . nurturing, yet angry—backward, yet strangely inspirational. I have often said you must leave Hamilton to realize just how wonderful it is.

And so, why did I write *The Coterian Retreat?* My conclusion is that I wrote it because it is an ongoing story that must not end. A storyteller usually weaves his tale as a fine tapestry. His craft involves borrowing from his experiences rather than recounting them. He trims his loose ends and edits out that which does not enhance his story. And yet life does not afford us this luxury—nor does it intend for us to neglect elements that at first appear insignificant or people who appear to be in the periphery.

People enter and exit our lives with frightening rapidity. And no matter how hard we try, we cannot cram all the infinite details of our lives into neat little compartments. They do not sort easily—and when finished, we will never be able to close the drawers. But all of life's experiences, little and large, leave their mark on us. And every living creature who draws our attention—be it for a fleeting moment or for a lifetime—influences our personalities.

Our coterian retreats are most often private treasures of universal ap-

277

peal. They are best friends and quality time spent with our children—our favorite vacation havens and intimate moments with lovers. When these memories cry out to us, they demand that we recognize their worth. Sometimes we recall their scent and taste—and if we want to badly enough, we can still reach out and touch them. I find them most easily in my own childhood, when my eyes were wide open and my passion near the skin's surface—when almost everyone I met could make a difference, and I had a supreme faith that I belonged.

Reality is not a formula drama, yet it can be every bit as agonizing—and uplifting. The recollections contained in this book begin and end only in the continuum of time. But they endure within me like a second heartbeat and survive in anyone who recalls the incidents or people I have described. Placing these memories into literary form allows for a new generation of life, as they are breathed into readers who might be touched by them. If the reader, in turn, rediscovers some misplaced pearls of his own—he becomes the keeper of their destiny. He decides with whom he wishes to share them and whom he may need to thank for his rediscovered jewels. I consider the stories contained within *The Coterian Retreat* a precious gift that it was my obligation to pass on.

The Coterian Retreat is a reconstructed diary of my youth, written at a time when my heart convinced me that I was able to do the remembrances justice. They resided within me in a language of untamed emotions until I was prepared to interpret them for others to hear. The places, faces and images are factual to the best of my memory. The stories are similar to those experienced by others—but are mine alone. My intention is to stir memories within readers that give them a sense of security and order, and a completeness that they have at some time felt.

And finally, to the many people who graced my childhood—I thank you profusely. I have been rescued by your unselfish deeds, and the deliverance continues years after your initial acts of kindness. You planted seeds within me where divine gardens grow. And your influence lives within every act of kindness that I now return to those who surround me. Your story will not end—your generosity will never be forgotten. You've touched so many more lives than you will ever realize.